WHO'S RUNNING AMERICA?

WHO'S RUNNING AMERICA?

Institutional Leadership in the United States

Thomas R. Dye

Florida State University

PRENTICE-HALL, INC., ENGLEWOOD CLIFFS, NEW JERSEY

Library of Congress Cataloging in Publication Data

Dye, Thomas R
Who's running America?

Includes bibliographical references and index.
1. Elite (Social sciences)—United States.
I. Title.
HN90.E4D93 301.44'92'0973 75-40421
ISBN 0-13-958397-1
ISBN 0-13-958389-0 pbk.

PRINTED IN THE UNITED STATES OF AMERICA

10 9 8 7 6 5 4 3 2 1

Prentice-Hall International, Inc., *London*
Prentice-Hall of Australia Pty. Limited, *Sydney*
Prentice-Hall of Canada, Ltd., *Toronto*
Prentice-Hall of India Private Limited, *New Delhi*
Prentice-Hall of Japan, Inc., *Tokyo*
Prentice-Hall of Southeast Asia Pte. Ltd., *Singapore*

CONTENTS

PART 2

PREFACE

Who's Running America? Institutional Leadership in the United States was *not* supported by any grant or contract from any institution, public or private. It grew out of a graduate seminar at the Florida State University on "Research on Power and Elites" in the spring of 1972. The biographical data for over 5000 institutional elites was painstakingly collected and coded by students. John W. Pickering, now Assistant Professor of Political Science at Memphis State University, made the most important contributions, and his Ph.D. dissertation, "The Concentration of Power and Authority in the American Political System," deserves independent reading by serious students of American elites. Others making significant contributions were Eugene R. DeClercq, now Assistant Professor of Political Science at George Washington University, and G. Edward Weston, Assistant Professor of Journalism at the University of Florida.

Two earlier articles appeared in social science journals, which were based on the same data collected for this volume:

> Thomas R. Dye, Eugene R. DeClercq, and John W. Pickering, "Concentration, Specialization, and Interlocking among Institutional Elites," *Social Science Quarterly* (June 1973), pp. 8–28.

Thomas R. Dye and John W. Pickering, "Governmental and Corporate Elites: Convergence and Specialization," *Journal of Politics* (November 1974), pp. 900–25.

We are grateful to the editors of these journals, Charles Bonjean and Donald Strong, for their assistance and encouragement. We are also indebted to a number of commentators who wrote us before and after publication of these articles, including G. William Domhoff, Suzanne Keller, John Walton, and Robert Lineberry.

The absence of any sources of support, and the magnitude of the data collection involved, slowed work on the volume and produced several problems that may disturb some readers. The most serious problem is the time lag between original data collection, which was based on 1970–71 sources, and the publication data of the volume, 1976. Individuals cited in this volume as holding certain positions in 1970–71 may no longer hold these positions. We do not believe this time lag affects any major findings (although we note in Chapter 7 the recent addition of a small number of women and blacks to top institutional positions); but there will be some discrepanices between our reported data for 1970–71 and institutional leadership today.

This volume is divided into three parts. Part I, "Power in American Society," sets forth our questions for research, defines terms and concepts, and explains our method of identifying the nation's institutional elite. Part II, "Institutional Leadership in America," describes concentration of power in industry, finance, insurance, utilities, government, the news media, the law, foundations, civic and cultural organizations, and universities. It also describes the type of person who occupies top institutional leadership positions in these various sectors of society: it "names names" and in doing so, makes use of brief biographical sketches. These sketches are designed to give us a general introduction to the characteristics of elites: the schools they attend, their early careers, their record of achievement, and the multiple positions of leadership that they occupy. These sketches are derived from a wide variety of sources—*Who's Who in America, Current Biography, Forbes, Fortune, Congressional Quarterly,* and individual articles and books collected by myself and my students over several years.[1] The sketches in Part II are designed to pave the way for more systematic analysis of biographical data, which follows in Part III.

[1] *Who's Who in America,* published biannually by Marquis Who's Who, Inc., Chicago; *Current Biography,* published monthly and annually by H. L. Wilson Co., New York; *Forbes,* published biweekly by Malcolm S. Forbes, New York; *Fortune,* published monthly by Time-Life, Inc., New York; *Congressional Quarterly Weekly Report,* published weekly by Congressional Quarterly, Inc., Washington.

Part III, "The Structure of Institutional Elites," is a systematic investigation of institutional elites: interlocking and specialization, overlapping elite membership, recruitment paths, socioeconomic backgrounds, previous experience, racial and sexual bias, club membership and life styles, attitudes and opinions, competition and consensus, factionalism, and patterns of interaction in policy-making. Part III relies heavily on computerized biographical files, which we compiled at Florida State University over an extended time period on several thousand top institutional elites. What is suggested in a general way about characteristics of America's elites in Part II, is subject to more careful systematic analysis in Part III.

The decision to "name names" was carefully considered. We knew that occupants of top institutional positions change over time, and that some of our information would be out of date by the time of publication. And with thousands of names, some mistakes are inevitable. But the biographical sketches provide "flesh and bones" to the statistical analysis—they "personalize" the numbers and percentages in our research. The men who run America *are* real people, and we know of no better way to impress our readers with this fact.

WHO'S RUNNING AMERICA?

PART 1

Power in American Society

One
MEN AT THE TOP

Great power in America is concentrated in a tiny handful of men. A few thousand individuals out of 200 million Americans decide about war and peace, wages and prices, consumption and investment, employment and production, law and justice, taxes and benefits, education and learning, health and welfare, advertising and communication, life and leisure. In all societies—primitive and advanced, totalitarian and democratic, capitalist and socialist—only a few men exercise great power. This is true whether such power is exercised in the name of "the people" or not.

Who's Running America? is about men at the top of the institutional structure in America—who they are, how much power they wield, how they came to power, and what they do with it. In a modern, complex, industrial society, power is concentrated in large institutions—corporations, banks, utilities, insurance companies, broadcasting networks, the White House, Congress and the Washington bureaucracy, the military establishment, the prestigious law firms, the foundations, and the universities. The men at the top of these institutions are the objects of our study in this book.

We want to ask such questions as: Who occupies the top positions of authority in America? How concentrated or dispersed is power in this nation? How do these institutional leaders attain their positions? What are their backgrounds, attitudes, and goals? What relationships exist among and between these men of power? How much cohesion or competition characterizes their relationships? Do they agree or disagree on crucial issues confronting the nation? How do they go about making important decisions or undertaking new programs or policies?

The Inevitability of Elites

An *elite* is the few who have power in society; the *masses* are the many who do not. We shall call our men of power "elites" because they possess formal authority over large institutions which shape the lives of all of us.

America is by no means unique in its concentration of great power in the hands of a few. The universality of elites is a prominent theme in the works of scholars throughout the ages. The Italian sociologist, Vilfredo Pareto, put it succinctly: "Every people is governed by an elite, by a chosen element of the population."[1]

Traditional social theorizing about elites views them as essential, functional components of social organization. The necessity of elites derives from the general need for *order* in society. Whenever human beings find themselves living together, they establish a set of ordered relationships so that they can know how others around them will behave. Without ordered behavior, it would be impossible to live in a social world. Among these ordered relationships is the expectation that a few people will make decisions on behalf of the group. Even in primitive societies, someone has to decide when the hunt will begin, how it will proceed, and what will be done with the catch.

Nearly two centuries ago Alexander Hamilton defended the existence of the elite by writing, "All communities divide themselves into the few and the many. The first are the rich and well-born, the other the masses of people. The voice of the people has been said to be the voice of God; and however generally this maxim has been quoted and believed, it is not true in fact. The people are turbulent and changing; they seldom judge or determine right."[2] The Italian political scientist Gaetano Mosca agreed, saying that the elite, "always the less numerous, performs all of the political functions, monopolizes power, and enjoys the advantages that power brings, whereas the second, the more numerous class, is directed and controlled by the first, in a manner that is now more or less

[1] V. Pareto, *Mind and Society* (New York: Harcourt, Brace, and Co., 1935), p. 246.

[2] A. Hamilton, *Records of the Federal Convention of 1797*.

legal, now more or less arbitrary and violent." [3] Contemporary social scientists have echoed the same theme. Sociologist Robert Lynd writes:

> It is the necessity in each society—if it is to be a society, not a rabble—to order the relations of men and their institutional ways of achieving needed ends. . . . Organized power exists—always and everywhere, in societies large or small, primitive or modern—because it performs the necessary function of establishing and maintaining the version of order by which a given society in a given time and place lives.[4]

Political scientists Harold Lasswell and Daniel Lerner are even more explicit: "The discovery that in all large-scale societies the decisions at any given time are typically in the hands of a small number of people," confirms a basic fact: Government is always government by the few, whether in the name of the few, the one, or the many." [5]

Elitism is *not* a result of inadequate education of the masses, or of poverty, or of a "military-industrial complex," or of capitalist control of the mass media, or of any special problem in society. The necessity for leadership in social organizations applies universally. Robert Michels, who as a student was active in socialist politics in Europe in the early 1900s, concluded that elitism was *not* a product of capitalism. *All* large organizations—political parties, labor unions, governments—are oligarchies, even radical *socialist* parties. In Michels' words, "He who says organization says oligarchy." Michels explains his famous "iron law of oligarchy" as a characteristic of *any* social system.[6]

Thus, the elitist character of American society is not a product of political conspiracy, capitalist exploitation, or any specific malfunction of democracy. *All* societies are elitist. There cannot be large institutions without great power being concentrated within the hands of the few at the summit of these institutions—the men at the top.

The Institutional Basis of Power

Power is not an attribute of individuals, but rather of social organizations. Power is not an individual act, but rather the potential for control in society that is achieved by occupying roles in the social system. This

[3] G. Mosca, *The Ruling Class* (New York: McGraw-Hill Book Co., 1939), p. 50.

[4] Robert Lynd, "Power in American Society," in Authur Kornhauser, ed., *Problems of Power in American Society* (Detroit: Wayne State University Press, 1957), pp. 3–4.

[5] Harold Lasswell and Daniel Lerner, *The Comparative Study of Elites* (Stanford: Stanford University Press, 1952), p. 7.

[6] Robert Michels, *Political Parties: A Sociological Study of the Oligarchical Tendencies of Modern Democracy* (1915) (New York: Free Press, 1962), p. 70.

notion reflects Max Weber's classic formulation of the definition of power:

> In general, we understand by "power" the *chance* of a man or of a number of men to realize their own will in a communal act even against the resistance of others who are participating in the action.[7]

"Chance" means that one must have the "capacity" to effect his will before he can be said to have power. Viewed in this fashion, power is not so much the *act* of control as the *potential to act*—the social expectation that such control is possible and legitimate—that defines power.

Power is simply the capacity or potential of persons in certain roles to make decisions that affect the conduct of others in the social system. Sociologist Robert O. Schultze puts it in these words:

> . . . a few have emphasized that *act as such* rather than the *potential to act* is the crucial aspect of power. It seems far more sociologically sound to accept a Weberian definition which stresses the potential to act. Power may thus be conceived as an inherently group-linked property, an attribute of social statuses rather than of individual persons. . . . Accordingly, power will denote the *capacity* or *potential* of persons *in certain statuses* to set conditions, make decisions, and/or take actions which are determinative for the existence of others within a given social system.[8]

Thus, elites are people who occupy power roles in society. In a modern, complex society, these roles are institutionalized; the elite are the individuals who occupy positions of authority in large institutions. Authority is the expected and legitimate capacity to direct, manage, and guide programs, policies, and activities of the major institutions of society.

It is true, of course, that not all power is institutionalized. Power can be exercised in transitory and informal groups and in interpersonal interactions. Power is exercised, for example, when a mugger stops a pedestrian on the street and forces him to give up his wallet, or when a political assassin murders a president. But great power is found only in institutional roles. C. Wright Mills, a socialist critic of the structure of power in American society, observed:

> No one . . . can be truly powerful unless he has access to the command of major institutions, for it is over these institutional means of power that the truly powerful are, in the first instance, powerful.[9]

[7] In Hans Gerth and C. Wright Mills, eds., *From Max Weber* (New York: Oxford University Press, 1946), p. 180.

[8] Robert O. Schultze, "The Bifurcation of Power in a Satellite City," in Morris Janowitz, ed., *Community Political Systems* (Glencoe: Free Press, 1961), p. 20.

[9] C. Wright Mills, *The Power Elite* (New York: Oxford University Press, 1956), p. 9.

Adolf A. Berle, who spent a lifetime studying private property and the American corporation, was equally impressed with the institutional basis of power:

> Power is invariably organized and transmitted through institutions.
> Top power holders must work through existing institutions, perhaps extending or modifying them, or must at once create new institutions. There is no other way of exercising power—unless it is limited to the range of the power holder's fist or his gun.[10]

Individuals do not become powerful simply because they have particular qualities, valuable skills, burning ambitions, or sparkling personalities. These assets may be helpful in gaining positions of power, but it is the position itself that gives an individual control over the activities of other individuals. This relationship between power and institutional authority in modern society is described by Mills:

> If we took the one hundred most powerful men in America, the one hundred wealthiest, and the one hundred most celebrated away from the institutional positions they now occupy, away from their resources of men and women and money, away from the media of mass communication . . . then they would be powerless and poor and uncelebrated. For power is not of a man. Wealth does not center in the person of the wealthy. Celebrity is not inherent in any personality. To be celebrated, to be wealthy, to have power, requires access to major institutions, for the institutional positions men occupy determine in large part their chances to have and to hold these valued experiences.[11]

Power, then, is an attribute of *roles* in a social system, not an attribute of individuals. People are powerful when they occupy positions of authority and control in social organizations. Once they occupy these positions, their power is felt as a result not only in their actions but in their failures to act as well. Both have great impact on the behaviors of others. Elites "are in positions to make decisions having major consequences. Whether they do or do not make such decisions is less important than the fact that they do occupy such pivotal positions: their failure to act, their failure to make a decision, is itself an act that is often of greater consequence than the decisions they do make."[12]

Political scientists Peter Bachrach and Morton S. Baratz have argued persuasively that individuals in top institutional positions exercise power whether they act overtly to influence particular decisions or

10 Adolf A. Berle, *Power* (New York: Harcourt, Brace and World, 1967), p. 92.
11 Mills, *The Power Elite*, p. 9.
12 Ibid., p. 4.

not.[13] They contend that when the social, economic, and political values of those people at the top, or more importantly, the structure of the institutions themselves, limit the scope of decision-making to only those issues which do not threaten top elites, then power is being exercised. Bachrach and Baratz refer to this phenomenon as "*non*–decision-making." A has power over B when he succeeds in suppressing issues that might in their resolution be detrimental to A's preferences. In short, the institutional structure of our society (and the people at the top of that structure) encourages the development of some kinds of public issues, but prevents other kinds of issues from ever being considered by the American public. Such "non-decision-making" provides still another reason for studying institutional leadership.

Power as Decision-Making: An Alternative View

It is our contention, then, that great power is institutionalized, that it derives from roles in social organizations, and that individuals who occupy top institutional positions possess power whether they act directly to influence particular decisions or not. But these views—often labeled as "elitist"—are not universally shared among social scientists. We are aware that our institutional approach to power conflicts with the approach of many scholars who believe that power can only be viewed in a decision-making context.

This alternative approach to power—often labeled as "pluralist" —defines power as *active participation in decision-making.* Persons are said to have power *only* when they participate directly in particular decisions. Pluralist scholars would object to our presumption that people who occupy institutional positions and who have formal authority over economic, governmental, or social affairs necessarily have power. Pluralists differentiate between the "potential" for power (which is generally associated with top institutional positions) and "actual" power (which assumes active participation in decision-making). Political scientist Robert A. Dahl writes:

> Suppose a set of individuals in a political system has the following property: there is a high probability that if they agree on a key political alternative, and if they all act in some specified way, then that alternative will be chosen. We may say of such a group that it has a high *potential* for control. . . . But a *potential* for control is not, except in a peculiarly Hobbesian world, equivalent to *actual* control.[14]

[13] Peter Bachrach and Morton S. Baratz, "Decisions and Non-Decisions," *American Political Science Review,* 57 (September 1963), 632–42.

[14] Robert A. Dahl, "Critique of the Ruling Elite Model," *American Political Science Review,* 52 (June 1958), 66. (Italics mine.)

Pluralists contend that the potential for power is not power itself. Power occurs in individual interactions: "A has power over B to the extent that he can get B to do something that B would not otherwise do." [15] Nothing categorical should be assumed about power in high office. Top institutional officeholders may or may not exercise power—their "power" depends upon their active participation in particular decisions. They may choose not to participate in particular decisions; their influence may be limited to particular kinds of decisions; they may be constrained by formal and informal checks on their discretion; they may be forced to respond to the demands of individuals or groups within or outside the institutions they lead; they may have little real discretion in their choice among alternative courses of action.

Pluralists would argue that research into institutional leadership can describe at best only the *potential* for control that exists within American society. They would insist that research on national leadership proceed by careful examination of a series of important national decisions—to identify the individuals who took an active part in these decisions and to obtain a full account of their behavior in the course of these decisions. Political scientist Nelson Polsby, a former student of Robert A. Dahl at Yale, reflects the interests of pluralists in observed decisional events:

> How can one tell, after all, whether or not an actor is powerful unless some sequence of events, competently observed, attests to his power? If these events take place, then the power of the actor is not "potential" but actual. If these events do not occur, then what grounds have we to suppose that the actor is powerful? [16]

And, indeed, much of the best research and writing in political science has proceeded by studying specific cases in the uses of power.

Pluralism, of course, is more than a definition of power and a method of study—it is an integrated body of theory that seeks to reaffirm the fundamental democratic character of American society. Pluralism arose in response to criticisms of the American political system to the effect that individual participation in a large, complex, bureaucratic society was increasingly difficult. Traditional notions of democracy had stressed individual participation of all citizens in the decisions that shape their own lives. But it was clear to scholars of all persuasions that relatively few individuals in America have any *direct* impact on national decision-making.

Pluralism developed as an ideology designed to reconcile the *ideals*

15 Robert A. Dahl, "The Concept of Power," *Behavioral Science*, 2 (1957), 202.

16 Nelson Polsby, *Community Power and Political Theory* (New Haven: Yale University Press, 1963), p. 60.

of democracy with the *realities* of a large scale, industrial, technocratic society. Jack L. Walker writes that the "principal aim" of the pluralists "has been to make the theory of democracy more realistic, to bring it into closer correspondence with empirical reality. They are convinced that the classical theory does not account for 'much of the real machinery' by which the system operates." [17]

Pluralists recognize that an elite few, rather than the masses, rule in America and that "it is difficult—nay impossible—to see how it could be otherwise in large political systems." [18] However, the pluralists reassert the essentially democratic character of America by arguing that:

1. While individuals do not participate directly in decision-making, they can join organized *groups* and make their influence felt through group participation.

2. There is competition between leadership groups that help protect the individual—countervailing centers of power, which check each other and guard against abuse of power.

3. Individuals can choose between competing groups in elections.

4. Leadership groups are not closed; new groups can be formed and gain access to the political system.

5. There are multiple leadership groups in society—"polyarchy." Leaders who exercise power over some kinds of decisions do not necessarily exercise power over other kinds of decisions.

6. Public policy may not be majority preference, but it is the rough equilibrium of group influence and therefore a reasonable approximation of society's preferences.

We are committed in this volume to the study of the institutional structure of American society, for the reasons cited earlier. It is *not* our purpose to assert the superiority of our approach to power in America over the approaches recommended by others. We do *not* intend to debate the merits of "pluralism" or "elitism" as political philosophies. Abstract arguments over conceptualizations, definitions, and method of study already abound in the literature on power. Rather we hope to learn what we can about *institutional* power in America. We intend to present systematic evidence about the concentration of resources in the nation's largest institutions, to find out who occupies top positions in these institutions, to explore interlocking and convergence among these top position-holders, to learn how they rose to their positions, to investigate the extent of their consensus or disagreement over the major issues con-

[17] Jack L. Walker, "A Critique of the Elitist Theory of Democracy," *American Political Science Review,* 60 (June 1966), 286.

[18] Robert A. Dahl, "Power, Pluralism and Democracy," paper delivered at the Annual Meeting of the American Political Science Association, 1966, p. 3.

fronting the nation, to explore the extent of competition and factionalism among various segments of the nation's institutional leadership, and to learn how institutional leadership interacts in national policy-making.

We hope to avoid elaborate theorizing about power, pluralism, and elitism. We propose to present what we believe to be interesting data on national institutional elites and to permit our readers to relate it to their own theory or theories of power.

Identifying Positions of Power

A great deal has been said about "the power elite," "the ruling class," "the liberal establishment," "the military-industrial complex," "the rich and the super-rich," and so on. But even though many of these notions are interesting and insightful, we never really encounter a systematic definition of precisely *who* these people are, how we can identify them, how they came to power, and what they do with their power.

Admittedly, the systematic study of power and elites is a frustrating task. Political scientists Herbert Kaufman and Victor Jones once observed:

> There is an elusiveness about power that endows it with an almost ghostly quality. It seems to be all around us, yet this is "sensed" with some sixth means of reception rather than with the five ordinary senses. We "know" what it is, yet we encounter endless difficulties in trying to define it. We can "tell" whether one person or group is more powerful than another, yet we cannot measure power. It is as abstract as time yet as real as a firing squad.[19]

We agree that power is elusive and that elites are not easy to identify, particularly in a society like ours. Scholars have encountered great difficulty in finding a specific working definition of a national elite—a definition that can be used to actually identify men of power. But this is the necessary starting place for any serious inquiry into power in America.

So our first task is to develop an operational *definition* of a national elite. We must formulate a definition that is consistent with our theoretical notions about the institutional basis of power that enables us to identify, by name and position, those individuals who possess great power in America.

Our "men at the top" will be individuals who occupy *the top*

19 Herbert Kaufman and Victor Jones, "The Mystery of Power," *Public Administration Review,* 14 (Summer 1954), 205.

positions in the institutional structure of American society. These are the individuals who possess the formal authority to direct, manage, and guide programs, policies, and activities of the major corporate, governmental, legal, educational, civic, and cultural institutions in the nation. Our definition of a national elite, then, is consistent with the notion that great power in America resides in large institutions.

For purposes of analysis in this book, we have divided society into three sectors—corporate, governmental, and public interest.

In the *corporate sector,* our operational definition of the elite is *those individuals who occupy formal positions of authority in institutions that control over half of the nation's total corporate assets.* The corporate sector includes industrial corporations; utilities, transportation, and communications; banking; and insurance. Our procedure in identifying the largest corporations was to rank corporations by the size of their assets, and then to cumulate these assets, moving from the top of the rankings down until roughly 50 percent of the nation's total assets in each field were included. (See Tables 2-1, 2-2, 2-3, and 2-4 in the next chapter.) Then we identified by name the presidents and directors of these corporations. This procedure produced a list of 3,572 names of individuals at the top of the corporate world in 1970.

In the *governmental sector,* the operational definition of the elite is *those individuals who occupy formal positions of authority in the major civilian and military bureaucracies of the national government.* Positions of authority in the governmental sector were defined as the president and vice-president; secretaries, under secretaries, and assistant secretaries of all executive departments; White House presidential advisers and ambassadors-at-large; congressional committee chairpersons and ranking minority committee members in the House and Senate; House and Senate majority and minority party leaders and Whips; Supreme Court justices; members of the Federal Reserve Board and the Council of Economic Advisers. This group totaled 227 in 1970. The military bureaucracy—because of its special theoretical interest and prominence in traditional elite literature—is included in the governmental sector. (The military is also treated separately where appropriate.) Positions of authority in the military include both civilian offices and top military commands: secretaries, under secretaries, and assistant secretaries of the Departments of the Army, Navy, Air Force; all four-star generals and admirals in the Army, Navy, Air Force, and Marine Corps, including the chairman of the Joint Chiefs of Staff, the chiefs of staff and vice-chiefs of staff of the Army and Air Force, the chief and vice-chief of Naval Operations, and the commanding officers of the major military commands. In 1970 there were 18 Army generals, 13 Air Force generals, 9 admirals, and 2 Marine generals, in addition to civilian officials, for a total of 59 positions.

In the *public interest sector,* our definition of the elite is *those individuals who occupy formal positions of authority in the mass media, the prestigious law firms, the major philanthropic foundations, the leading universities, and the recognized national civic and cultural organizations.* The identification of these institutions involves some subjective judgments. These judgments can be defended, but we recognize that other judgments could be made. In the *mass media* we include the three television networks: CBS, NBC, and ABC; *The New York Times; Time, Inc.; Washington Post-Newsweek;* Associated Press and United Press International wire services; and ten newspaper chains which account for one-third of the nation's daily newspaper circulation. There are 213 presidents and directors of these institutions. Because of the rapidly growing influence of the mass media in America's elite structure, we have devoted a special chapter to "The Newsmakers." Other "public interest" elites are considered together under the general heading of "The Civic Establishment." *In education,* the twelve colleges and universities identified in our study do not control any significant proportion of *all* higher education resources in the nation. However, they do control 50 percent of all *private endowment funds* in higher education (this was the formal basis of their selection), and they are consistently ranked among the most "prestigious" private colleges and universities. Their presidents and trustees numbered 656 in 1970. *Foundations:* according to *The Foundation Directory,* the nation's top twelve foundations control 38.6 percent of all foundation assets. The Directory does not identify foundations by size of assets beyond these twelve leading institutions. There are a total of 121 directors of these top foundations. Identifying top positions in the field of *law* is an even more subjective task. Our definition of positions of authority includes the 176 senior partners of twenty-eight top New York and Washington law firms. Top positions in *civic and cultural affairs* can only be identified by qualitative evaluation of the prestige and influence of various well-known organizations. We have identified twelve leading organizations, including the Brookings Institution, Council on Foreign Relations, and the Committee on Economic Development, among civic associations; and the Metropolitan Museum of Art, the Metropolitan Opera, the Lincoln Center for the Performing Arts, and the Smithsonian Institution among cultural institutions. In 1970 these twelve organizations were legally governed by 392 individuals.

Any effort to operationalize a concept as broad as a national institutional elite is bound to generate discussion over the inclusion or exclusion of specific sectors, institutions, or positions. (Why law, but not medicine? Why not religious institutions, or labor unions? Why not governors or mayors of big cities?) *Systematic* research on national elites is still very exploratory, and there are no explicit guidelines. Our choices involve many subjective judgments. But let us see what we can learn about concentration, specialization, and interlocking using the definitions above; perhaps other researchers can improve upon our attempt to operationalize this elusive notion of a national institutional elite. In the analysis to follow, we will present findings for our aggregate corporate, governmental, and public interest elites, and for specific sectors of these elites. Findings for specific sectors will be free of whatever bias might exist in the aggregate elite, owing to our judgments about the inclusion or exclusion of specific sectors.

Dimensions of America's Elite: The Top Five Thousand

Our definition of a national institutional elite results in the identification of 5,416 elite positions:

Corporate Sector	
Industrial Corporations	1534
Utilities, Communications, Transportation	476
Banking	1200
Insurance	362
Total	3572
Governmental Sector	
U.S. Government	227
Legislative, Executive, Judicial, Military	59
Total	286
Public Interest Sector	
Mass Media	213
Education	656
Foundation	121
Law	176
Civic and Cultural	392
Total	1558
Total	5416

These top positions, taken collectively, control half of the nation's industrial assets; half of all assets in communication, transportation, and utilities; half of all banking assets, two-thirds of all insurance assets. They control the television networks, the influential news agencies, and the major newspaper chains. They control nearly 40 percent of all the assets of private foundations and half of all private university endowments. They direct the nation's largest and best-known New York and Washington law firms. They direct the nation's major civic and cultural organizations. They occupy key federal governmental positions in the executive, legislative, and judicial branches. And they occupy all the top command positions in the Army, Navy, Air Force, and Marines.

These aggregate figures—roughly 5000 positions—are themselves important indicators of the concentration of authority and control in American society. Of course, these figures are the direct product of our specific definition of top institutional positions. Yet these aggregate statistics provide us, for the first time, with an explicit definition and quantitative estimate of the size of the national elite in America.

Some Questions for Research

Our definition of America's institutional elite provides a starting place for exploring some of the central questions confronting students of power. How concentrated are institutional resources in America? How much concentration exists in industry and finance, in government, in the mass media, in education, in the foundations, and in civic and cultural affairs? Who are the people at the top of the nation's institutional structure? How did they get there? Did they inherit their positions or work their way up through the ranks of the institutional hierarchy? What are their general attitudes, beliefs, and goals? What do they think about their own power? Do elites in America generally agree about major national goals and the general directions of foreign and domestic policy, and limit their disagreements to the *means* of achieving these goals and the details of policy implementation? Or do leaders disagree over fundamental *ends* and values and the future character of American society?

Are institutional elites in America "interlocked" or "specialized"? Is there convergence at the "top" of the institutional structure in America, with the same group of people dominating decision-making in industry, finance, education, government, the mass media, foundations, and civic and cultural affairs? Or is there a separate elite in each sector of society with little or no overlap in authority? Are there opportunities to rise to the top of the leadership structure for individuals from both sexes, all classes, races, religious, and ethnic groups, through multiple career paths in different sectors of society? Or are opportunities to acquire key leadership roles generally limited to white, Anglo-Saxon, Protestant, upper- and upper-middle class males whose careers are based primarily in industry and finance? Is the nation's institutional leadership recruited primarily from private "name" prep schools and "Ivy League" universities? Do leaders join the same clubs, intermarry, and enjoy the same lifestyles? Or is there diversity in educational backgrounds, social ties, club memberships, and lifestyles among the elite?

How much competition and conflict takes place among America's institutional elite? Are there clear-cut factions within the nation's leadership struggling for pre-eminence and power, and if so, what are the underlying sources of this factionalism? Do different segments of the nation's institutional elite accommodate each other in a system of bargaining, negotiation, and compromising based on a widely shared consensus of values?

How do institutional elites make national policy? Are there established institutions and procedures for elite interaction, communication, and consensus-building on national policy questions? Or are such questions decided in a relatively unstructured process of competition, bargaining, and compromise among a large number of diverse interested groups and individuals? Do the "proximate policy-makers"—the president, Congress, courts—respond to mass opinion, or do they respond primarily to initiatives originating from elite organizations, foundations, and civic associations?

These are the questions that we will tackle in the pages to follow. In Part II, "Institutional Leadership in America," we will describe the concentration of power in a limited number of institutions in various sectors of society. We will also describe in general terms the men who occupy top positions in these institutions; we will provide a number of brief biographical sketches suggestive of the characteristics of these elites —who they are and how they got there. These sketches are designed to "personalize" the statistical analysis that follows. In Part III, "The Structure of Institutional Elites," we will examine the questions posed above in a more systematic fashion, employing computerized data files on our top five thousand elites.

PART 2

Institutional Leadership in America

Two

THE CORPORATE DIRECTORS

A great deal of power is organized into large economic institutions—industrial corporations, banks, utilities, and investment firms. Control of economic resources provides a continuous and important base of power in any society. Economic organizations decide what will be produced, how it will be produced, how much will be produced, how much it will cost, how many people will be employed, who will be employed and what their wages will be. They determine how goods and services will be distributed, what technology will be developed, what profits will be made and how they will be distributed, how much money will be available for loans, what interest rates will be charged, and many similarly important questions.

Obviously, these decisions affect our lives as much as or perhaps even more than those typically made by governments. We cannot draw inferences about a "national power structure" from studies of governmental decision-making alone. Studies of power in society must include economic power.

The Concentration of Economic Power

Economic power in America is highly concentrated. Indeed, only about 3500 individuals—two one-thousandths of one percent of the population—exercise formal authority over half of the nation's industrial assets, nearly half of all banking assets, half of all assets in communications, transportation and utilities, and two-thirds of all insurance assets. These individuals are the presidents and directors of the largest corporations in these fields. The reason for this concentration of power in the hands of so few people is found in the concentration of industrial and financial assets in a small number of giant corporations. The following statistics can only suggest the scale and concentration of modern corporate enterprise in America.

There are more than 200,000 *industrial corporations* in the United States with total assets in 1970 of $554 billion. But the 100 corporations listed in Table 2-1 control 50 percent ($290 billion) of all industrial assets. The five largest industrial corporations—Exxon (Standard Oil of New Jersey), General Motors, Texaco, Ford Motors, and Gulf Oil—control 10 percent of all industrial assets themselves.

Concentration of resources among industrial corporations is increasing over time. In a twenty-year period the proportion of all industrial assets controlled by the top 100 corporations grew as follows:

1950	1955	1960	1965	1970
39.8%	44.3%	46.4%	46.5%	52.3%

Concentration in *transportation, communications, and utilities* is even greater than in industry. Thirty-three corporations (see Table 2-2), out of 67,000 in these fields, control 50 per cent of the nation's assets in airlines and railroads, communications, and electricity and gas. This sector of the nation's economy is dominated by the American Telephone and Telegraph Company (AT&T)—by total assets the single largest corporation in the U.S.

The financial world is equally concentrated. The fifty largest banks (see Table 2-3), out of 13,500 *banks* serving the nation control 48 percent of all banking assets. Three banks (Bank America, First National City, and Chase Manhattan) control 14 percent of all banking assets themselves. In the *insurance* field, 18 companies (see Table 2-4) out of 1,790 control two-thirds of all insurance assets. Two companies (Prudential and Metropolitan) control over one-quarter of all insurance assets.

Control over the resources of these corporations rests in their presi-

Table 2-1. Largest Industrial Corporations, by Size of Assets, 1970

Rank	Name	Assets	Cumulative Percent
01	Standard Oil (N.J.) (Exxon)	19.2	3.4
02	General Motors	14.2	5.8
03	Texaco	9.9	7.6
04	Ford Motor	9.9	9.3
05	Gulf Oil	8.7	10.8
06	IBM	8.5	12.3
07	Mobil Oil	7.9	13.7
08	Gen. Telephone	7.7	15.0
09	ITT	6.7	16.2
10	Standard Oil (Calif.)	6.6	17.3
11	U. S. Steel	6.3	18.4
12	General Electric	6.3	19.5
13	Standard Oil (Ind.)	5.4	20.5
14	Chrysler	4.8	21.3
15	Shell Oil	4.6	22.1
16	Atlantic Richfield	4.4	22.9
17	Tenneco	4.3	23.6
18	Western Electric	3.7	24.3
19	E. I. DuPont	3.6	24.9
20	Union Carbide	3.6	25.5
21	Westinghouse Electric	3.4	26.1
22	Bethlehem Steel	3.3	26.7
23	Phillips Petroleum	3.1	27.2
24	Eastman Kodak	3.0	27.8
25	Continental Oil	3.0	28.3
26	Goodyear	3.0	28.8
27	RCA	2.9	29.3
28	Dow Chemical	2.8	29.8
29	Sun Oil	2.8	30.3
30	Alcoa	2.6	30.8
31	Boeing	2.6	31.2
32	Ling-Temco-Vought	2.6	31.7
33	Occidental	2.6	32.1
34	Union Oil of Calif.	2.5	32.6
35	Boise Cascade	2.3	33.0
36	International Harvester	2.2	33.3
37	Cities Service	2.2	33.7
38	Gulf & Western	2.2	34.1
39	Monsanto	2.1	34.5
40	Firestone	2.1	34.8
41	International Paper	2.0	35.2
42	Honeywell	2.0	35.5
43	American Brands	2.0	35.9
44	Armco Steel	2.0	36.2
45	Getty Oil	1.9	36.6
46	Litton Industries	1.9	36.9
47	R. J. Reynolds	1.9	37.2
48	Xerox	1.9	37.6
49	Procter & Gamble	1.9	37.9
50	Reynolds Metals	1.8	38.2
51	Republic Steel	1.8	38.5
52	Caterpillar Tractor	1.8	38.8
53	Weyerhaeuser	1.8	39.2

Rank	Name	Assets	Cumulative Percent
54	Anaconda	1.8	39.5
55	McDonnell Douglas	1.8	39.8
56	Standard Oil (Ohio)	1.7	40.1
57	Kennecott Copper	1.7	40.4
58	Georgia-Pacific	1.7	40.7
59	Rapid-American	1.7	41.0
60	National Cash Register	1.6	41.2
61	Singer	1.6	41.5
62	Kaiser Aluminum	1.6	41.8
63	Celanese	1.6	42.1
64	Allied Chemical	1.6	42.4
65	W. R. Grace	1.6	42.6
66	National Steel	1.6	42.9
67	United Aircraft	1.5	43.2
68	Continental Cars	1.5	43.4
69	N. American Rockwell	1.5	43.7
70	Lykes-Youngstown	1.5	44.0
71	Deere	1.5	44.2
72	Minn. Mining & Mfg.	1.5	44.5
73	American Can	1.5	44.8
74	Burroughs	1.4	45.0
75	Sperry Rand	1.4	45.2
76	Burlington Industries	1.4	45.5
77	Inland Steel	1.4	45.7
78	General Foods	1.4	46.0
79	Marathon Oil	1.3	46.2
80	Signal Companies	1.3	46.4
81	Avco	1.3	46.7
82	Owens-Illinois	1.3	46.9
83	Uniroyal	1.3	47.1
84	B. F. Goodrich	1.3	47.3
85	Control Data	1.3	47.6
86	PPG Industries	1.3	47.8
87	Ill. Central Ind.	1.3	48.0
88	International Utilities	1.2	48.2
89	American Standard	1.2	48.4
90	Philip Morris	1.2	48.6
91	Greyhound	1.2	48.9
92	Borden	1.2	49.1
93	U.S. Plywood	1.2	49.3
94	City Investing	1.2	49.5
95	Amerada Hess	1.1	49.7
96	Olin	1.1	49.9
97	General Dynamics	1.1	50.1
98	United Brands	1.1	50.3
99	TRW	1.1	50.4
100	American Metal Climax	1.1	50.6
		290.1	

Total Number of Manufacturing Corporations 202,920

Total Manufacturing Assets in United States $572.9 billion

Table 2-2. Largest Transportation, Utilities, and Communication Corporations, by Size of Assets, 1970

Rank	Name	Assets	Cumulative Percent
01	AT & T	49.6	19.0
02	Penn. Central	6.9	21.6
03	Consolidate Edison	4.4	23.3
04	Pacific Gas & Elec.	4.3	25.0
05	Commonwealth Edison	3.4	26.3
06	American Electric	3.2	27.5
07	Southern Cal. Edison	3.2	28.7
08	Southern Co.	3.1	29.9
09	Southern Pacific	3.1	31.1
10	Burlington Northern	2.9	32.3
11	Norfolk & W. Ry.	2.8	33.3
12	Union Pacific	2.8	34.4
13	Chesapeake & Ohio Ry.	2.7	35.4
14	PSE & G	2.6	36.4
15	Santa Fe Industries	2.3	37.3
16	United Airlines	2.2	38.1
17	General Public Utilities	2.1	38.9
18	Philadelphia Electric	2.1	39.7
19	Columbia Gas System	2.1	40.5
20	Consumers Power	2.0	41.3
21	Detroit Edison	2.0	42.1
22	El Paso Natural Gas	1.9	42.8
23	Pan American World Airway	1.8	43.5
24	Virginia Elec. & Power	1.8	44.2
25	Duke Power	1.9	44.9
26	Texas Eastern Trans.	1.8	45.6
27	Middle South Utilities	1.7	46.2
28	Pennzoil United	1.7	46.9
29	Texas Utilities	1.7	47.5
30	American Natural Gas	1.7	48.2
31	Niagara Mohawk Power	1.6	48.8
32	Southern Railroad	1.6	49.4
33	American Airlines	1.5	50.0
		31.4	

Total Number of Corps. 67,311

Total Assets of Trans. & Service Industries $261.0 billion

dents and directors and the holders of what are called "control blocks" of stock. Corporate power does not rest in the hands of the masses of corporate employees, or even in the hands of the millions of middle- and upper-class Americans who own corporate stock. A. A. Berle, Jr., a corporation lawyer and corporate director who has written extensively on the modern corporation, states,

> The control system in today's corporations, when it does not lie solely in the directors as in the American Telephone and Telegraph Company, lies in a combination of the directors of a so-called control block [of stock]

Table 2-3. Largest Commercial Banks, by Size of Assets, 1970

Rank	Name	Assets	Cumulative Percent
01	Bank America	29.7	5.2
02	First National City Corp.	25.8	9.6
03	Chase Manhattan	24.5	13.9
04	Mfrs. Hanover	12.7	16.1
05	J. P. Morgan	12.1	18.2
06	Western Bancorp.	11.4	20.2
07	Chemical N. Y. Corp.	11.1	22.1
08	Bankers Trust	9.9	23.8
09	Conill Corp.	9.0	25.4
10	Security Pacific	8.0	26.8
11	First Chicago Corp.	8.0	28.1
12	Marine Midland	7.6	29.5
13	Charter New York	6.3	30.6
14	Wells Fargo	6.2	31.6
15	Crocker Nat'l.	6.0	32.7
16	Mellon Nat'l. B&T	5.7	33.7
17	Nat'l. Bank of Detroit	5.2	34.6
18	First Nat'l. of Boston	4.7	35.4
19	First Bank (Minn.)	4.4	36.1
20	N. W. Bancorp.	4.3	36.9
21	Franklin N.Y.	3.5	37.5
22	First Pennsylvania	3.3	38.1
23	Bank of New York	3.1	38.6
24	Unionamerica	2.7	39.1
25	Cleveland Trust	2.6	39.5
26	Rep. Nat'l. Bank of Dallas	2.6	40.0
27	PNB (Philadelphia)	2.6	40.4
28	Seattle—First Nat'l. Bank	2.5	40.9
29	Girard Co. (Philadelphia)	2.5	41.3
30	Wachovia (Win. Sal.)	2.3	41.7
31	Detroit Bank & Trust	2.3	42.1
32	First Wisconsin	2.2	42.5
33	Nat'l. Bank of N. America	2.2	42.9
34	Mfrs. Nat'l. Bank	2.2	43.2
35	Nortrust (Chicago)	2.1	43.6
36	First Nat'l., Dallas	2.1	44.0
37	Harris Trust	2.1	44.3
38	Pittsburgh National	2.0	44.7
39	Lincoln First	2.0	45.0
40	Bank of Calif. (S.F.)	2.0	45.4
41	Valley National	1.9	45.7
42	Citizens & Southern Nat'l. (Atlanta)	1.9	46.0
43	U. S. Bancorp. (Port.)	1.8	46.3
44	BancOhio	1.8	46.7
45	Shawmut (Bos.)	1.7	47.0
46	NCNB (Charlotte)	1.7	47.2
47	Fidelity Penn. (Phil.)	1.7	47.5
48	Nat'l. City (Cleveland)	1.6	47.8
49	Marine BkCorp. (Seattle)	1.5	48.1
50	Commonwealth (Detroit)	1.5	48.3
		278.6	

Total Number of Banks in United States 13,511

Total Banking Assets in United States $576.3 billion

Table 2-4. Largest Insurance Companies, by Size of Assets, 1970

Rank	Name	Assets	Cumulative Percent
01	Prudential Insurance Co.	29.1	14.0
02	Metropolitan Life	27.9	27.5
03	Equitable Life	14.4	34.4
04	New York Life	10.7	39.6
05	John Hancock	10.0	44.4
06	Aetna Life	7.2	47.9
07	Northwestern Mutual	6.1	50.8
08	Connecticut General Life	5.1	53.3
09	Travelers Insurance Co.	4.7	55.6
10	Mass. Mutual Life	4.3	57.6
11	Mutual Life of New York	3.7	59.4
12	New England Mutual Life	3.5	61.1
13	Connecticut Mutual	2.8	62.5
14	Mutual Benefit Life	2.6	63.7
15	Penn. Mutual Life	2.4	64.9
16	Teachers Ins. & Ann.	2.3	66.0
17	Lincoln National Life	2.3	67.1
18	Bankers Life	2.0	68.1
		141.1	

Total Number of Life Insurance Companies 1,790
Total Life Insurance Assets in United States $207.3 billion

> plus the directors themselves. For practical purposes, therefore, the control or power element in most large corporations rests in its group of directors, and it is autonomous—or autonomous if taken together with a control block. . . . This is a self-perpetuating oligarchy.[1]

The power of stockholders over corporations is a legal fiction. Stockholders are seldom able to replace management. When confronted with mismanagement, stockholders simply sell their stock rather than try to challenge the powers of management. Berle describes this situation as follows:

> Management control is a phrase meaning merely that no large concentrated stockholding exists which maintains a close working relationship with the management or is capable of challenging it, so that the board of directors may regularly expect a majority, composed of small and scattered holdings, to follow their lead. Thus, they need not consult with anyone when making up their slate of directors, and may simply request their stockholders to sign and send in a ceremonial proxy. They select their own successors. . . . Nominal power still resides in the stockholders; actual power in the board of directors.[2]

[1] A. A. Berle, Jr., *Economic Power and a Free Society* (New York: Fund for the Republic, 1958), p. 10.

[2] A. A. Berle, Jr., *Power Without Property* (New York: Harcourt, Brace & World, 1959), p. 73.

The Corporate Directors

Who are the men at the top of the nation's corporate structure? Let us begin with some brief sketches of a few selected corporate leaders. Later in this volume we will examine recruitment patterns, interlocking and specialization, social backgrounds, attitudes and opinions, cohesion and competition, and patterns of interaction. But let us first get a general notion of *who the men at the top are.*

David Rockefeller. Chairman of the board of the Chase Manhattan Bank. Youngest of five sons of John D. Rockefeller, Jr.; heir of the Standard Oil Co. (Exxon) fortune; grandson of John D. Rockefeller, Sr., who founded the company that made the Rockefeller family one of the richest in the world. Attended Lincoln School in New York, Harvard, The London School of Economics, and the University of Chicago (Ph.D. degree in economics). Also a member of the board of directors of the B. F. Goodrich Co., Rockefeller Bros., Inc., Equitable Life Insurance Co. Is a trustee of Rockefeller Institute of Medical Research, Council on Foreign Relations, Museum of Modern Art, Rockefeller Center, and Harvard College. One of the nation's richest men.

Richard King Mellon. Chairman of the board of Mellon National Bank and Trust Co.; a director of Aluminum Co. of America (Alcoa), General Motors Corp., Gulf Oil Corp., Koppers Co., Pennsylvania Co., and the Penn Central Railroad (before its bankruptcy). Attended Culver Military Academy and Princeton. Only son of Richard Beatly Mellon and grandson of Thomas Mellon, who established a fortune in Alcoa and Gulf Oil and banking. Uncle, Andrew Mellon, was secretary of the treasury under Presidents Harding, Coolidge, and Hoover. Mellon started as a messenger in father's bank; after the death of his father, accepted 34 directorships of major corporations as "head of the Mellon clan." Personally responsible for Pittsburgh's urban renaissance, principal creator of the "Golden Triangle" of that city. A trustee of Carnegie-Mellon University, Mellon Institute, and University of Pittsburgh. Personal wealth exceeds one-half billion dollars.

Amory Houghton. Chairman of the board, First National City Corp. Attended St. Paul's School and Harvard. Descendant of four generations of owners of Corning Glass Works. Father was ambassador to Germany under President Harding and ambassador to Great Britain under President Coolidge. Sometimes confused with his cousin, Arthur Amory Houghton, who now serves as chairman of the board of Corning Glass (and is also director of New York Life Insurance, United States Steel Corp., J. Pierpont Morgan Library, New York Philharmonic, Lincoln Center for Performing Arts, Metropolitan Museum of Art, and the New York Public Library). Served as president of Corning Glass before World War II, then switched to banking—first as a director and later chairman of the board of nation's second largest bank. Devoted a great deal of attention to the Boy Scouts of America (served as national president). Also served briefly as ambassador to France. Is a director of Metropolitan Life Insurance and Dow Corning Corp.; trustee of the University of Rochester, Brookings Institution, St. Paul's School, and Harvard University. Both he and his cousin Arthur are centimillionaires.

Henry Ford II. Chairman and chief executive of the Ford Motor Co. Eldest son of Edsel Bryan Ford (president of the company from 1918 to his death in 1943); grandson of Henry Ford, founder of the company. Attended Hotchkiss School and Yale University. Started in the automobile industry at age 25 as vice-president of Ford Motors; took over the presidency one year later. Is a director of General Foods Corp., trustee of the Ford Foundation. Brother, Benson Ford, is also a director of Ford Motor Co. and the Ford Foundation, and serves as a director of the American Safety Council and United Community Funds of America. Another brother, William Clay Ford, is president of the Detroit Lions professional football club and a director of the Girl Scouts of America and the Henry Ford Hospital. All of the Fords rank at top of nation's individual wealth-holders.

H. I. Romnes. Chairman of the board, AT&T. Attended public schools and the University of Wisconsin. Served as an engineer in Bell Laboratories for twenty-five years. Later, served as chief engineer, vice-president for operations and engineering, and president of Western Electric Co., before being named chairman of the board at age 59. Romnes is also a director of Chemical Bank of New York, United States Steel, Cities Service, Mutual Life Insurance of New York.

Ellmore C. Patterson. Chairman of the board of Morgan Guaranty Trust Co. Attended Lake Forest Academy and University of Chicago. Married to Ann Hude Choate, daughter of a prominent investment banker who was associate of J. P. Morgan & Co. Became vice-president of Morgan Guaranty Trust in 1951; executive vice-president in 1959, president in 1969, and chairman of the board in 1971. Also a director of Canadian Life Assurance Co., International Nickel, the Atcheson, Topeka & Sante Fe Railroad, and Standard Brands, Inc. Member of the New York State Banking Board; trustee of the Alfred P. Sloan Foundation, Sloan-Kettering Cancer Institute, Carnegie Endowment for International Peace, University of Chicago, and Council on Foreign Relations.

Albert L. Williams. President, IBM. Attended public schools and spent two years at Berkeley College. Spent six years as an accountant for state of Pennsylvania before becoming a salesman for IBM in 1936. Rose to the position of controller in 1942, treasurer in 1947, executive vice-president in 1954, and president in 1961. A director of General Motors Corp., Mobil Oil, First City Bank of New York, Eli Lilly and Co., and General Foods. Also a trustee of the Alfred P. Sloan Foundation.

It is clear from these sketches that some individuals gain corporate power through inheritance, while others come up through the ranks of corporate management. Men such as Rockefeller, Ford, Mellon, and Houghton largely inherited their position and power. Others, such as Romnes, Patterson, and Williams, rose to power through the ranks of management. In fact, we will see that a surprising percentage of top corporation leaders achieved their power that way.

The Managers: Climbing the Corporate Ladder

The top echelons of American corporate life are occupied primarily by men who have climbed the corporate ladder from relatively obscure and powerless bottom rungs. It is our rough estimate that only 12 percent of the 3500 presidents and directors of the top 100 corporations are heirs of wealthy families. The rest—the "managers"—owe their rise to power not to family connections, but to their own success in organizational life. Of course, these managers are overwhelmingly upper-middle-class and upper-class in social origin, and most attended "Ivy League" colleges and universities. (The social origin and background of top elites is discussed in Chapter 8.) The rise of the managers is a recent phenomenon. As recently as 1950, we estimate that 30 percent of the top corporate elite were heirs of wealthy families, compared to our figure of 12 percent for 1970. How can we explain the rise to power of the corporate managers?

Today the requirements of technology and planning have greatly increased the need in industry for specialized talent and skill in organization. Capital is something that a corporation can now supply to itself. There is little need for the old-style "tycoon." Thus, there has been a shift in power in the American economy from capital to organized intelligence, and we can reasonably expect that this shift will be reflected in the deployment of power in society at large. This is reflected in the decline of individual and family controlled large corporations and an increase in the percentage of large corporations controlled by management (see Table 2-5).

Table 2-5. Increase in Management Control of the 200 Largest Industrial Corporations and the Decline in Family Ownership

	1929		1963	
	Number of Corporations	*Percent of 200 Largest*	*Number of Corporations*	*Percent of 200 Largest*
Individual or Family:				
Private Ownership	12	6	0	0
Majority Ownership	10	5	5*	2.5
Minority Control	47	23.5	18	9
Control by Legal Device	41	20.5	8	4
Management Control	88	44	169	84.5
Receivership	2	1	0	0

*A&P, Duke, Power, Kaiser Industries, Sun Oil, TWA.

Source: Derived from figures supplied by Robert J. Larner, "Ownership and Control in the 200 Largest Nonfinancial Corporations, 1929 and 1963," *American Economic Review,* 66 (September, 1966), 777-87.

Individual capitalists are no longer essential to the accumulation of capital for investment. Approximately *three-fifths* of industrial capital now comes from retained earnings of corporations rather than from the investments of individual capitalists. Another *one-fifth* of industrial capital is borrowed, chiefly from banks. Even though the remaining *one-fifth* of the capital funds of industry comes from "outside" investments, the bulk of these funds are from large insurance companies, mutual funds, and pension trusts, rather than from individual investors. Thus, the individual capitalist investor is no longer in a position of dominance in American capital formation.

American capital is primarily administered and expended by managers of large corporations and financial institutions. Stockholders are supposed to have ultimate power over management, but as we have noted, individual stockholders seldom have any control over the activities of the corporations they own. Usually "management slates" for the board of directors are selected by management and automatically approved by stockholders. Occasionally banks and financial institutions and pension trust or mutual fund managers will get together to replace a management-selected board of directors. But more often than not, banks and trust funds sell their stock in corporations whose management they distrust rather than use the voting power of their stock to replace management. Generally, banks and trust funds vote their stock for the management slate. The policy of nonaction by institutional investors means that the directors and management of corporations whose stock they hold become increasingly self-appointed and unchallengeable; and this policy freezes absolute power in the corporate managements.

Most of the capital in America is owned not by individuals but by corporations, banks, insurance companies, mutual funds, investment companies, and pension trusts. Adolf A. Berle writes:

> Of the capital flowing into non-agricultural industry, 60 percent is internally generated through profits and depreciation funds (within corporations). Another 10 or 15 percent is handled through the investment staffs of insurance companies and pension trusts. Another 20 percent is borrowed from banks. Perhaps 5 percent represents individuals who have saved and chosen the application of their savings. This is the system. . . . The capital system is not in many aspects an open market system. It is an administered system.[3]

Liberal economist John Kenneth Galbraith summarizes the changes in America's economic elite:

> Seventy years ago the corporation was the instrument of its owners and a

[3] Ibid., p. 45.

projection of their personalities. The names of these principals—Carnegie, Rockefeller, Harriman, Mellon, Guggenheim, Ford—were well known across the land. They are still known, but for the art galleries and philanthropic foundations they established and their descendants who are in politics. The men who now head the great corporations are unknown. Not for a generation did people outside Detroit in the automobile industry know the name of the current head of General Motors. In the manner of all men, he must produce identification when paying by check. So with Ford, Standard Oil, and General Dynamics. The men who now run the large corporations own no appreciable share of the enterprise. They are selected not by the stockholders but, in the common case, by a board of directors which narcissistically they selected themselves.[4]

How do you climb the corporate ladder? It is not easy, and most who begin the climb fall by the wayside at some point in their career before reaching the top. Howard Morgens, president of Procter & Gamble, is a successful manager. He climbed his organization to succeed its president, Neil McElroy (who left to be secretary of defense), and headed the corporation for over fifteen years. In an interview with this executive, *Forbes* magazine described the qualities of a corporate career-riser:

> Just to be in the running, a career riser must discipline himself carefully. He must become a seasoned decision-maker. He must cultivate an aura of success and sustain his upward momentum on the executive ladder. He must be loyal to a fault, tolerably bright, fairly creative, politically agile, always tough, sometimes flexible, unfailingly sociable and, in the minds of his company's directors, seem superior to a dozen men who are almost as good. He must also be lucky.[5]

Over time, the organization man accepts the goals of the organization as his own, and the procedures of the bureaucracy as a way of life:

> In staying, however, the career riser must accept the necessarily bureaucratic ways and the shared beliefs of a huge organization. He must be willing to follow prescribed procedures and behavioral norms. He must do things the P&G way or the IBM way or the General Motors way. Moreover, he must find it in himself to believe in the essential goodness of the company, in its traditions and in his co-employees. He must be willing to accept a good deal on faith. He must, in short, conform.[6]

Getting to the top by climbing the ladder of the giant corporation is not only difficult; it is also risky. The percentage chances of any one individual making it to the top are infinitesimal.

[4] John Kenneth Galbraith, *The New Industrial State* (Boston: Houghton Mifflin, 1967), p. 323.

[5] "Proud to Be An Organization Man," *Forbes,* May 15, 1972, p. 241.

[6] Ibid.

> Yet hundreds of thousands of executives willingly devote entire careers to working their way up through these giant corporations. On the lower rungs of the ladder, when they are in their 20's, all of them dream of reaching the top. As they advance into their 30's, and receive more responsibility and more money, the dream flowers brightly. Some time in their 40's and 50's, however, most realize they aren't going to make it. They are sorely disappointed, but it's too late to change. Comfortable and secure, they stay. Then each year there are perhaps a dozen or so—the lucky men who go all the way.[7]

It might be instructive to sketch briefly the career of one of "the lucky men" who went "all the way."

H. I. Romnes: Up the Organization

In 1970 the chairman of the board of the world's largest corporation, American Telephone and Telegraph Company, was H. I. Romnes. The son of Norwegian immigrants, tall, ruggedly handsome "Hi" Romnes rose to great power through the ranks of corporate management. He worked in his father's bakery in Stoughton, Wisconsin to support himself while he was in public school and later while he attended the University of Wisconsin. His boyhood hobby was building crystal radios, and he received his B.A. in electrical engineering in 1927. Upon graduation he joined the Bell Telephone Laboratories in New York City, and spent the next seven years patiently designing electrical circuits. Romnes' progress in the labyrinths of AT&T's giant engineering department was slow. His specialty became long-distance toll transmissions. By 1952 he had put in 25 years of work on long-distance transmissions, and was assistant chief engineer for AT&T. But then, in a series of rapid promotions, Romnes became chief engineer, vice-president for operations and engineering, and in 1959, president of Western Electric Company, the equipment manufacturing subsidiary of AT&T. Undoubtedly his rise to the top in these years was aided by the fact that AT&T chose to introduce direct dialing—a major technological transition involving the integration of telephone lines throughout the United States in one vast switching facility. Fortunately, Romnes' years in the engineering laboratories paid off in his mastery of a significant technological innovation.

Romnes obviously proved his management skills as Western Electric president. In 1964 he was named vice-chairman of the board of directors of AT&T, and in 1966 he replaced retiring Federick R. Kappel as chairman of the board. Romnes was 59 years old when he took over this key post.

[7] Ibid., p. 244.

Romnes' public statements have reflected liberal establishment values. Even before the passage of the Civil Rights Act of 1964, he initiated an equal employment opportunity program, one of the first in the nation. "The businessman's responsibility for advancing equality of opportunity does not stop at the factory gate," he declared. His participation in the Urban League and the United Negro College Fund bore out his beliefs—"No company is an island; its fortunes are bound up with the community around it."[8] Because he believed that the future would be greatly influenced by technological developments, this top-level manager was committed to keeping AT&T in the forefront of new technology. But he expressed a public-regarding attitude toward technological change:

> Surely we can never forget—in applying new technology to our business practices—that the ultimate test of everything we do is the satisfaction and convenience of the customer. He is the one who shouldn't be folded, spindled, or mutilated.

Romnes did *not* oppose governmental regulation; he consistently expressed an attitude of accommodation toward the Federal Communications Commission, which regulates long-distance telephone rates.

> If we in business can say of the bureaucrat that "he never met a payroll," it can also be said with equal justice about us that "we never carried a precinct!" We have a lot to learn from each other.

Romnes is also a director of the Chemical Bank of New York, United States Steel Corporation, Cities Service, and Mutual Life Insurance Company of New York. But these directorships came to him *after* his rise in AT&T.

Of course, Romnes is active in cultural, educational, and charitable organizations. He is a director of the American Cancer Society, the Downtown–Lower Manhattan Association (with friend David Rockefeller), the National Citizens Committee on the United Community Campaigns of America, the Presbyterian Hospital of New York City, the National Safety Council, the Alexander Graham Bell Association for the Deaf, and so forth. He is a member of the M.I.T. Corporation as well as the Wisconsin Alumni Research Foundation. He is a member of the University Club in New York, and more importantly, the Links Club.

Romnes' personal success story is testimony to the opportunities for upward mobility in the corporate structure. Of course, there was a crucial element of good fortune in Romnes' mastery of a key technological development—long distance direct dialing—at the point in time that the development was introduced.

[8] Quotations from *Current Biography,* 1968, pp. 334–36.

The Inheritors: Starting at the Top

Unquestionably, the Rockefellers, Fords, duPonts, Mellons, and other families still exercise great power over America's corporate resources. For example, the Mellon family's personal control of Alcoa is legendary:

> When Gulf executives speak reverently of "The Board," they are normally referring to a single man, diffident Richard King Mellon, senior member of one of the world's richest families. The only Mellon on Gulf's board, Dick Mellon looks after his family's two billion, 32 percent interest in Gulf—though he rarely is concerned with the day-to-day operations.[9]

The Ford family maintains control of Ford Motor Company, and of course the Rockefellers continue their dominant interest in Chase Manhattan Bank, First National City Bank, Standard Oil (Exxon), Equitable Life Assurance Society, Eastern Airlines, and other key banks and industries. The duPonts continue to control E. I. duPont de Nemours Corporation through their family holding company, Christiana Securities.

Research on family holdings in large corporations is not easy. Table 2-6 lists major family holdings of large corporations as revealed by Securities and Exchange Commission's *Official Summary of Security Transactions and Holdings*. Each month the SEC reports stock transactions by offices and directors of corporations, and by stockholders owning 10 percent or more of any corporation. Ferdinand Lundberg painstakingly studied monthly reports for five years in the 1960s to obtain this list.[10] We have updated it from *Fortune Magazine* and other sources.

Many members of the corporate elite "start at the top." *Fortune Magazine* suggests that 150 of the largest 500 industrial corporations are controlled by one or more members of a single family. True, most of these individual- or family-controlled corporations are ranked *below* the top 100. But if indeed 30 percent of American industrial corporations are controlled by individuals or family groups, then the claimed disappearance of the traditional American capitalist may have been exaggerated. *Fortune* concludes:

> After more than two generations during which ownership has been increasingly divorced from control, it is frequently assumed that all large

9 *Forbes,* May 1, 1964, p. 22.

10 Ferdinand Lundberg, *The Rich and the Super-Rich* (New York: Lyle Stuart, 1968).

Table 2-6. Family Dominance in Corporations

Corporation	Family
E. I. duPont de Nemours	duPont
Remington Arms Co., Inc.	Dodge, Rockefeller
Ford Motor Co.	Ford
Aluminum Co. of America	Mellon
Carborundum Co.	Mellon
Gulf Oil Co.	Mellon, Scaife
Sun Oil Co.	Pew
Pittsburgh Plate Glass	Pitcairn
Standard Oil (Exxon)	Rockefeller
Sears, Roebuck & Co.	Rosenwald
Reynolds Metals	Reynolds
The Singer Company	Clark
Inland Steel Co.	Block
Allegheny Corp.	Kirby
Scott Paper Co.	McCabe
Minnesota Mining & Mfg. Co.	Ordway, McKnight
Polaroid Corp.	Land
IBM	Watson, Fairchild
Dow Chemical Co.	Dow
Corning Glass Works	Houghton
International Paper Co.	Phipps
W. R. Grace & Co.	Grace, Phipps
Weyerhaeuser	Weyerhaeuser
Winn-Dixie, Inc.	Davis
Georgia-Pacific	Cheatharn
General Tire & Rubber Co.	O'Neil
Campbell Soup Company	Dorrance
H. J. Heinz Co.	Heinz
Wm. Wrigley Jr. Co.	Wrigley
Firestone Tire & Rubber	Firestone
National Steel	Hanna
Columbia Broadcasting Co. (CBS)	Paley
Olin Chemical	Olin
Ralston Purina Co.	Danforth
Crown-Zellerbach Corp.	Zellerbach
Texas Eastern Transmission	Brown
Fairchild Camera	Fairchild
Smith Kline & French Laboratories	Valentine
Allied Chemical Corp.	Burden
Merck & Co., Inc.	Rogengarten
American Metal Climax	Hochschild, Dodge
W. T. Grant Co.	Grant
E. J. Korvette	Ferkauf
Hilton Hotels	Hilton
Howard Johnson Co.	Johnson
Great Atlantic & Pacific Tea Co. (A&P)	Hartford
S. S. Kresge Co.	Kresge
Beech Aircraft Corp.	Beech
McDonnell Douglass Aircraft	McDonnell
General Dynamics Corp.	Crown
Hess Oil & Chemical	Hess
Eli Lilly & Co.	Lilly
Duke Power Co.	Duke

Corporation	Family
Kaiser Industries	Kaiser
Rockwell Mfg. Co.	Rockwell
Gerber Products Co.	Gerber
Deere & Company	Deere
Jos. Schlitz Brewing Co.	Uihlein
George A. Hormel & Co.	Hormel
Oscar Mayer & Co.	Mayer

Sources: Ferdinand Lundberg, *The Rich and the Super-rich* (New York: Lyle Stuart Inc., 1968); *Fortune Magazine,* June 15, 1967; updated to *Fortune,* "Directory of the Largest 500 Corporations" May, 1975.

> U.S. corporations are owned by everybody and nobody, and are run and ruled by bland organization men. The individual entrepreneur or family that holds onto the controlling interest and actively manages the affairs of a big company is regarded as a rare anachronism. But a close look at the 500 largest industrial corporations does not substantiate such sweeping generalizations. . . . The demise of the traditional American proprietor has been slightly exaggerated and the much advertised triumph of the organization is far from total.[11]

Nonetheless, even family-controlled corporations recruit professional managers from the ranks. Indeed, a majority of the directors of Ford, Alcoa, Gulf, Standard Oil, Chase Manhattan, E. I. duPont, and other such corporations are professional managers recruited from outside the family.

It really does not matter a great deal whether the "inheritors" or the "managers" really control America's largest corporations; the end policies appear to be the same. Management is motivated by considerations of growth, stability, and profit, and so are prudent family stockholders. Moreover, "managers" themselves usually acquire sizable blocks of stock in their own companies as they move up through the ranks. For example, Charles E. Wilson, former president of General Motors, had accumulated $2.5 million in stock in that company before he was appointed secretary of defense by President Eisenhower; and Robert McNamara, president of Ford Motors, had accumulated $1.5 million in Ford stock before he was appointed secretary of defense by President Kennedy. Both men had come up through the ranks of management. It is doubtful that the decisions of "managers" and "inheritors" differ a great deal. *Fortune Magazine* agrees:

> It was expected that the demise of the owner-manager would markedly affect the conduct and performance of business. Some have predicted that

[11] Robert Sheehan, "Family Run Corporations: There Are More of Them Than You Think," *Fortune,* June 15, 1967, p. 179.

> the new managerial brass, as essentially non-owners, would lack the self-interested maximization of profits that inspired proprietors, would be inclined to curb dividends, and would be tempted to provide themselves with disproportionately large salaries and bonuses. . . .
>
> Despite these theories, it is extremely doubtful that ownership or the lack of it motivated the conduct of executives in such a direct way. Very few executives agree that the managers of a widely held company run their business any differently from the proprietors of a closely held company. Competition is a great leveler, and both managers and proprietors respond to its pressures with equal spirit and objectivity.[12]

Henry Ford II: The Inheritor as Boss

"The first thing you have to understand about the company is that Henry Ford is the boss. . . . He *is* the boss, he always was the boss since the first day I came in and he always will be the boss." These are the words of Arjay Miller, who spent 23 years climbing the rungs of Ford management to become president of the company, only to find that Henry Ford II actually ran things. Miller eventually resigned to become Dean of the Graduate School of Business at Stanford University.

Henry Ford II grew up in a very narrow society—he was a member of a rich, insulated family that was dominated by his grandfather, known to be an exceedingly suspicious, prejudiced, and willful man. Young Ford attended Hotchkiss School and later Yale University. But he failed to graduate in 1940 after admitting that he had cheated on a term paper. He enlisted in the Navy and served until his father died in 1943; President Roosevelt directed the secretary of Navy to release Ford to return to the family business.

Ford started in the automobile industry at the age of 25 as vice-president of Ford Motors, serving under his aged grandfather. A year later he took over the presidency. His initial decisions were to replace the one-man autocratic rule of the company with a modern management structure, recruiting bright young management types (the famous Ford "Whiz Kids" including Robert S. MacNamara, who later resigned as Ford president to become Secretary of Defense). He also initiated a modern labor relations program and ended the company's traditional hostility toward labor unions. As commonplace as these policies appear today, they were considered advanced, enlightened, and liberal for the Ford Motor Company at the time.

Over the years Ford proved himself a capable director of the com-

12 Ibid., p. 183.

pany, despite some occasional and even colossal mistakes. (The Edsel fiasco cost the company over $300 million.) Ford works long hours at the company headquarters in Detroit. He personally approves style changes in Ford cars and test-drives them himself. He is active on the board of the Ford Foundation, and conscientiously reviews research and grant proposals with other board members.

In recent years Ford's energies have increasingly turned to public service programs. He helped launch the National Urban Coalition and organized the National Alliance of Businessmen to provide more jobs for minorities. He heads the National Center for Voluntary Action (frequently advertised in spot commercials featuring popular athletes on TV sports programs), which tries to bring volunteer workers into social welfare projects. He has been a prime mover in Detroit's urban renewal and redevelopment program.

Ford explained his leadership in public-regarding programs to a Yale University audience in 1969: "To hire a man because he needs a job rather than because the job needs him is to assure him that he is useless. On the other side of the coin, to help a man because it is in your own interest to help him is to treat him as an equal." Ford supported Lyndon Johnson in 1964 and Hubert Humphrey in 1968; he supported Nixon in 1972 but afterward became "bluntly and profanely" critical of Nixon's performance.

Ford is particularly concerned with energy policy: "I'm more worried about it than any other problem. I'm not worried about gasoline for automobiles, but the whole infra-structure of the U.S. We've got to heat our homes, and run our plants to employ people. People want air conditioning and a lot of other things that they're used to, and I don't see the power system of this country meeting the needs. . . . We need something like the Manhattan Project to solve this energy crisis." [13] His notion of a Manhattan Project (the World War II code name for the crash program to develop an atomic bomb) was quickly picked up by Richard Nixon, who announced Project Independence to make America self-sufficient in energy by 1980.

Like many men born to wealth and power, Ford's personal style is far from that of the bland organizational man. He is frequently unpredictable, sometimes abrasive, often profane; he expresses his opinions directly. His public and private actions are often controversial (he divorced his wife of many years and married a beautiful young Italian actress); but his preeminence in America's elite structure is unquestioned.

[13] *Fortune,* May 1973, p. 191.

Personal Wealth and Economic Power

It is a mistake to equate *personal* wealth with economic power. Men with relatively little personal wealth can exercise great power if they occupy positions that give them control of huge institutional resources. A president of a large company who came through the ranks of management may receive an income of only $200,000 or $300,000 a year, and possess a net worth of $1 or 2 million. Yet these amounts are small when you consider that he may control a corporation with annual revenues of $2 *billion* and assets worth $10 or 20 *billion*. (The contrast is even greater in government where $40,000-a-year bureaucrats manage government expenditures of $50 *billion* a year!) The important point is that personal wealth in America is insignificant in comparison to corporate and governmental wealth.

One must occupy top *positions* in large corporate *institutions* to exercise significant economic power. The mere possession of personal wealth, even $100 million, does not guarantee economic power. Indeed, among America's 150 "centimillionaires"–individuals with personal wealth in excess of $100 million–there are many people such as widows, retired persons, and other inheritors who have never played any role in the family business. There are also many "independent operators," who have acquired great wealth in, say, independent oil operations or land speculation, but who do not occupy high positions in the corporate world. Of course, there are many centimillionaires whose personal wealth has come to them through their personal ownership of corporate shares. Familiar names–Ford, Rockefeller, duPont, Mellon–are liberally sprinkled among the nation's top personal wealth-holders. But their personal wealth is a *by-product* of their role, or their ancestor's role, in the corporate structure.

Socialist critics of America usually do not comprehend the insignificance of personal wealth in relation to corporate and governmental resources. They direct their rhetoric against inequality in personal income in the nation, when in fact the greatest inequities occur in the comparisons between corporate and government resources and the resources of individuals.

Let us illustrate our point: If the personal wealth of every one of America's 150 centimillionaires were *completely confiscated* by the government, the resulting revenue (about $3 billion) would amount to less than *one percent* of the federal budget for a *single year!*

The relationship between personal wealth and institutional power is described well by economist Adolf Berle:

> As of now, in the United States and in Western Europe, the rich man has little power merely because he is rich. . . . [He] amounts to little unless he connects himself with effective institutions. He must master past institutions or must create new ones. . . . However large his bank account, he can do nothing with it but consume. He can build or buy palaces, amuse himself at Mediterranean or Caribbean resorts, become a figure in Monte Carlo, Miami, or Las Vegas. He can amuse himself by collecting books or purchasing bonds. He can give libraries or laboratories to universities and have his name put on them. He can receive the pleasant but powerless recognition of decorations, honorary degrees, and even titles of nobility. None of these things entitle him to make decisions affecting other men or to give orders (outside his household) with any likelihood they will be fulfilled. Even when he seeks to give his son a career in business, he must ask the assistance of acquaintances and friends who will give the boy a fair chance—and can give him little more. Beyond that, he can leave his son nothing but the ability to live without work and to waste as long as his wealth holds out. All of this does not add up to power.
>
> So, if he wishes a power position, he must find it outside his bank account. He can, it is true, use the bank account to buy into, or possibly create, an institution. He can buy control of a small corporation. (Few rich men are left who are capable of buying individual control of really large ones.) He can undertake the management of that corporation. Then he can derive power from the institution—if, and only if, he is capable of handling it. Whatever power he has comes from the corporation or other institutions, and from such intellectual or organizing skill as he may have—not from his wealth, which is largely irrelevant. He at once discovers that he is subordinate to the institution. It operates under, and in conditions accepted or laid down or directed by, the paramount political power. Then he is tested, not by the dollar value of his wealth, but by his performance as director or manager of the institution.[14]

Of course, income inequality is and has always been a significant component of American social structure.[15] The top fifth of income recipients in America accounts for over 40 percent of all income in the nation, while the bottom fifth accounts for only about 5 percent (see Table 2-7). However, the income share of the top fifth has declined since the pre–World War II years. The income share of the top 5 percent of families has declined dramatically from 30 to 14.4 percent. But the bottom fifth of the population still receives a very small share of the national income. The significant rise in income shares has occurred among the middle classes, in the second, third, and fourth income fifths.

Nonetheless, it is interesting to observe who the top personal

[14] From *Power,* copyright © 1967, 1968, 1969 by Adolph A. Berle. Reprinted by permission of Harcourt Brace Jovanovich, Inc.

[15] See Gabriel Kolko, *Wealth and Power in America* (New York: Praeger, 1962); see also Clair Wilcox, *Toward Social Welfare* (Homewood, Ill.: Richard D. Irwin, 1969), pp. 7–24.

Table 2-7. The Distribution of Family Income in America

By Quintiles and Top 5 Percent

Quintiles	1929	1936	1944	1950	1956	1962	1972
Lowest	3.5	4.1	4.9	4.8	4.8	4.6	5.5
Second	9.0	9.2	10.9	10.9	11.3	10.9	12.0
Third	13.8	14.1	16.2	16.1	16.3	16.3	17.4
Fourth	19.3	20.9	22.2	22.1	22.3	22.7	23.5
Highest	54.4	51.7	45.8	46.1	45.3	45.5	41.6
Total	100.0	100.0	100.0	100.0	100.0	100.0	100.0
Top 5 Percent	30.0	24.0	20.7	21.4	20.2	19.6	14.4

Source: U.S. Bureau of the Census, *Current Population Reports* Series P-60 No. 80; data for early years from Edward C. Budd, *Inequality and Poverty* (New York: W. W. Norton and Co., 1967).

wealth-holders in America are. The editors of *Fortune* report that in 1957, 45 persons in the United States had fortunes of over $100 million. In the following ten years, this "centimillionaire" population tripled, and 66 persons were estimated to have $150 million or more. (These 66 are listed on Table 2-8.)

Even if personal wealth is not the equivalent of power, the list of top wealth-holders is worthy of study. It includes at least two categories —old and established, Eastern families with wealth derived from corporate ownership; and newly rich, self-made Southern and Western centimillionaires whose wealth is derived from "independent" oil operations, real estate speculations, aerospace industries, or technological inventions. (Further contrasts between new wealth and established wealth are found in Chapter 8.) Representative of new-rich, self-made wealth are the first four names on the list—America's wealthiest men: J. Paul Getty and H. L. Hunt, whose fabulous fortunes were amassed in independent oil operations; Howard Hughes, whose fortune was made in the aerospace industry and is now invested in Las Vegas real estate; and Edwin H. Land, an inventor whose self-developing "Land" camera was the foundation of the giant Polaroid Corporation. Representative of established Eastern wealth derived from stable corporate enterprise are the Mellons, duPonts, Fords, Rockefellers, and others whose wealth extends back through several generations.

It is our judgment that twelve (18 percent) of the 66 richest Americans in Table 2-8 are *self-made* men of wealth.[16] The remaining 54 (82 percent) are connected to established sources of corporate wealth.

[16] Getty, Hughes, Hunt, Land, Smith, Hess, Hewlitt, Packard, Carlson, Hope, Kiewit, McDonnell.

Table 2-8. America's Centimillionaires*

1. J. Paul Getty (oil)
2. Howard Hughes (Hughes Tool Co., real estate)
3. H. L. Hunt (oil)
4. Edwin H. Land (Polaroid)
5. Daniel K. Ludwig (shipping)
6. Alisa Mellon Bruce (Mellon)
7. Paul Mellon (Mellon)
8. Richard King Mellon (Mellon)
9. N. Bunker Hunt (oil, son of H. L. Hunt)
10. John D. MacArthur (Bankers Life and Casualty)
11. William L. McKnight (Minnesota Mining and Manufacturing)
12. Charles S. Mott (General Motors)
13. R. E. (Bob) Smith (oil)
14. Howard F. Ahmanson (Home Savings & Loan Association)
15. Charles Allen, Jr. (investment banking)
16. Mrs. W. Van Alan Clark, Sr. (Avon Products)
17. John T. Dorrance, Jr. (Campbell Soup)
18. Mrs. Alfred I. Du Pont (duPont)
19. Charles W. Englehard, Jr. (mining and metal fabricating)
20. Sherman M. Fairchild (Fairchild Camera, IBM)
21. Leon Hess (Hess Oil & Chemical)
22. William R. Hewlett (Hewlett-Packard)
23. David Packard (Hewlett-Packard)
24. Amory Houghton (Corning Glass Works)
25. Joseph P. Kennedy (banking, real estate, investments; father of John F. Kennedy)
26. Eli Lilly (Eli Lilly & Co.)
27. Forrest E. Mars (Mars candy)
28. Samuel I. Newhouse (newspapers)
29. Marjorie Merriweather Post (General Foods)
30. Mrs. Jean Mauze (Abby Rockefeller)
31. David Rockefeller
32. John D. Rockefeller III
33. Laurance Rockefeller
34. Nelson Rockefeller
35. Winthrop Rockefeller
36. Cordelia Scaife May (Mellon)
37. Richard Mellon Scaife (Mellon)
38. DeWitt Wallace (Reader's Digest)
39. Mrs. Charles Payson (Joan Whitney)
40. John Hay Whitney
41. James S. Abercrombie (oil, iron)
42. William Benton (Encyclopaedia Britannica)
43. Jacob Blaustein (Standard Oil of Indiana)
44. Chester Carlson (inventory of xerography)
45. Edward J. Daly (World Airways)
46. Clarence Dillon (investment banking)
47. Doris Duke (tobacco)
48. Lammot Du Pont Copeland (duPont)
49. Henry B. Du Pont (duPont)
50. Benson Ford (Ford Motor)
51. Mrs. W. Buhl Ford II (Ford Motor)
52. William C. Ford (Ford Motor)
53. Helen Clay Frick (steel)
54. William T. Grant (variety stores)
55. Bob Hope (entertainment)
56. Arthur A. Houghton, Jr. (Corning Glass)
57. J. Seward Johnson (Johnson & Johnson)

58. Peter Kiewit (construction)
59. Allan P. Kirby (Woolworth heir, Allegheny Corp.)
60. J. S. McDonnell, Jr. (McDonnell Douglas, aircraft)
61. Mrs. Lester J. Norris
62. E. Claiborne Robins (A. H. Robins, drugs)
63. W. Clement Stone (insurance)
64. Mrs. Arthur Hays Sulzberger (New York Times)
65. S. Mark Taper (First Charter Financial Corp.)
66. Robert W. Woodruff (Coca-Cola)

*In descending order of approximate wealth, from $1.5 billion to $150 million. These assessments include holdings of spouses and minors, of trusts, and of foundations established by the individuals or their spouses.

Source: *Fortune,* May 1968.

The Corporate Conscience

Today those at the top of the corporate world are far more liberal and public-regarding in their attitudes and decisions than the robber-baron, industrial capitalists of a few decades ago. Radical critics of American business who portray top corporate elites as reactionary, repressive, narrow-minded, or short-sighted vastly underestimate their chosen enemy.

Rugged individualism, laissez-faire, "public-be-damned" business attitudes are far more characteristic of new-rich, self-made men than of established corporate leaders. The people who head the nation's large corporations—both "inheritors" and up-from-the-ranks "managers"—are generally sympathetic to liberal, public-regarding, social welfare ideas. They are concerned with the public interest and express a devotion to the "corporate conscience." The corporate conscience is, in Adolph Berle's words,

> the existence of a set of ideas, widely held by the community and often by the organization itself and the men who direct it, that certain uses of power are "wrong," that is, contrary to the established interest and value system of the community. Indulgence of these ideas as a limitation on economic power, and regard for them by the managers of great corporations, is sometimes called—and ridiculed as—the "corporate conscience." The ridicule is pragmatically unjustified. The first sanction enforcing limitations imposed by the public consensus is a lively appreciation of that consensus by corporate managements. This is the reality of the "corporate conscience." [17]

These top leaders place great value on social prestige and popular esteem. Although the public has no direct economic control over man-

[17] Adolph A. Berle, *Power Without Property,* pp. 90–91.

agement, and government control is more symbolic than real, the deprivation of prestige is one of the oldest methods by which any society enforces its values upon individuals and groups. Moreover, most of the values of the prevailing liberal consensus have been internalized by corporate managers themselves; that is, they have come to believe in a public-regarding philosophy.

Corporate elites are by no means hostile to big governments. Indeed, in his popular book, *The New Industrial State,* John K. Galbraith argues effectively that we are experiencing a gradual blurring of the distinction between the corporate and governmental enterprise and the giant, bureaucratic "techno-structure." Corporate planning and governmental planning are replacing market competition in America. Corporations avoid vigorous price competition, and the government also endeavors to fix overall prices. Both corporations and governments seek stable relations with large labor unions. Solid, prosperous growth is the keynote of the planned economy, without undue, disruptive, old-style competition. Wars, depressions, or overheated inflations are to be avoided in the interest of stable growth. Big government, big industry, and big labor organizations share in this consensus. Within it, the big quietly grow bigger and more powerful. Government protects this secure, stable world of corporate giants, unless they abuse the accepted standards of behavior or openly try to improve their positions.

Thus the interests of the government and the corporate world come together on behalf of a consensus for stable planned growth:

> The state is strongly concerned with the stability of the economy. And with its expansion or growth. And with education. And with technical and scientific advance. And, most notably, with the national defense. These are *the* national goals; they are sufficiently trite so that one has a reassuring sense of the obvious in articulating them. All have their counterpart in the needs and goals of the techno-structure. It requires stability in demand for its planning. Growth brings promotion and prestige. It requires trained manpower. It needs government underwriting of research and development. Military and other technical procurement support its most developed form of planning. At each point the government has goals with which the techno-structure can identify itself.[18]

The new jargon in the board room is "corporate responsibility," "social consciousness," "affirmative action." These notions are more prevalent in larger corporations than smaller ones, but it is the larger corporations that control the greatest share of America's economic resources. Only a few "classic" economists—most notably, University of Chicago's Milton Friedman—continue to argue that America's corpora-

[18] Galbraith, *The New Industrial State,* p. 316.

tions best serve the nation by concentrating on business alone, allocating resources on the basis of profit alone, and striving for optimum efficiency and productivity. In contrast, most top corporate elites are advocates of corporate responsibility—they want a larger social role for industry and generally are willing to sacrifice some profits to perform such a role. They believe that business should undertake positive efforts to expand minority opportunities, abate pollution, assist in the renewal and redevelopment of the nation's cities, and, in general, *do good.*

Consider, for example, the case of General Motors. The men at the top of GM are aware of the charges against the company; they are concerned with air pollution, congestion in cities, the ugliness of used-car scrap heaps, employment opportunities for blacks, and, of course, the safety record of their cars. In 1970, GM created a Public Policy Committee within its board of directors and elected its first black, Reverend Leon Sullivan, a leader in the creation of on-the-job minority training centers, to its board.[19] The Policy Committee recommended a series of steps to increase safety and pollution-control engineering efforts, speed up minority promotion practices, and improve GM relations with the mass media. When GM engineers wanted to inform the public that pollution control costs rise exponentially when attempts are made to control the last few grams of pollutants, the Committee vetoed the effort. The engineers argued that spilling half a cup of gasoline at the pump puts more pollutants in the air than burning an entire tankful. They wanted to make public the fact that the added cost of meeting unreasonably high anti-pollution standards ($300 to $600 per car) was not worth the amount of pollutants involved. The GM directors agreed, but they were so sensitive to possible charges of economic self-interest and lack of concern for the environment that they decided *not* to tell the public of the unfavorable cost-benefit tradeoffs involved.

The cost of GM's annual social effort is estimated to be in excess of $600 million, or about one-third of its $2 billion before-tax profits.[20] In other words, earnings could be increased by one-third if GM dropped its "social" efforts. This figure represents a significant commitment to "corporate responsibility," but not a serious threat to the profit motive. Other factors—volume of sales, worker productivity, plant utilization, etc.—affect profits more significantly than corporate social efforts. But it is wrong to believe that GM directors or other top corporate leaders are unconcerned with social problems.

Of course, the profit motive is still important to the corporate

[19] Peter Vanderwicken, "GM: The Price of Being Responsible," *Fortune Magazine* (January 1972).

[20] Ibid.

elites, because profits are the basis of capital formation within the corporation. Increased capital at the disposal of corporate managers means increased power; losses mean a decrease in the capital available to the managers, a decrease in their power, and perhaps eventual extinction for the organization. But a certain portion of profits can be sacrificed for social concerns. The prudent corporate leader views such expenditures as being in the long-run interest of his corporation and himself.

Summary

In later chapters, we will examine interlocking, recruitment, conflict, and consensus, as well as corporate involvement in national policy-making, in greater detail. Let us now summarize our initial observations regarding the corporate directors as key elites in the institutional structure in the U.S.

Economic power in America is highly concentrated. For example, a small number of corporations control over half the nation's industrial assets; half of all assets in communications, transportation, and utilities; and two-thirds of all insurance assets. This concentration of economic power is increasing gradually over time, as the nation's largest corporations gain ever-larger shares of total corporate assets.

Power over corporate assets rests in the hands of about 3500 presidents and directors. These directors, not the stockholders or employees, decide major policy questions, choose the people who will carry out these decisions, and even select their own replacements. However, most of these presidents and directors have climbed the corporate ladder to their posts. These "managers" owe their rise to power to their skill in organizational life, and to their successful coping with the new demands for expertise in management, technology, and planning. Individual capitalists are no longer essential in the formation of capital assets. In fact, four-fifths of industrial capital is raised within the corporation itself or from institutional borrowing.

It is true that the Rockefellers, Fords, duPonts, Mellons, and other great entrepreneurial families still exercise great power over corporate resources. But a majority of the directors of family-dominated firms have been brought in from outside the family; and only about 150 of the 500 largest corporations are family-dominated.

Personal wealth is insignificant in relation to corporate (or governmental) wealth. Individuals may own millions, but institutions control billions. Thus it is necessary for individuals to achieve top corporate positions in order to exercise significant economic power.

Top corporate leaders generally display moderately liberal, socially responsible attitudes and opinions on public issues. They are not necessarily hostile to government, but generally share with government an interest in stable growth, the avoidance of disruption, and planned scientific and technological development. The notion of "corporate responsibility" involves a willingness to sacrifice some profits to exercise a larger role in social policy-making. Profits, however, remain essential to the accumulation of capital and the continued existence of the corporation.

Three

THE GOVERNING CIRCLES

If there ever was a time when the powers of government were limited—when government did no more than secure law and order, protect individual liberty and property, enforce contracts, and protect against foreign invasion—that time has long passed. Today it is commonplace to observe that governmental institutions intervene in every aspect of our lives—from the "cradle to the grave." Government in America has the primary responsibility for providing insurance against old age, death, dependency, disability, and unemployment; for providing medical care for the aged and indigent; for providing education at the elementary, secondary, collegiate, and post-graduate levels; for providing for public highways and regulating water, rail, and air transportation; for providing police and fire protection; for providing sanitation services and sewage disposal; for financing research in medicine, science, and technology; for delivering the mail; for exploring outer space; for maintaining parks and recreation; for providing housing and adequate food for the poor; for providing for job training and manpower programs; for cleaning the air and water; for rebuilding central cities; for maintaining full employment and a stable money supply; for regulating business practices and labor relations; for eliminating racial and sexual discrimination. Indeed, the list of government responsibilities seems endless, yet each year we manage to find additional tasks for government to do.

The Concentration of Governmental Power

Governments do many things that cannot be measured in terms of dollars and cents. Nonetheless, government expenditures are the best available measure of the dimensions of government activity. Such expenditures in the United States amount to about one-third of the gross national product. This is an increase from about 8 percent of the GNP at the beginning of the century. (Years ago, the German economist Adolph Wagner set forth the "law of increasing state activity"; in effect, this law states that government activity increases faster than economic output in all developing societies.) Today taxes amount to over $2,000 each year for every man, woman, and child in the nation. The largest governmental cost is "income maintenance"—social security, welfare, and related social services. Defense spending is the second largest governmental cost, followed by education.

Of course, the observation that government expenditures now account for one-third of the nation's GNP actually understates the great power of government over every aspect of our lives. Government regulatory activity cannot be measured in government expenditures. Indeed, large segments of the economy come under direct federal regulation, notably transportation and utilities; yet these are officially classified as private industries and are not counted in the governmental proportion of the GNP.

Concentration of governmental resources is also evidenced in the growing proportion of *federal* expenditures in relation to *state* and *local* government expenditures. There are approximately 80,000 separate governmental units operating in the United States today. (U.S. government—1; state governments—50; counties—3,044; municipalities—18,517; townships—16,991; school districts—15,781; special districts—23,885.) But only one of these, the U.S. government, accounts for *two-thirds* of all governmental expenditures. This means that approximately 21 percent of the GNP is accounted for by federal expenditures alone. This centralization of governmental activity is a twentieth-century phenomenon: seventy years ago the federal government accounted for only one-third of all governmental expenditures; local governments carried on the major share of governmental activity.

We have defined our governmental elite as the top executive, congressional, military, and judicial officers of the *federal* government: the president and vice-president; secretaries, undersecretaries, and assistant secretaries of executive departments; White House presidential advisers; congressional committee chairmen and ranking minority members; congressional majority and minority party leaders in the House and Senate; Supreme Court justices; and members of the Federal Reserve Board and the Council of Economic Advisers. In the pages that follow we will try to describe some members of the governmental elite, as well as to discuss the power they exercise, and how they came to power.

The Politicians: Style and Image

The politician is a professional office-seeker. He knows how to run for office—but not necessarily how to run the government. After victory at the polls, the prudent politician turns to "serious men" to run the government. Pulitzer Prize-winning writer David Halberstam reports a revealing conversation between newly elected President John F. Kennedy and Robert A. Lovett in December 1960, a month before Kennedy was to take office:

> On the threshold of great power and great office, the young man seemed to have everything. He was handsome, rich, charming, candid. The candor was part of the charm: he could beguile a visitor by admitting that everything the visitor proposed was right, rational, proper—but he couldn't do it, not this week, this month, this term. Now he was trying to put together a government, and the candor showed again. He was self-deprecating with the older man. He had spent the last five years, he said ruefully, running for office, and he did not know any real public officials, people to run a government, *serious men*. The only ones he knew, he admitted, were politicians.. . . Politicians *did* need men to serve, to run the government. The implication was obvious. Politicians could run Pennsylvania and Ohio, and if they could not run Chicago they could at least deliver it. But politicians run the world? What did they know about the German, the French, the Chinese?[1]

Robert Lovett was "the very embodiment of the Establishment." His father had been chairman of the board of Union Pacific Railroad and a partner of the great railroad tycoon, E. H. Harriman. Lovett attended Hill School and Yale, married the daughter of James Brown, the senior partner of the great banking firm of Brown Brothers, and formed a new and even larger Wall Street investment partnership, Brown

[1] David Halberstam, *The Best and the Brightest* (New York: Random House, 1969), pp. 3–4. Italics added.

Brothers, Harriman, & Co. Lovett urged Kennedy to listen to the advice of Averell Harriman; to see "Jack McCloy at Chase," and "Doug Dillon too"; to look up a "young fellow over at Rockefeller, Dean Rusk," to head up the State Department; and to get "this young man at Ford, Robert McNamara," to run the Defense Department. Kennedy gratefully accepted the advice: he turned to these "serious men" to run the government.

Of course, not all politicians are shallow, superficial, office-seekers. Some are "serious men" themselves—that is, they would be influential even if they never won elective office. Following are a few examples of such individuals.

> *Nelson A. Rockefeller.* Vice-president of the United States, four-term governor of New York. Son of John D. Rockefeller. Attended Lincoln School and Dartmouth College. Former president and chairman of the Rockefeller Center of New York City. Former assistant secretary of state, special assistant to the president for International Development, under secretary of Health, Education and Welfare. Chairman of the board of the Museum of Modern Art, trustee of the Rockefeller Brothers Fund, Government Affairs Foundation, Inc., member of Century, University, Knickerbocker, and Metropolitan Clubs.
>
> *Charles Percy.* U.S. Senator (R. Illinois). Attended University of Chicago. Former president and chairman of the board of Bell & Howell Corporation. Director of Harris Trust and Savings Bank, Outboard Moving Corporation. Former chairman of National Finance Committee of the Republican Party. Trustee of the University of Chicago, Illinois Institute of Technology, California Institute of Technology. Member of Chicago, Executives, Economic, and Commonwealth Clubs.

The backgrounds of these men suggest that they can run a government as well as run for office. But the great majority of politicians—elective officeholders—have had little or no experience in heading major enterprises. Most have devoted their lives to running for public office. They are specialists in vote-getting, public relations, image-making, bargaining and compromise, and coalition-building.

Most politicians in America are lawyers. But they are not usually top professional lawyers. (We will examine these "super-lawyers" later.) Instead, the typical politician-lawyer uses his law career as a means of support—one that is compatible with political office-holding. Woodrow Wilson said, "The profession I chose was politics; the profession I entered was the law. I entered one because I thought it would lead to the other." [2] The legal profession provides the free time, the extensive public contacts, and the occupational prestige required for political campaign-

[2] Quoted in Heinz Eulau and John Sprague, *Lawyers in Politics* (Indianapolis: Bobbs-Merrill Co., 1964), p. 5.

ing. The lawyer's occupation is the representation of clients, so he makes no great change when he moves from representing clients in private practice to representing constituents in public office.

A significant number of top politicians have inherited great wealth. The Roosevelts, Rockefellers, Kennedys, Lodges, Harrimans, and others have used their wealth and family connections to support their political careers. *But it is important to note that a majority of the nation's top politicians have climbed the ladder from relative obscurity to political success.* Many have acquired some wealth in the process, but most started their climb from very middle-class circumstances. In fact, only one of the last five presidents (John F. Kennedy) was born to great wealth. Thus, as in the corporate world, one finds both "inheritors" and "climbers" in the world of politics.

Gerald R. Ford: From the Rose Bowl to the White House

Gerald Ford has always been a team player—from his days as an All-American lineman at the University of Michigan, through his long service and rise to leadership in the Congress, during his years of service and support for the Republican Party, to his presidency. He projects the image of an open, accessible, and consensus-building presidency. Ford is the nation's first president not selected by popular vote (or by vote of presidential electors). He is a man whose career was built in the Congress of the United States. His colleagues there have described him as "solid, dependable, and loyal—a man more comfortable carrying out the programs of others than initiating things on his own." [3] As president, he is thrust into the role of leadership, but there is ample evidence that he acts only after extensive consultation with leaders in Congress, the Cabinet, industry, finance, labor, and the mass media.

Gerald Ford was born Leslie King, Jr., but his mother divorced and remarried Gerald R. Ford, a Grand Rapids, Michigan paint store owner. Ford attended public schools in Grand Rapids, and received his B.A. from the University of Michigan and his law degree from Yale University. He was a star lineman on the University of Michigan's national championship and Rose Bowl football teams in 1932 and 1933, and was the team's most valuable player in 1934. He turned down the opportunity to play professional football in order to take a coaching job at Yale that would permit him to attend law school at the same time. Upper-social-class member U.S. Senator William Proxmire, whom Ford coached at

[3] *Congressional Quarterly,* October 20, 1973, p. 2762.

Yale says, "Ford is the same kind of man now as he was then—solid and square. He has the kind of wholesome sincerity, the kind of loyal consistency that many voters may be looking for." Ford graduated in the top third of his Yale Law School class in 1941. Following service with the Navy in World War II in the South Pacific, Ford returned home to Grand Rapids and, capitalizing on his football reputation and war service, won election to the House in 1948.

Ford served 25 years in the House as a loyal Republican, winning recognition for his integrity, sincerity, and common sense, rather than his intelligence, initiative, or imagination. He was also careful to cultivate his home constituents with minor services, favors, and visits. In 1965, Wisconsin Congressman Melvin Laird, later to become secretary of defense, led a movement among House Republicans to replace the aging Charles Halleck as Minority Leader with the younger, likable Gerald Ford. Ford developed into an excellent House Leader through his engaging personality, honesty, and ability to establish close personal relationships with both allies and opponents. A House colleague explained: "Jerry is an open tactician. He doesn't look for clever ways to sneak in behind you. He does the obvious, which is usually common sense." [4]

Ford's voting record was moderately conservative. He voted *for* the Civil Rights Act of 1964, the Voting Rights Act of 1965, and the Fair Housing Act of 1968. But he opposed many aspects of the "war on poverty" and other social welfare spending measures. He supported defense spending, and supported both Presidents Johnson and Nixon in their conduct in the Vietnam War. Ford denounced ultraliberal Supreme Court Justice William O. Douglas after the Justice wrote an article in the left-wing *Evergreen Review* sanctioning violent revolution in America.

In 1973, as the Watergate Affair expanded and Vice-President Spiro Agnew resigned and pleaded guilty to the charge of tax evasion, President Nixon sought to bring into his administration men of recognized personal integrity who could improve presidential relations with Congress. Nixon's ultimate decision to make Gerald Ford vice-president under the 26th Amendment was widely applauded in Congress and the news media. But in a sense, Ford was Congress' choice for the vice-presidency, not Richard Nixon's. Nixon personally preferred former Texas governor John Connally. Ford was quickly confirmed by the Democratic-controlled Congress.

Ford's style is candid, folksy, unpretentious. His long years in the Congress have developed in him a tolerance of differing views, a desire to accommodate, and a willingness to compromise differences. In his first

[4] *Time*, August 19, 1974, p. 32.

speech to the nation as president he said, "I have had lots of adversaries, but no enemies that I can remember."

When Ford spoke at the Harvard Club of Boston, he was asked to comment on the exile of the world-renowned Russian novelist Alexander Solzhenitsyn. Ford simply said: "Well I've never read anything Solzhenitsyn has written, but I understand he's quite superb." [5] Doubtlessly there were many others at the Harvard Club who had never read Solzhenitsyn, but to admit such a fact in these circles is unheard of. Such openness has contributed immeasurably to his rise to the top. Whether this is a sufficient quality to govern a nation remains a crucial question. But after the years of Watergate, and a notable absence of candor in the White House, Ford's most visible quality appealed to the Congress, the news media, and the general public.

Ted Kennedy: Crown Prince

John F. Kennedy once said of his brothers, "Just as I went into politics because Joe [the oldest Kennedy brother, killed in World War II] died, if anything happened to me tomorrow Bobby would run for my seat in the Senate. And if Bobby died, our young brother Ted would take over for him."

Edward M. "Ted" Kennedy's major qualifications for public office are his style, appearance, accent, and name. He is the image of his late brothers, John and Robert. Their deaths by assassins' bullets make the youngest Kennedy brother the sentimental favorite of millions of Americans—the last guardian of the Camelot legend. The Kennedy charisma attaches to "Ted" despite tragedy, scandal, and defeat at the hands of fellow Democratic senators (Kennedy was unceremoniously ousted as Senate Democratic Whip in 1971). The Kennedy wealth is another major political asset. Ted Kennedy's public tax returns reveal an income of $.5 million per year from interest on his inheritance, suggesting a personal net wealth of at least $10 million. Total family wealth probably exceeds $100 million.

The Kennedy dynasty began with the flamboyant career of Joseph P. Kennedy, son of a prosperous Irish saloon-keeper and ward boss in Boston. Joseph Kennedy attended Boston Latin School and Harvard, receiving his B.A. in 1912. He started his career in banking, moved into stock market operations, dabbled in shipbuilding, formed a movie-making company (RKO and later Paramount), and married the daughter of the

5 Saul Friedman, "In Praise of Honest Ignorance," *Harpers* (August 1974), p. 16.

mayor of Boston. "Old Joe" made the major part of his fortune in stock market manipulations. With his associate, William Randolph Hearst, Kennedy provided key financial backing for the 1932 presidential campaign of Franklin D. Roosevelt. FDR later made Kennedy head of the Securities and Exchange Commission. But making a market speculator head of a commission that was designed to protect investors caused such public outcry that he was forced to resign after one year. FDR then appointed Kennedy head of the Maritime Commission, but rumors of extravagant subsidies to shipbuilding friends forced his resignation after only two months on the job. In 1937, FDR appointed him ambassador to England. His diplomatic career lasted three years and ended over differences with FDR regarding U.S. assistance to the Allies. Old Joe is said to have advised FDR of the likelihood of German victory and the advantages of placating Hitler.

Joseph P. Kennedy, Sr., was a family man, a prominent Catholic, and the father of nine children. (Joseph P., Jr., was killed as a World War II Navy Pilot; President John F. Kennedy was assassinated; Senator Robert F. Kennedy was assassinated; Kathleen died in a plane crash; Rosemary is living in an institution for the mentally retarded; Eunice is married to Sargent Shriver, former director of the Peace Corps and the War on Poverty and replacement for Senator Thomas Eagleton as the Democratic vice-presidential nominee in 1972; Patricia, formerly married to actor Peter Lawford; Jean, wife of Stephen Smith; and the youngest, Edward M. "Ted" Kennedy.)

Although born to great wealth and accustomed to an upper-class style of living (he received his first communion from Pope Pius XII), Ted Kennedy acquired the sense of competition fostered in the large Kennedy household. In 1951, suspended from Harvard for cheating on a Spanish examination, he joined the Army and served two years in Germany. He was readmitted to Harvard, where he played on the Harvard football team and graduated in 1956.

Despite his family background, Harvard Law School rejected Ted Kennedy's application for admission. So he enrolled in the University of Virginia Law School and completed his law degree in 1959. Following graduation and work on his brother's 1960 presidential campaign, he was appointed assistant district attorney for Suffolk County, Massachusetts.

In 1962, when he was just 30 years old, the minimum age for a U.S. Senator, he announced his candidacy for the Massachusetts Senate seat formerly held by his brother, who was then president. In the Democratic primary he faced Edward J. McCormack, nephew of the then Speaker of the House, John W. McCormack. During a televised debate, McCormack said to Kennedy, "You never worked for a living. You never held elective office. You lack the qualifications and maturity of judgment. . . . If your name were not Kennedy, your candidacy would be a joke." But Kennedy won overwhelmingly and went on to defeat the Republican candidate George Cabot Lodge. (George Cabot Lodge was the son of U.S. Ambassador to South Vietnam and former U.S. Senator Henry Cabot Lodge, Jr. In 1916, Kennedy's grandfather, Boston Mayor, John F. Fitzgerald had been defeated in a race for the same Senate seat by Lodge's great-grandfather, Senator Henry Cabot Lodge.) Kennedy's campaign slogan was "I can do more for Massachusetts," which undoubtedly carried the implication to some of political patronage from his brother the president.

Kennedy performed better in the Senate than many had expected. He cultivated Senate friends, appeared at fund-raising dinners, and informed himself about several important policy fields. He worked hard learning about national health problems and eventually became chairman of the Subcommittee on Health of the Senate Labor and Public Welfare Committee. He also devoted considerable attention to problems of the elderly and to the activities of the National Science Foundation. In 1969 he was elected Senate Democratic Whip by his colleagues.

But his personal life was marred by accident, tragedy, and scandal. He nearly died in a 1964 plane crash in which he suffered a broken back. An athletic and handsome 6 foot 2 inches, Kennedy was frequently the object of romantic gossip at Washington cocktail parties. On July 19, 1969, a young woman, Mary Jo Kopechne, died when the car Kennedy was driving plunged off a narrow bridge on Chappaquiddick Island after a late-night party. Missing for ten hours after the accident, Kennedy later made a dramatic national television appearance, saying that the tragedy had been an accident, that he had tried unsuccessfully to save Miss Kopechne, and that he had been too confused to report the tragedy until the next day. The official inquest has been kept secret, and many feel that there are still unresolved discrepancies in Kennedy's story.[6] Kennedy pled guilty to the minor charge of leaving the scene of an accident.

Senate Democrats removed Kennedy from his position of Majority Whip. But the national news media never pressed the Chappaquiddick incident and continued favorable reporting of the still charismatic Senator. He recovered quickly in public opinion polls and generally leads all other Democrats in presidential preference polling. Kennedy deliberately avoided the Democratic presidential nomination in 1972 and announced that he would not be a candidate in 1976. But most observers believe he can have the Democratic Party's presidential nomination if and when he wants it.

[6] See Robert Sherrill, "Chappaquiddick + 5," *New York Times Magazine,* July 14, 1974.

Like his brothers before him, Ted Kennedy's political stance has been typically liberal and public-regarding. He has generally reflected current liberal concerns as they surfaced in the news media—racial discrimination, the poor, the elderly, the sick, ecology, migrant labor, women's rights, the plight of the Indians. Kennedy is a trustee of the Joseph P. Kennedy, Jr. Foundation, Boston Children's Hospital, Boston Museum, Boston University, John F. Kennedy Library, the Fletcher School of Tufts University, Emmanuel College, and Northeastern University.

Executive Decision-Makers: The Serious Men

The responsibility for the initiation of national programs and policies falls primarily upon the president, top White House staff, and the heads of executive departments. Generally, Congress merely responds to policy proposals initiated by the executive branch. The president and his key advisors and administrators have a strong incentive to fulfill their responsibility for decision-making: in the eyes of the American public, they are responsible for everything that happens in the nation regardless of whether or not they have the authority or capacity to do anything about it. There is a general expectation that every administration, even one committed to a "caretaker" role, will put forth some sort of policy program.

The president and vice-president, White House presidential advisors and ambassadors-at-large, cabinet secretaries, under secretaries, and assistant secretaries constitute our executive elite. Let us examine some of the people who have served in key cabinet positions in recent presidential administrations.

DEFENSE

Charles E. Wilson. Secretary of defense, 1953–1957; president and member of the board of directors of General Motors.

Neil H. McElroy. Secretary of defense, 1957–1959; former president and member of the board of directors of Procter & Gamble; member of the board of directors of General Electric, of Chrysler Corp., and of Equitable Life Assurance Co.; member of the board of trustees of Harvard University, of the National Safety Council, and of the National Industrial Conference.

Thomas S. Gates. Secretary of defense, 1959–1960, and secretary of the Navy, 1957–1959; chairman of the board and chief executive officer, Morgan Guaranty Trust Co.; member of the board of directors of General Electric, Bethlehem Steel, Scott Paper Co., Campbell Soup Co., Insurance

Co. of North America, Cities Service, Smith Kline and French (pharmaceuticals), and the University of Pennsylvania.

Robert S. McNamara. Secretary of defense, 1961–1967; president and member of the board of directors of the Ford Motor Co.; member of the board of directors of Scott Paper Co.; president of the World Bank, 1967 to date.

Clark Clifford. Secretary of defense, 1967–1969; senior partner of Clifford & Miller (Washington law firm); member of board of directors of the National Bank of Washington, and of the Sheridan Hotel Corp.; special counsel to the president, 1949–1950; member of board of trustees of Washington University in St. Louis.

Melvin Laird. Secretary of defense, 1969–1973; former Wisconsin Republican Congressman and chairman of Republican Conference in the House of Representatives.

James R. Schlesinger. Secretary of defense, 1973 to date; former director, Central Intelligence Agency; former chairman of Atomic Energy Commission; formerly assistant director of Office of Management and Budget, economics professor, and research associate of the RAND Corp.

STATE

John Foster Dulles. Secretary of state, 1953–1960; partner of Sullivan & Cromwell (one of 20 largest law firms on Wall Street); member of the board of directors of the Bank of New York, Fifth Avenue Bank, American Bank Note Co., International Nickel Co. of Canada, Babcock and Wilson Corp., Shenandoah Corp., United Cigar Stores, American Cotton Oil Co., United Railroad of St. Louis, and European Textile Corp. Was a trustee of New York Public Library, Union Theological Seminary, Rockefeller Foundation, and the Carnegie Endowment for International Peace; also a delegate to the World Council of Churches.

Dean Rusk. Secretary of state, 1961–1968; former president of Rockefeller Foundation.

William P. Rodgers. Secretary of state, 1969–1973; U.S. Attorney General during Eisenhower administration; senior partner in Royall, Koegal, Rogers, and Wells (one of the 20 largest Wall Street law firms).

Henry Kissinger. Secretary of state, 1973 to date; former special assistant to the president for National Security Affairs; former Harvard Professor of International Affairs, and project director for Rockefeller Brothers Fund and for the Council on Foreign Relations.

TREASURY

George M. Humphrey. Secretary of the treasury, 1953–1957; former chairman of the board of directors of the M. A. Hanna Co.; member of board of directors of National Steel Corp.; Consolidated Coal Co. of Canada and Dominion Sugar Co.; trustee of M.I.T.

Robert B. Anderson. Secretary of the treasury, 1957–1961; secretary of the Navy, 1953–1954; deputy secretary of defense, 1954–1955; member of board of directors of Goodyear Tire and Rubber Co. and Pan-American Airways; member of the executive board of the Boy Scouts of America.

Douglas Dillon. Secretary of the treasury, 1961–1963; chairman of the board of Dillon, Reed, and Co., Inc. (one of Wall Street's largest investment firms); member of New York Stock Exchange; director of U.S. and Foreign Securities Corp. and U.S. International Securities Corp.; member of board of governors of New York Hospital and Metropolitan Museum.

David Kennedy. Secretary of the treasury, 1969–1971; president and chairman of the board of Continental Illinois Bank and Trust Co.; director of International Harvester Co., Commonwealth Edison, Pullman Co., Abbott Laboratories, Swift and Co., U.S. Gypsum, and Communications Satellite Corp.; trustee of the University of Chicago, the Brookings Institution, the Committee for Economic Development, and George Washington University.

John B. Connally. Secretary of the treasury, 1971–1972; former secretary of Navy, governor of Texas, administrative assistant to Lyndon B. Johnson; attorney for Murcheson Brothers Investment (Dallas); former director of New York Central Railroad.

George P. Schultz. Secretary of the treasury, 1972–1974; former secretary of labor and director of the Office of Management and Budget; former dean of the University of Chicago Graduate School of Business; former director of Borg-Warner Corp., General American Transportation Co., and Stein, Roe & Farnham (investments).

William E. Simon. Secretary of the treasury, 1974 to date; former director, Federal Energy Office, and former deputy secretary of the treasury; formerly a senior partner of Salomon Brothers (one of Wall Street's largest investment firms–specialization in municipal bond trading).

It makes relatively little difference whether a president is a Democrat or a Republican: he must call on the same type of "serious men" to run the government.

Henry Kissinger: The Intellectual in Power

One of the most powerful men in the world today is Henry A. Kissinger. His achievements in world diplomacy are legendary: he negotiated the U.S. withdrawal from the Vietnam War; established a new détente between the United States and the Soviet Union; engineered the SALT agreement, the world's first attempt at limiting the development of strategic nuclear weapons; opened U.S. relations with China; and negotiated a series of difficult agreements between Arabs and Israelis in the Middle East.

Heinz Alfred Kissinger (he changed his name to Henry after coming to the United States) was born in Furth in Bavaria, Germany, in

1923. His father was a teacher in the local gymnasium, or prep school. The Kissingers were an educated middle-class German Jewish family. When the Nazis came to power in the early 1930s, the Kissingers were subjected to increasing persecution. Young Henry was denied entrance to the gymnasium and forced to attend an all-Jewish school. He and his fellow Jewish students were frequently beaten up on their way to and from school. His father was humiliated and then dismissed from his teaching post. At his mother's urging, the family emigrated to New York City in 1938. His father found work as a clerk and bookkeeper and his mother worked as a cook. Henry attended George Washington High School in New York; he was a straight-A student, but his heavy accent and unhappy experiences in Germany caused him to be withdrawn.

After graduation, Kissinger took a job in a shaving brush factory and took evening courses at the City University of New York in hopes of becoming an accountant. He was drafted in 1943, and as a private in the 84th Infantry Division saw action in France and Germany. But his comrades still described him as "totally withdrawn."

Kissinger once observed about his own early career: "Living as a Jew under the Nazis, then as a refugee in America, and then as a private in the Army, isn't exactly an experience that builds confidence." But it was in the Army that Kissinger first made his mark. When his division moved into Germany, he was made interpreter for the division's commanding general. Later he was placed in charge of the military government of the small German town of Drefeld, and promoted to staff sergeant. One of his officers urged him to return home after his service and complete his college education. He also advised him that *"gentlemen* do not go to the College of the City of New York." Kissinger took the advice, returned home, won a New York State scholarship, and was admitted to Harvard University.

Kissinger graduated as a Phi Beta Kappa, summa cum laude, government major in 1950, and continued his studies at the Harvard Graduate School. He received his M.S. (1952), and Ph.D. (1954), writing his dissertation on the efforts of conservative statesmen to create a new world balance of power at the Conference of Vienna in 1815. (This was later published as *A World Restored: Castlereagh, Metternich, and the Problems of Peace* [1957].)

Kissinger reportedly turned down a professorship at the University of Chicago to stay at Harvard as a temporary instructor. But shortly thereafter he was appointed to head an important study by the Council on Foreign Relations to develop methods short of all-out war for coping with the perceived Soviet challenge to Western Europe. Key members of this influential Council had become disenchanted with the "massive retaliation" doctrine of then Secretary of State John Foster Dulles. In 1957

Kissinger produced his major work, *Nuclear Weapons and Foreign Policy,*[7] which argued persuasively that strategy must determine weapons rather than vice versa, and that the U.S. should strive for greater flexibility in weapons development, including tactical nuclear weapons.

The book established Kissinger as a leading "defense intellectual." He was named associate professor (1959) and professor (1962) in Harvard's Government Department and director of Harvard's Defense Studies Program. He became a consultant to the Joint Chiefs of Staff, the National Security Council, Arms Control and Disarmament Agency, and the State Department, as well as the RAND Corporation. His close association with the Rockefellers began when Nelson A. Rockefeller asked him to direct a Rockefeller Brothers Foundation special study of foreign policy. The resulting book, *The Necessity of Choice; Prospects of American Foreign Policy* (1961), warned against undue optimism about U.S.–Soviet relations but also recommended ways of avoiding the ultimate confrontation between these superpowers. Later Kissinger became foreign policy adviser to Nelson Rockefeller and drafted his key statements on world affairs during the New York governor's unsuccessful bid for the presidency in 1968.

Although Nixon viewed himself as an expert on world affairs, when he won the presidency in 1968 he asked for assistance from the Rockefellers, the Council of Foreign Affairs, and the Harvard University intellectuals. They recommended Kissinger and even though Nixon had only met him once, Kissinger was appointed special assistant to the president for national security affairs.

Kissinger's performance as the president's national security adviser and special emissary can only be described as spectacular. He met secretly with North Vietnamese representatives over a prolonged period in negotiations which eventually ended the Vietnam War. He undertook his now-celebrated clandestine trip to Peking to arrange the president's historic visit to that nation. In trips to Moscow he paved the way for the president's visit and the establishment of a new Soviet-American détente. He played the major role in the Strategic Arms Limitation Talks (SALT), which resulted in the world's first agreement to limit strategic nuclear weapons. His performance overshadowed that of Secretary of State William P. Rodgers. In 1974, upon the resignation of Rodgers, Kissinger was appointed secretary of state.

Kissinger's power and reputation generally survived the demise of the Nixon presidency. The new president, Gerald Ford, with little experience in foreign policy, seemed to rely on Kissinger as much or more

[7] Henry Kissinger, *Nuclear Weapons and Foreign Policy* (New York: Council on Foreign Relations, 1957). Published also as an Anchor Book by Doubleday, 1958.

than had Nixon. As secretary of state, Kissinger continued to engage in personal travel and face-to-face diplomacy. He did not retreat within the State Department bureaucracy. But with the presidency weakened by Watergate, with a Democratic Congress suspicious of presidential power, and with the mass media increasingly critical of foreign commitments, the power of America has waned in world affairs. Kissinger's efforts to maintain American influence were frustrated not only by communist victories in Southeast Asia but also by internal politics, which placed domestic concerns ahead of national defense and international affairs.

Kissinger's diplomacy reflects his fundamental belief in balance-of-power politics. While voicing respect for the U.S. and other international bodies, Kissinger has concentrated attention on relationships among the big powers. He recognizes the role of military power at the conference table. His approach to world politics might have been predicted from a careful reading of his Harvard Ph.D. dissertation in 1954:

> Whenever peace—conceived as the avoidance of war—has been the primary objective of a group of powers, the international system has been at the mercy of the most ruthless member of the international community. Whenever the international order has acknowledged that certain principles should not be compromised, even for the sake of peace, stability based on an equilibrium of forces was at least conceivable.[8]

Note that Kissinger's rise to power depended more upon his affiliation with Nelson Rockefeller, the Rockefeller Foundation, and the Council on Foreign Relations, than his intellectual attachments.

The Professional Bureaucrats

The federal bureaucracy, comprised of nearly three million people, and the professional federal executives who supervise it, occupy a uniquely influential position in American society. They advise the president on decisions he must make; they present and defend legislative recommendations before the Congress; and they supervise the day-to-day decisions of the hundreds of departments, agencies, commissions, and boards that influence the lives of every American. A powerful bureaucratic elite is comprised of these federal executives—particularly the secretaries, assistant secretaries, and under secretaries of the twelve federal departments (State, Treasury, Defense, Justice, Post Office, Interior, Agriculture, Commerce,

[8] Henry A. Kissinger, *A World Restored: Castlereagh, Metternich, and the Restoration of Peace, 1812–1822.*

Labor, HEW, Housing and Urban Development, and Transportation); the same officials for the Army, Navy, and Air Force departments; administrators of important independent agencies in the executive office of the president (including the Office of Management and Budget, the National Security Council, and the Council of Economic Advisers); and members of key regulatory commissions and boards (Federal Reserve Board, Civil Aeronautics Board, Federal Communications Commission, Federal Power Commission, Federal Trade Commission, Interstate Commerce Commission, National Labor Relations Board, and Securities and Exchange Commission). Nearly all of these top federal executive positions are filled by presidential appointment with Senate confirmation.

What kind of men head the federal bureaucracy? In an interesting study[9] of over 1000 men who occupied the positions listed above during the presidential administrations of Roosevelt, Truman, Eisenhower, Kennedy and Johnson, the Brookings Institution reports that 36 percent of these top federal executives came up through the ranks of the government itself, 26 percent were recruited from law, 24 percent from business, 7 percent from education, and 7 percent from a variety of other fields. A plurality of top federal executives are *career bureaucrats*. Moreover, most of these people have served in only one government agency,[10] slowly acquiring seniority and promotion in the agency in which they eventually served in a top post. A total of 63 percent of the top federal executives were federal bureaucrats at the time of their appointment to a top post; only 37 percent had no prior experience as federal bureaucrats.[11] (If experience in *state* bureaucracies is counted, a total of 69 percent of the top federal executives can be said to have been government bureaucrats at the time of their appointment.)

Thus, a majority of top federal executives are themselves career bureaucrats. The federal bureaucracy itself is producing its own leadership, with some limited recruitment from business and law. (Later in this volume, we will compare our own data for the early 1970s on governmental and military elites with the earlier Brookings Institution's data; but we can say now that our figures are roughly comparable.) The federal bureaucracy, then, is an independent channel of recruitment to positions of governmental power in America. Consider, for example, the careers of the following individuals.

Elliot Richardson. Former secretary of Department of Health, Education and Welfare, secretary of defense, and U.S. Attorney General. Attended

[9] David T. Stanley, Dean E. Mann, and Jameson W. Doig, *Men Who Govern* (Washington: Brookings Institution, 1967).

[10] Ibid., p. 8.

[11] Ibid., p. 45.

Harvard College, Harvard Law School. Millionaire descendant of six generations of Boston doctors (father was chief of surgery at Massachusetts General Hospital) and to the Boston Brahmin family of Shattuck, which had played a key role in the history of Harvard University. Richardson graduated cum laude from Harvard Law School and edited the *Harvard Law Review*. He did his law clerkship under Supreme Court Justice Felix Frankfurter, then joined a prestigious Boston law firm. He served briefly as an assistant to Republican U.S. Senator Leverett Saltonstall of Massachusetts, and was assistant secretary of Health, Education and Welfare in the Eisenhower Administration. Richardson ran successfully for lieutenant governor of Massachusetts in 1964 and for state attorney general in 1966. Nixon appointed Richardson as Secretary of Health, Education and Welfare in 1971. The appointment was based more on Richardson's proven administrative abilities than on his political association with Nixon. Richardson managed well, despite pressure upward from a liberal and Democratic HEW bureaucracy and pressure downward from a conservative and Republican White House staff. Richardson's upper-class, Eastern, liberal convictions set him apart from the Nixon team, but improved his relations with Congress. In 1973 Nixon asked Richardson to take over the Defense Department to rebuild it after the Vietnam debacle. But Watergate events soon overtook the White House and Nixon found himself in need of an attorney general whose integrity was unchallenged and who had the confidence of Eastern liberals in the news media and Congress. In an apparent agreement with congressional leaders, Nixon appointed Richardson as attorney general, who in turn appointed his old Harvard Law Professor Archibald Cox as special Watergate prosecutor. But Cox recruited a staff of young liberals as prosecutors, expanded his investigations of the White House far beyond the original Watergate break-in, and finally went to court to subpeona the president to produce the famous White House tapes. Nixon fired Cox, and Richardson resigned his office in protest. The ejection of Richardson and Cox from his administration initiated the impeachment movement which eventually led to Nixon's resignation. President Ford thereafter appointed Richardson Ambassador to Great Britain and Richardson remains a powerful figure in Washington. Richardson is a trustee of Massachusetts General Hospital, Radcliffe College, and Harvard University.

Joseph J. Sisco. Assistant secretary of state. Attended Knox College, University of Chicago, Ph.D. Son of an Italian immigrant tailor in Chicago, Sisco largely financed his own education through work at odd jobs. Upon completion of his B.A. in 1941, he entered the Army and served as a first lieutenant in the infantry in the Pacific. After the war, he entered graduate school at the University of Chicago, completing his Ph.D. in Soviet Studies and International Affairs in 1950. He served with the CIA in 1950 and 1951 and then transferred to the State Department. He rose gradually in the State Department bureaucracy, serving in such positions as specialist in U.N. affairs, deputy director and later director of the State Department's Office of U.N. Affairs, deputy assistant secretary of the Bureau of International Organization Affairs, and finally in 1965, assistant secretary of state for International Organization Affairs. While this fifteen-year sojourn in the labyrinths of the State Department bureaucracy may seem like a long apprenticeship to outsiders, actually Sisco's climb was considered unprecedented among the old hands at the State Department. After the Arab-Israeli Six-Day War in 1967, Sisco was given key responsibilities in mediating negotiations between Arabs and Israelites. (Ordinarily this task would fall to the Near Eastern Bureau of the State Department, but this bureau was widely recognized as pro-Arab in outlook; hence Sisco was brought into Middle Eastern Affairs.) In 1969, President Nixon named him assistant secretary of state for Near Eastern Affairs. Sisco has been the chief U.S. negotiator in the Middle East, and next to Henry Kissinger, the most influential figure shaping U.S. foreign policy in recent years.

Note that these men rose to prominence primarily in government service. They were not recruited from the corporate or financial world. Of course, top federal bureaucrats are recruited primarily from the middle- and upper-middle-class segments of the population, as are leaders in other sectors of society. The Brookings Institution reports that the percentage of college-educated top executive bureaucrats rose from 88 percent in the Roosevelt Administration to 99 percent in the Johnson Administration. Morover, 68 percent had advanced degrees—44 percent in law, 17 percent with earned master's degrees, and 11 percent with earned doctorates. But the class composition of the top bureaucrats is better reflected in information on *which* schools and colleges were attended. The Brookings Institution reports that the Ivy League schools plus Stanford, Chicago, Michigan, and Berkeley educated over 40 percent of the top federal executives, with Yale, Harvard, and Princeton leading the list.[12] Moreover, this has increased over time; there were larger proportions of Ivy Leaguers in top posts in 1965 than in 1945. Perhaps more importantly, the Brookings study reports that 39 percent of the top federal executives attended *private* schools (compared to only 6 percent of the U.S. population); and 17 percent went to one of only eighteen "name" prep schools.[13] The Brookings Institution study also reports that most top federal executives come from large Eastern cities.

There is little difference between Republican and Democratic administrations in the kind of men who are appointed to top executive posts. It is true, of course, that Republican presidents tend to appoint Republicans to top posts, and Democratic presidents tend to appoint Democrats; only about 8 percent of the top appointments cross party lines. However, the Brookings study reports few discernible differences in the class backgrounds, educational levels, occupational experiences, or previous public service of Democratic or Republican appointees.

One troublesome problem at the top of the federal bureaucracy is

[12] Ibid., p. 21.

[13] Avon Old Farms, Choate, Deerfield, Groton, Hill, Hotchkiss, Kent, Lawrenceville, Loomis, Middlesex, Milton, Phillips Andover, Phillips Exeter, St. George's, St. Mary's, St. Paul's, Taft, Thatcher.

the shortness of tenure of federal executives. *The median tenure in office of top federal executives is only two years.*[14] Only on the regulatory commissions do we encounter significantly longer tenure. Of course, top federal executives have had significant federal bureaucratic experience before coming to their posts. But such a short tenure at the top has obvious disadvantages; it is generally estimated that a top federal executive needs a year or more to become fully productive, to learn the issues, programs, procedures, technical problems, and personalities involved in his work. If he resigns after his second year, the federal bureaucracy is not getting continuous, knowledgeable direction from its top officials. According to the Brookings study, of the top bureaucrats who leave office, 60 percent go into private law practice or private business, 25 percent stay in the federal service in some other capacity, and 15 percent retire or die.[15] The data on short tenure suggests that we have created too many conflicting pressures on top federal executives—from the White House, Congress, interest groups, other government agencies, and particularly the mass media. Top federal executive positions are becoming less attractive over time.

The Military Establishment

In his farewell address to the nation in 1961, President Dwight D. Eisenhower warned of "an immense military establishment and a large arms industry." He observed:

> In the councils of government, we must guard against the acquisition of unwarranted influence, whether sought or unsought, by the military-industrial complex. The potential for the disastrous rise of misplaced power exists and will persist. We must never let the weight of this combination endanger our liberties or democratic processes. We should take nothing for granted. Only an alert and knowledgeable citizenry can compel the proper meshing of the huge industrial and military machinery of defense with our peaceful methods and goals, so that security and liberty may prosper together.

These words were prepared by political scientist Malcolm Moos, an Eisenhower adviser who was later to become president of the University of Minnesota. But they accurately reflect Eisenhower's personal feelings about the pressures that had been mounting during his administration from the military and from private defense contractors for increased

14 Stanley et al., *Men Who Govern,* p. 57.

15 Ibid.

military spending. The "military-industrial complex" refers to the Armed Forces, the Defense Department, military contractors, and congressmen who represent defense-oriented constituencies.

While radicals view the military-industrial complex as a conspiracy to promote war and imperialism, it is not really anything like that. Economist John K. Galbraith portrays the military-industrial complex as a far more subtle interplay of forces in American society:

> It is an organization or a complex of organizations and not a conspiracy. . . . In the conspiratorial view, the military power is a coalition of generals and conniving industrialists. The goal is mutual enrichment; they arrange elaborately to feather each other's nests. The industrialists are the *deus ex machina;* their agents make their way around Washington arranging the payoff. . . .
>
> There is some enrichment and some graft. Insiders do well. . . . Nonetheless, the notion of a conspiracy to enrich the corrupt is gravely damaging to an understanding of military power. . . .
>
> The reality is far less dramatic and far more difficult of solution. The reality is a complex of organizations pursuing their sometimes diverse but generally common goals. The participants in these organizations are mostly honest men. . . . They live on their military pay or their salaries as engineers, scientists, or managers, or their pay and profits as executives, and would not dream of offering or accepting a bribe. . . .
>
> The problem is not conspiracy or corruption, but unchecked rule. And being unchecked, this rule reflects not the national need but the bureaucratic need. . . .[16]

What are real facts about the military-industrial complex? Military spending runs about $100 billion per year—less than 30 percent of the federal government's budget and only about *6 percent of the gross national product.* The 100 largest industrial corporations in the United States depend on military contracts for *less than 10 percent of their sales.* In other words, American industry does *not* depend upon war or the threat of war for any large proportion of its income or sales.

Nonetheless, there are a few powerful companies that depend heavily on defense contracts—Lockheed Aircraft, General Dynamics, McDonald Douglass, Boeing Co., Martin-Marietta Co., Grumman Aircraft, Thiokol, and Newport News Shipbuilding. But in the world of corporate giants, these firms are considered only medium-sized. None appears in the list of the top 100 corporations in America (see Table 3-1). While General Electric and American Telephone and Telegraph, among the real corporate giants, appear near the top of defense contract lists, their military sales are only *a small proportion of total sales.* Yet there is enough military business to make it a real concern of certain companies,

[16] John Kenneth Galbraith, *How to Control the Military* (New York: Signet Books, 1969), pp. 23–31.

Table 3-1. Companies Awarded Military Contracts Totaling in Excess of $1 Billion

	Ranking by Total Dollar Amounts of Military Contracts	Percent of Total Sales
1.	Lockheed Aircraft	88%
2.	General Dynamics	67
3.	McDonnell-Douglas	75
4.	Boeing Co.	54
5.	General Electric	19
6.	North American-Rockwell	57
7.	United Aircraft	57
8.	AT & T	9
9.	Martin-Marietta	62
10.	Sperry-Rand	35
11.	General Motors	2
12.	Grumman Aircraft	67
13.	General Tire	37
14.	Raytheon	55
15.	AVCO	75
16.	Hughes Tool Co. (Howard Hughes)	u
17.	Westinghouse Electric	13
18.	Ford (Philco)	3
19.	RCA	16
20.	Bendix	42
21.	Textron	36
22.	Ling-Temco-Vought	70
23.	Internat. Tel. & Tel.	19
24.	IBM	7
25.	Raymond International*	u
26.	Newport News Shipbuilding	90+
27.	Northrop	61
28.	Thiokol	96
29.	Standard Oil of N.J.	2
30.	Kaiser Industries	45
31.	Honeywell	24
32.	General Tel.	25
33.	Collins Radio	65
34.	Chrysler	4
35.	Litton	25
36.	Pan-Am. World Air.	44
37.	FMC	21
38.	Hercules	31

u-Unavailable
*Includes Morrison-Knudsen, Brown & Root, and J. A. Jones Construction Co.

Source: Dr. Ralph E. Lapp, *The Weapons Culture* (New York: Norton 1968), pp. 187-88.

the people who work for them, the communities in which they are located, and the congressmen and other public officials who represent these communities.

But American business in general is not interested in promoting war or international instability. The defense industry is considered an unstable enterprise—a feast or famine business for industrial companies. The price-earnings ratios for military-oriented companies are substantially lower than for civilian-oriented companies. More importantly, corporate America seeks planned stable growth, secure investments, and guaranteed returns. These conditions are disrupted by war. The stock market, reflecting the aspirations of businessmen, goes *up* when peace is announced, not *down*.

A frequent criticism of the military-industrial complex is that defense-oriented industries have become dependent on military hardware orders. Any reduction in military spending would result in a severe economic setback for these industries, so they apply great pressure to keep defense spending high. This is particularly true of the industries that are almost totally dependent upon defense contracts. The military, always pleased to receive new weapons, joins with defense industries in recommending to the government that it purchase new weapons. Finally, congressmen from constituencies with large defense industries and giant military bases can usually be counted on to join with the armed forces and defense industries in support of increased defense spending for new weapons.

But the "military-industrial complex" has been notably *unsuccessful* in recent years in federal budget-making. Federal spending for defense has *declined* from 49.8 percent of the budget in 1960, to 40.8 percent in 1970, and down to 27 percent of the budget in 1976. Federal spending for social security and welfare surpassed defense spending, even in a Republican administration committed in principle to a strong national security posture. This indicates that the American military-industrial complex is *not* a powerful conspiracy.

How many top federal executives come to Washington from employment by large defense contractors? The Brookings Institution reports that of 1,000 top federal executives studied from 1954 through 1965, *only 4 percent* had been employed by major defense contractors before their employment by the federal government.[17] Of course, there were slightly more people with defense industry backgrounds in the Defense Department itself, but even here, the Brookings study reports that only 12 percent of all top executives in the Defense Department and the Departments of the Army, Navy, and Air Force had had previous employment with defense contractors.

It seems clear in retrospect that C. Wright Mills placed too much importance on the military in his description of *The Power Elite*.[18] Mills was writing in the early 1950s when military prestige was high following

[17] Ibid., p. 38.

[18] C. Wright Mills, *The Power Elite* (New York: Oxford, 1956).

victory in World War II. After the war a few top military men were recruited to top corporate positions: General Douglas MacArthur became chairman of the board of Remington-Rand (now Sperry-Rand Corporation). General Lucius D. Clay, who commanded American troops in Germany after the war, became board chairman of Continental Can Company; General James H. Doolittle, head of the Air Force in World War II, became vice-president of Shell Oil. General Omar M. Bradley, Commander of the 12th Army Group in Europe in World War II, became board chairman of Bulova Research Laboratories. General Leslie R. Groves, head of the Manhattan Project, which developed the atomic bomb, became vice-president of Remington-Rand. General Walter Bedell Smith, Eisenhower's Chief of Staff, became vice-president of the board of directors of American Machine and Foundry Company. General Matthew B. Ridgeway, Army Chief of Staff during the Korean War, became chairman of the board of the Mellon Institute of Industrial Research.

But as sociologist Morris Janowitz points out, "The practice of appointing military personnel to politically responsible posts, although it continues, has declined sharply since 1950. Much of the political debate about military personnel in government policy positions centers on a few conspicuous cases where civilian leadership sought to make use of prestigious military officers to deal with difficult political problems."[19] Indeed, the contrast between the political prestige of the military in the 1950s and the 1970s is striking: the Supreme Allied Commander in Europe in World War II, Dwight D. Eisenhower, was elected president of the United States; the U.S. Commander in Vietnam, William Westmoreland, was defeated in his bid to become governor of South Carolina!

Moreover, in contrast with corporate and governmental elites, military officers do *not* come from the "upper classes" of society. Janowitz reports that a general infusion of persons from lower- and lower-middle-class backgrounds has occurred in all branches of the Armed Services (particularly the Air Force). He also reports that military leaders are more likely to have rural and Southern backgrounds than corporate or governmental elites: "In contrast with almost 70 percent of contemporary military leaders with social backgrounds with rural settings, only 26 percent of business leaders have rural backgrounds." [20]

The Congressional Establishment

While national policies are developed outside Congress, Congress is no mere "rubber stamp." Key congressmen do play an independent role in

19 Morris Janowitz, *The Professional Soldier* (New York: Free Press, 1960), p. 378.
20 Ibid., p. 87.

national decision-making; top congressional leaders must be included in any operational definition of a national elite.

But the congressional role is essentially a deliberative one. Congress accepts, modifies, or rejects the policies and programs developed by the president and White House staff, executive departments, influential interest groups and the mass media.

Many important government decisions, particularly in foreign and military affairs, are made without any direct participation by Congress. The president, with the support of top men in his administration, the mass media, the foundations, and civic associations, can commit the nation to foreign policies and military actions that Congress can neither foresee, prevent, or reverse. Congress had little or no role in the Korean War and the Vietnam War, other than to appropriate the necessary funds. Détente with the Soviet Union, new relationships with Communist China, the U.S. role in the Middle East, and similarly important policy directions are decided with little congressional participation. Often congressional leaders are told of major foreign policy decisions or military actions only a few minutes before they are announced on national television.

Congress is more influential in domestic affairs than in foreign or military policy. It is much freer to reject presidential initiatives in education, welfare, health, urban affairs, civil rights, agriculture, labor, business, or taxing and spending. Executive agencies—for example, the Office of Education, the Social Security Administration, the Housing Assistance Administration, the Department of Agriculture, the Office of Economic Opportunity—must go to Congress for needed legislation and appropriations. Congressional committees can exercise power in domestic affairs by giving or withholding the appropriations and the legislation wanted by these executive agencies.

Finally, congressional committees are an important communication link between governmental and nongovernmental elites; they serve as a bridge between the executive and military bureaucracies and the major nongovernmental elites in American society. Congressional committees bring department and agency heads together with leading industrial representatives—bankers, cotton producers, labor leaders, citrus growers, government contractors.

Political scientists have commented extensively on the structure of power *within* the Congress. They generally describe a hierarchical structure in both houses of the Congress—a "congressional establishment" which largely determines what the Congress will do. This "establishment" is composed of the Speaker of the House and President Pro Tempore of the Senate; House and Senate Majority and Minority Leaders and Whips; and committee chairmen and ranking minority members of House and Senate standing committees. Party leadership roles in the House and Senate are major sources of power in Washington. The Speaker of the House and the Majority and Minority Leaders of the House and Senate direct the business of Congress. Although they share this task with the standing committee chairmen, these leaders are generally "first among equals" in their relationships with committee chairmen. But the committee system also creates powerful congressional figures, the chairmen of the most powerful standing committees—particularly the Senate Foreign Relations, Appropriations, and Finance Committees, and the House Rules, Appropriations, and Ways and Means Committees.

"Policy clusters"—alliances of leaders from executive agencies, congressional committees, and private business and industry—tend to emerge in Washington. Committee chairmen, owing to their control over legislation in Congress, are key members of these policy clusters. One policy cluster might include the chairmen of the House and Senate committees on agriculture, the secretary of agriculture, and the leaders of the American Farm Bureau Federation. Another vital policy cluster would include the chairmen of the House and Senate Armed Services Committees; the secretary and under secretaries of defense; key military leaders, including the Joint Chiefs of Staff; and the leadership of defense industries such as Lockheed and General Dynamics. These alliances of congressional, executive, and private elites determine most public policy within their area of concern.

Senators and prominent reporters have described a Senate "establishment" and an "inner club" where power in the Senate and in Washington is concentrated (see Table 3-2). Ralph K. Huitt describes the Senate "establishment" type as

> a prudent man, who serves a long apprenticeship before trying to assert himself, and talks infrequently even then. He is courteous to a fault in his relations with his colleagues, not allowing political disagreements to affect his personal feelings. He is always ready to help another Senator when he can, and he expects to be repaid in kind. More than anything else he is a Senate man, proud of the institution and ready to defend its traditions and prerequisites against all outsiders. He is a legislative workhorse who specializes in one or two policy areas. . . . He is a man of accommodation who knows that "you have to go along to get along"; he is a conservative, institutional man, slow to change what he has mastered at the expense of so much time and patience.[21]

But viewed within the broader context of a *national elite,* congressional leaders appear "folksy," parochial, and localistic. Because of

[21] Ralph K. Huitt, "The Outsider in the U.S. Senate: An Alternative Role," *American Political Science Review,* 65 (June, 1961), 568.

Table 3-2. The Congressional Establishment 1975-76

Senate Leadership	
President Pro Tempore	James O. Eastland (D. Miss.)
Majority Leader	Mike Mansfield (D. Mont.)
Majority Whip	Robert C. Byrd (D. W. Va.)
Minority Leader	Hugh Scott (R. Pa.)
Minority Whip	Robert P. Griffin (R. Mich.)
House Leadership	
Speaker	Carl Albert (D. Okla.)
Majority Leader	Thomas P. O'Neill, Jr. (D. Mass.)
Majority Whip	John J. McFall (D. Calif.)
Minority Leader	John J. Rhodes (R. Ariz.)
Minority Whip	Robert H. Michel (R. Ill.)
Senate Committees	
Appropriations	John L. McClellan (D. Ark.)
Armed Services	John C. Stennis (D. Miss.)
Labor and Public Welfare	Harrison A. Williams (D. N.J.)
Banking, Housing and Urban Affairs	William Proxmire (D. Wis.)
Foreign Relations	John Sparkman (D. Ala.)
Government Operations	Abraham Ribicoff (D. Conn.)
Judiciary	James O. Eastland (D. Miss.)
Finance	Russell B. Long (D. La.)
Agriculture	Herman E. Talmadge (D. Ga.)
House Committees	
Rules	Ray J. Madden (D. Ind.)
Ways and Means	Al Ullman (D. Ore.)
Interstate Commerce	Harley O. Staggers (D. W.Va.)
Judiciary	Peter W. Rodino (D. N.J.)
Government Operations	Jack Brooks (D. Texas)
Foreign Affairs	Thomas E. Morgan (D. Pa.)
Banking and Currency	Henry S. Reuss (D. Wis.)
Armed Services	Melvin Price (D. Ill.)
Appropriations	George Mahon (D. Texas)
Agriculture	Thomas S. Foley (D. Wash.)

the local constituency of a congressman, he is predisposed to concern himself with local interests. Congressmen are part of local elite structures "back home"; they retain their local businesses and law practices, club memberships, and religious affiliations. Congressmen represent many small segments of the nation, rather than the nation as a whole. Even top congressional leaders, from safe districts, with many years of seniority, cannot completely shed their local interests. Their claim to *national* leadership must be safely hedged by attention to their local constituents. Consider, for example, the parochial backgrounds of these top congressional leaders.

Mike Mansfield. (D. Montana) Senate Majority Leader. Left home in Missoula, Montana at age 14 to join the Navy in World War I. Served in the Navy 1918–19, the Army 1919–20, and was in China with the Marines 1920–22. Returned to Montana to work in the copper mines and study nights for a high school education. Later enrolled at Montana State University and received B.A. (1933) and M.A. (1934) degrees in history. Taught Latin American and Far Eastern history at Montana State until elected to the House in 1942. Spent 10 years in the House and then defeated a Republican incumbent for his Montana Senate seat in 1952. Attracted attention defending the then Majority Leader Lyndon B. Johnson against attacks by Senators opposed to his dominance of legislative affairs; was immediately placed on the Foreign Relations Committee, where he was a strong supporter of the United Nations—even serving briefly as a U.S. delegate. Is very quiet-spoken and modestly liberal in expressed views—generally seeking consensus and compromise within his party. Was elected Majority Leader in 1961, succeeding Lyndon B. Johnson.

Carl B. Albert. (D. Oklahoma) Speaker of the House. Son of a small cotton farmer and coal miner, the diminutive Albert (5′4″, 120 pounds) attended public schools in McAlester, Oklahoma, where he was a national debate team champion. Attended the University of Oklahoma, was elected student council president. Was a Phi Beta Kappa and a Rhodes Scholar; obtained his law degree from Oxford on his Rhodes scholarship. Returned to Oklahoma in the midst of the Depression and his career stagnated. Worked as an accountant for Sague Oil Co. and Ohio Oil Co. and moved briefly to Illinois; failed in attempts to start a successful private law practice. Served as a Pentagon legal officer during World War II. Returned to McAlester, Oklahoma and in 1946 won a close upset victory in a race for his district's House seat. Was 38 when he won election in the House and may never have achieved leadership except for one fortunate circumstance: his Oklahoma district bordered on the Texas district of the powerful Speaker Sam Rayburn. Albert became Rayburn's protégé, performing chores for Speaker Rayburn and Majority Leader McCormack. Albert was made Whip in 1954. When Rayburn died in 1962, McCormack became Speaker and Albert moved up to Majority Leader. When McCormack retired, Albert became Speaker in 1971.

Robert C. Byrd. (D. W.Virginia) Majority Whip. Chairman, Senate Judiciary Committee. Attended Berkeley College and Marshall College (W.Virginia) for three years. Elected to W.Virginia legislature in 1946, and to U.S. House of Representatives in 1952. After three terms in the House, ran successfully for the U.S. Senate in 1958.

Henry M. Jackson. (D. Washington) U.S. Senator, chairman of Senate Internal Affairs Committee, member of Senate Government Operations and Armed Services committees. Son of Norwegian immigrants in Everett, Washington. Attended the University of Washington and received law degree in 1935. Was popularly elected Snohomish County Prosecuting Attorney, and four years later (1940) was elected to the House of Representatives. Served in the House until election to the Senate in 1952. Has never lost an election, and has been re-elected to the Senate by record margins of over 80 percent. Is the leading spokesman in the Senate on national defense. Boeing Aircraft, a major defense contractor, is a major employer in his district; however, a fellow congressman once remarked: "If the State of Washington did not have a single defense contract or a single military base, Jackson would still be strong for defense." Is co-author of the Environmental Protection Act and leading advocate of environmental protection. Belongs to the Everett, Washington American Legion, Elks, Eagles, Masons, and Sons of Norway.

John J. Rhodes. (R. Arizona) House Minority Leader. Kansas State University and Harvard Law School. Opened law practice in Mesa, Arizona after service in the Air Force. First elected to House of Representatives in 1952. Served three terms before appointment to the Appropriations Committee in 1959 Developed an important specialty on that Committee—defense appropriations—and rose in power within Republican ranks in Congress. In 1965, became chairman of the House Republican Policy Committee. In same year, helped swing crucial support behind Gerald Ford in his successful bid to unseat aging Charles Halleck as House Republican Leader. In 1973, when Ford became vice-president under the 26th Amendment to the Constitution, Rhodes won easy election as House Republican Leader. "Johnny won because of his close ties with Ford and the ranking members. He's had his little group in the policy committee. He's been easy to get along with. He's been very patient, almost overdue. So he was ready to roll." [22] Rise to congressional leadership fits the traditional mold of the loyal, hard-working, friendly, patient party man who eventually rises in seniority and influence. Political views are generally labeled as "independently conservative." Member of Mesa, Arizona Masons, Elks, Rotary, Mesa Junior Chamber of Commerce, American Legion, and Sons of the American Revolution.

Hugh Scott. (R. Pennsylvania) Senate Minority Leader. Attended Randoph-Macon College, University of Virginia Law School. Entered law practice in Philadelphia in 1922 at the age of 21. In 1926 became assistant district attorney for Philadelphia, then under control of a strong Republican party "machine." After 15 years of service in the Philadelphia Republican Party organization, elected to the U.S. House of Representatives in 1940. A loyal Republican party-line voter in the House. During World War II served aboard U.S. Merchant Marine ships and later was on active duty with the Navy in the Pacific (both while still a congressman). In 1948 after defeat of Republican presidential candidate Thomas E. Dewey, was given task of rebuilding the defeated party organization; eminently successful in this post. Provided Eisenhower with crucial support in his successful bid for the Republican nomination and the presidency in 1952. Gradually moved toward the liberal wing of his party, and won election as a Republican in an increasingly Democratic Philadelphia. In 1958, after 18 years of service in the House, won election to the U.S. Senate from Pennsylvania. Prominence in Republican party affairs before accession to the Senate assisted in rise to power within that body. Quickly became the recognized head of Republican leaders in the Senate. In 1969, elected Republican Senate Whip. In same year, upon the death of Senate Republican Leader Everett McKinley Dirkson, Scott succeeded to this top post. Was opposed by some of the more conservative Senators in his own party;

[22] *Congressional Quarterly,* December 15, 1973, p. 3293.

defeated Senator Howard Baker of Tennessee by a fairly close 24–19 vote in the 1969 intraparty election for Senate Minority Leader. Style and voting record differed from his more colorful and conservative predecessor, Everett Dirksen. Scott publicly disagreed with Republican President Nixon on many issues. Generally maintains an independent and politically moderate stance on most public issues.

The Judges

Nine men—none of whom is elected and all of whom serve for life—possess ultimate authority over all the other institutions of government. The Supreme Court of the United States has the authority to void the acts of popularly elected presidents and Congresses. There is no appeal from their decision about what is the "supreme law of the land," except perhaps to undertake the difficult task of amending the Constitution itself. Only the good judgment of the justices themselves—their sense of "judicial self-restraint"—limits their power over government elites. It was the Supreme Court, rather than the president or the Congress, that took the lead in such important issues as eliminating segregation from public life, insuring voter equality in representation, limiting the powers of police, and declaring abortion to be a fundamental right of women.

Social scientists have commented on the class bias of Supreme Court justices. John R. Schmidhauser reports that over 90 percent of the Supreme Court justices serving on the Court between 1789 and 1962 were from socially prominent, politically influential, upper-class families.[23] Over two-thirds of the Supreme Court justices ever serving on the Court attended well-known or Ivy League Law Schools (Harvard, Yale, Columbia, Pennsylvania, N.Y.U., Michigan, Virginia, etc.). No Negroes served on the Supreme Court until the appointment of Associate Justice Thurgood Marshall in 1967. Henry Abraham depicts the typical Supreme Court justice: "White; generally Protestant. . . ; fifty to fifty-five years of age at the time of his appointment; Anglo-Saxon ethnic stock. . . ; high social status; reared in an urban environment; member of a civic-minded, politically active, economically comfortable family; legal training; some type of public office; generally well educated."[24] Of course, social background does not necessarily determine judicial philosophy. But as Schmidhauser observes: "If . . . the Supreme Court is the keeper of the American conscience, it is essentially the conscience of the Ameri-

23 John R. Schmidhauser, *The Supreme Court* (New York: Holt, Rinehart and Winston, 1960), p. 59.

24 Henry Abraham, *The Judicial Process* (New York: Oxford University Press, 1962), p. 58.

can upper-middle class sharpened by the imperative of individual social responsibility and political activism, and conditioned by the conservative impact of legal training and professional legal attitudes and associations." [25]

But not all justices conform to this upper-class portrait. Indeed, the current justices of the Supreme Court are middle-class rather than upper-class in social origin. Their appointments to the Supreme Court have been more closely related to their political activities than either their social backgrounds or their accomplishments in the law.

Warren E. Burger. Chief Justice, U.S. Supreme Court. Son of a successful Swiss-German farmer near St. Paul, Minnesota. Worked his way through the University of Minnesota and St. Paul College of Law, receiving law degree in 1931. Developed a successful 22-year private practice in Minneapolis–St. Paul with a wide range of civil and criminal cases. An early political associate of Minnesota Republican Governor Harold E. Stassen, brought himself to the attention of Eastern Republicans in national GOP conventions in 1940 and 1952. President Eisenhower appointed him assistant attorney general in 1953, then to U.S. Court of Appeals in 1956. Served on the Court of Appeals until appointed Chief Justice by President Nixon in 1969 on the resignation of Earl Warren.

Byron R. White. U.S. Supreme Court Justice. Son of the mayor of Wellington, Colorado. Attended public schools and University of Colorado. At Colorado, was Phi Beta Kappa, a Rhodes Scholar, and an All-American Halfback. Attended Yale Law School while playing halfback for the Pittsburgh Steelers and Detroit Lions; was the NPL leading ground gainer in 1938. In World War II served in Navy in the Pacific, where he met John F. Kennedy. After the war, completed law degree at Yale, served legal clerkship under U.S. Supreme Court Chief Justice Fred M. Vinson, and opened a law practice in Denver, Colorado. His law practice was undistinguished, but in 1960 the Kennedys called on him to organize Colorado for JFK's presidential campaign. White was credited with delivering Colorado's convention votes to Kennedy. Was JFK's only appointment to the Supreme Court.

Thurgood Marshall. U.S. Supreme Court Justice. Son of a Pullman car steward. Educated at Lincoln University and Howard University Law School. Shortly after graduation in 1933, became counsel for Baltimore chapter of NAACP. From 1940 to 1961, served as director and chief counsel of NAACP's semi-autonomous Legal Defense and Educational Fund. During that period, he argued 32 cases before the Supreme Court, winning 29. His notable victory (indeed, perhaps the black man's most notable judicial victory) came in *Brown v. Board of Education of Topeka* in 1954.

President Kennedy chose Marshall as a judge for the U.S. Circuit Court of Appeals in 1961; President Johnson appointed him U.S. Solicitor General in 1965. As the latter, Marshall argued 19 more cases before the U.S. Supreme Court. When President Johnson announced Marshall's ap-

[25] Schmidhauser, *The Supreme Court,* p. 59.

pointment to the Supreme Court in 1967, he accurately noted that "probably only one or two other living men have argued as many cases before the court—and perhaps less than half a dozen in all the history of the nation."

The Political Contributors

Political campaign financing provides important linkage between corporate and personal wealth and the political system. Campaigns for public office cost money—a great deal more than candidates themselves are willing or able to spend. President Richard Nixon spent an estimated $60 million in his 1972 re-election campaign and his "poorer" opponent, Senator George McGovern, spent an estimated $30 million. Even an unsuccessful presidential *primary* campaign can cost $5 to $10 million. Few candidates can even begin a political career for state or local office without first securing financial support from wealthy "angels." Farsighted men of wealth may choose to back a promising young congressman or senator early in his career and continue this support over many years. Richard Nixon has been supported by W. Clement Stone since young Nixon's early days as a California congressman, and Stewart Mott has likewise supported the political career of Senator George McGovern. There are few in the Congress or Senate who do not have wealthy financial sponsors.

Top political contributors are drawn from the corporate and financial world and the nation's wealthiest strata of the population. Lists of top political campaign contributors contain many familiar names—Rockefellers, Fords, duPonts, Mellons, etc. These names are found on *both* Republican and Democratic lists. In 1972, Richard Nixon's top financial backers included:

W. Clement Stone. President and chairman of the board of Combined Insurance Co. of America, and a director of Alberto-Culver Co. Publisher of *Success Unlimited* magazine, and president of Religious Heritage of America, Inc. A director of Boy's Club of America, Chicago Mental Health Assn., National Center for Voluntary Action, and the Richard Nixon Foundation. A centimillionaire. (Contributed $2 million.)

Richard Mellon Scaife. Director of Mellon Bank and Trust, and Gulf Oil Corp. An heir of the Mellon fortune, a centimillionaire, and a trustee of Carnegie-Mellon University. (Contributed $1 million.)

Arthur K. Watson. Former president and chairman of board, IBM A director of Pan-American World Airways, Continental Insurance, Carnegie Endowment of International Peace, Hotchkiss School, Metropolitan Museum of Art, and Yale University. (Contributed $300,000.)

Cornelius Vanderbilt Whitney. President of Whitney, Inc., Hudson Bay

Mining and Smelting, and Whitney Farms. A director of Churchill Downs racetrack, and New York Philharmonic Symphony. Heir to Vanderbilt and Whitney family fortunes. (Contributed $300,000.)

Other large Nixon contributors included John duPont (duPont Corporation), Harvey Firestone (Firestone Tire & Rubber), Henry Ford II (Ford Motors), J. Paul Getty (oil), Howard Hughes, Walter Annenberg (ambassador to England), J. Willard Marriot (motels), Elmer Bobst (Warner-Lambert Pharmaceuticals), Henry J. Heinz II (ketchup), Bob Hope, and Frank Sinatra.

Democrats do not usually receive as much money from the corporate world as do Republicans, although about half of Democratic funds come from this source. The Xerox Corporation, for example, has been a major source of support for Democratic candidates. Traditionally, Democrats have turned to big labor for support, notably the Committee on Political Education (COPE) of the AFL-CIO and the larger international unions—United Automobile Workers, United Steel Workers, etc. Democrats have also relied on wealthy Jewish investment interests including Wall Street investment firms (Lehman Brothers; Goldman, Sachs; and Kuhn, Loeb), and conservative Democratic oil and gas money from the Southwest.

Liberal Democrats also have been supported by upper-class liberal philanthropists. These "limousine liberals" provided much of the financial support for the civil rights movement, the peace movement, the ecology movement, and other liberal causes.

In 1972, Senator George McGovern's "liberalism," for example, was backed by, among others:

Stewart Mott. President Compo Industries. Heir to General Motors fortune of his father Charles Stewart Mott, who was president and chairman of the board of General Motors and U.S. Sugar Corp. Young Mott is also a director of U.S. Sugar Corp., Michigan National Bank, Rubin Realty, Planned Parenthood, Urban League of New York, United Peace Foundation, Center for the Study of Democratic Institutions. (Contributed $725,000.)

Max Palevsky. Chairman of Board of the Xerox Corp. (Contributed $310,000.)

Nicholas and Daniel Noyes. Students who are heirs to Eli Lilly pharmaceutical fortune. (Contributed $400,000.)

Richard Saloman. President, Charles of the Ritz, Inc. of New York (fashions, cosmetics). A director of Federation of Jewish Philanthropies and trustee of Brown University. (Contributed $137,000.)

It is difficult to systematically identify top political contributors—if for no other reason than the fact that they do not usually welcome identification. Political scientist Herbert Alexander provides a list of 424 contributors of $20,000 or more to the 1968 presidential campaigns of candidates Nixon and Humphrey. The *Congressional Quarterly* published a list of 50 contributors of $50,000 or more (obtained from the U.S. General Accounting Office) to the 1972 presidential campaigns of candidates Nixon and McGovern. And an out-of-court settlement of a suit by the lobbying group Common Cause against the Committee to Re-Elect the President produced a list of 105 additional Nixon contributors. But discrepancies in these listings are numerous, contributions are often listed under the names of wives and relatives; large contributions are frequently split into smaller unidentified gifts to numerous separate campaign committees and organizations; and finally, some contributions have remained secret by design.

Nonetheless, we have made a composite listing of the heavy political contributors in the 1968 and 1972 presidential elections.[26] About one-third of these contributors were presidents or directors of the nation's largest corporations and banks. (These were the same top economic elites identified in Chapter 2.) Another third were inheritors of large fortunes.[27] The remainder appeared to be wealthy, upper-middle-class, successful people whose names were not directly linked to large corporations or recognized great family fortunes.

Political contributors cannot buy themselves *top* governmental positions. Only one major contributor became a *top* government official after the 1968 election: David Packard, who became deputy secretary of defense. Packard is a centimillionaire who was formerly president of Hewitt-Packard Company and a director of National Airlines, Pacific Gas and Electric, Systems Development Corporation, and a former trustee of Stanford University. However, some top contributors were given government positions of *lesser* importance: J. William Middendorf II, ambassador to the Netherlands; John C. Pritzlaff, ambassador to Malta; Fred J. Russell, deputy director of Emergency Preparedness.

What then, do contributors get for their money? Perhaps the most important payoff is simply *access* to the political officeholder—in the presidency, Senate, Congress, or state government. The big contributor can expect to see and talk with the officeholder to discuss general issues confronting the nation as well as the contributor's specific problems with the government. This access assures that the views of top contributors will at least be heard. Another payoff is *assistance* with government-related problems. Large contributions generally insure speedy considera-

[26] Using the sources listed above: 424 contributors of $20,000 or more in 1968, and 150 contributors of $50,000 or more in 1972.

[27] Half of the nation's 66 known centimillionaires listed in Chapter 2 turned up as top political contributors.

tion of requests, applications, contracts, bids, etc., by government bureaucracies. Assistance does not necessarily mean favoritism, but it does mean a reduction of standard red tape, bureaucratic delays, and cumbersome and time-consuming administrative reviews. Of course, *favoritism* itself is a frequent motive for large contributions by individuals and corporations who are dependent upon government contracts, licenses, or regulatory decisions. But despite occasional sensational cases, blatant favoritism is a politically dangerous game avoided by most officeholders.[28] Generally it is only when the contributor's contract, bid, or license application is substantially equal to that of the noncontributor that favoritism plays a decisive role. Another motive of contributors is the *status* a large contribution provides—the opportunity to rub shoulders with the great and near-great in American politics, to be invited to the president's inaugural ball, to visit the White House for dinner and tell one's friends about it, and even to boast of the size of one's contribution at cocktail parties.

Perhaps the most important motive in campaign contributions, however, is *political ideology*. Most of the top contributors, including conservatives W. Clement Stone, Richard Mellon Scaife, Arthur K. Watson, Cornelius Vanderbilt Whitney, John duPont, and Bob Hope, and liberals Stewart Mott, Max Palevsky, Averell Harriman, and Jacqueline Onassis, expect no direct personal gain from their contributions. They believe their contributions are helping to guide the nation's government in the proper direction.

Summary

Governmental power may be even more concentrated than corporate power in America. One indicator of its growing concentration is the increasing proportion of the Gross National Product produced by government. All governmental expenditures now account for one-third of the GNP and *federal* expenditures account for two-thirds of these. Fewer than 250 people occupy *all* of the influential posts in the com-

[28] For example, the jury found in the trial of former Attorney General John Mitchell and former Republican Campaign Chairman Maurice Stans that the contribution of financier Robert Vesco merely bought the assistance of John Mitchell in presenting Vesco's argument to the Security and Exchange Commission. The SEC actually decided *against* Vesco, despite his secret $100,000 contribution to President Nixon's re-election. It was Vesco himself who expected White House intervention on his behalf and when he did not get it, threatened to "blow the lid" on his secret contribution. Vesco's top lieutenant attempted to implicate Mitchell and Stans by charging their complicity in bribery. But the jury decided their actions did not constitute illegal acts.

bined executive, legislative, and judicial branches of the federal government.

Presidents must depend upon "serious men" to run the government, for skill in vote-getting does not necessarily prepare individuals for the responsibility of governing. Key government executives must be recruited from industry, finance, the law, the universities, and the bureaucracy itself. These "serious men" do not appear to differ much in background or experience from one administration to another.

The federal bureaucracy, an independent channel of recruitment to positions of power, is now producing its own leadership. The declining percentage of federal expenditures devoted to the military and the small percentage of corporate sales devoted to arms suggest that the "military-industrial complex" has been notably *un*successful in recent years. There has been a sharp decline since the 1950s in the exchange of military and corporate personnel, and a sharp decline in the power and prestige of the military generally.

Congress seldom initiates programs, but rather responds to the initiatives of the president, the executive departments, influential interest groups, and the mass media. Power *within* Congress is concentrated in the House and Senate leadership and the chairmen and ranking minority members of the standing committees. Compared to other national elites, congressional leaders appear localistic. Their claim to national leadership must be safely hedged by attention to their local constituencies. Congressmen are frequently recruited from very modest, middle-class backgrounds.

Nine men on the Supreme Court have the authority to void the acts of popularly elected presidents and Congresses. It was the Supreme Court, rather than the president or Congress, which took the lead in eliminating segregation from public life, insuring voter equality in representation, limiting the powers of police, and declaring abortion to be a fundamental right of women. Although most justices have been upper-class in social origin, their appointment has generally been related to their political activities rather than to their experience in the law.

Political contributions are important linkages between corporate wealth and the political system. About one-third of the heavy political contributors in presidential elections are presidents or directors of large corporations and banks; one-third are inheritors of large fortunes; and one-third are wealthy upper-middle-class individuals who are not directly linked to large corporations or great family fortunes. Their contributions are usually given in support of their political views rather than for direct personal gain.

Four THE NEWSMAKERS

Television is the major source of information for the vast majority of Americans, and the people who control this flow of information are among the most powerful in the nation. Indeed, today the leadership of the mass media has successfully established itself as equal in power to the nation's corporate and governmental leadership.

The rise of the mass media leadership to a position of pre-eminence among men of power is a relatively recent phenomenon. It is a direct product of technological change: the development of a national television communication network extending to nearly every home in America. (In 1952 only 19.8 percent of all American homes had TV sets, compared to 99.8 percent in 1972.)[1] Newspapers had always reported wars, riots, scandals, and disasters, just as they do today. But the masses of Americans did not read them—and fewer still read the editorials on these topics. But today television reaches the masses: it is really the first form of mass communication devised by man. And it presents a *visual* image, not merely a printed word. Nearly everyone watches TV, and over two-thirds of the American public testify that

[1] *Statistical Abstract of the United States, 1973,* p. 693.

television provides "most of [their] views about what's going on in the world today." [2] Over two-thirds of the American people say that television is the best way to follow candidates for national office.[3]

Network television news not only reaches a larger audience than newspapers, but perhaps more importantly, it reaches children, functional illiterates, the poor, and the uneducated. The television viewer *must* see the news, or else turn off his set; the newspaper reader can turn quickly to the sports and comics without confronting the political news. But the greatest asset of television is its *visual* quality—the emotional impact that is conveyed in pictures. Scenes of burning and looting in cities, sacks of dead American GIs being loaded on helicopters, pathetic bodies of dead Vietnamese children, all convey *emotions* as well as *information.*

Concentration of Power in the Mass Media

The power to determine what the American people will see and hear about their world is vested in three private corporations—the American Broadcasting Company (ABC), the National Broadcasting Corporation (NBC), and the Columbia Broadcasting System, Inc. (CBS). These networks determine what will be seen by the mass viewing audience; there is *no* public regulation whatsoever of network broadcasting. Individual television stations are privately owned and licensed to use public broadcast channels by the Federal Communications Commission. But these stations are forced to receive news and programming from the networks because of the high costs involved in *producing* news or entertainment at the local station level. The top officials of these corporate networks, particularly the people in charge of the news, are indeed "a tiny, enclosed fraternity of privileged men." [4] Nicholas Johnson, a member of the Federal Communications Commission, and a self-professed liberal, has said:

> The networks, in particular . . . are probably now beyond the check of any institution in our society. The President, the Congress of the United States, the FCC, the foundations, and universities are reluctant even to

[2] The Roper Organization, *What People Think of Television and Other Mass Media: 1959–1972* (New York: Television Information Office, 1973), p. 2.

[3] Ibid.

[4] The phraseology is courtesy of former Vice-President Spiro Agnew, who also used the more colorful description of the network top brass—"super-sensitive, self-anointed, supercilious electronic barons of opinion." See *Newsweek,* November 9, 1970, p. 22.

get involved. I think they may now be so powerful that they're beyond the check of anyone.[5]

The men at the top of the news media do not doubt their own power. They generally credit themselves with the success of the civil rights movement: the dramatic televised images of the nonviolent civil rights demonstrators of the early 1960s being attacked by police with night-sticks, cattle prods, and vicious dogs, helped to awaken the nation and its political leadership to the injustices of segregation. These leaders also credit TV with "decisively changing America's opinion of the Vietnam War," and forcing Lyndon Johnson out of the presidency. The director of CBS News in Washington proudly claims:

> When television covered its "first war" in Vietnam, it showed a terrible truth of war in a manner new to mass audiences. A case can be made, and certainly should be examined, that this was cardinal to the disillusionment of Americans with this war, the cynicism of many young people towards America, and the destruction of Lyndon Johnson's tenure of office.[6]

Television news, together with the Washington press corps, also lays claim, of course, to the expulsion of Richard Nixon from the presidency. The *Washington Post* conducted the "investigative reporting" that produced a continuous flow of embarrassing and incriminating information about the president and his chief advisers. But, it was the television networks that maintained the continuous nightly attack on the White House for nearly two years because of the Watergate Affair. Richard Nixon's approval rating in public opinion polls dropped from an all-time high of 68 percent in January 1973 following the Vietnam Peace Agreement to a low of 24 percent less than one year later.

Yet the leadership of the mass media frequently claim that they do no more than "mirror" reality. Although the "mirror" argument contradicts many of their more candid claims to having righted many of America's wrongs (segregation, Vietnam, Watergate), the leadership of the three television networks claim that television "is a mirror of society." Frank Stanton, president of CBS, told a House committee: "What the media does is hold a mirror up to society and try to report it as factually as possible." When confronted with charges that television helped to spread urban rioting in the late 1960s, Julian Goodman, president of NBC, told the National Commission on the Cause and

[5] Quoted by Edward Jay Epstein, *News from Nowhere* (New York: Random House, 1973), p. 6.

[6] Ibid., p. 9.

Prevention of Violence that "the medium is being blamed for the message." [7]

Of course, the mirror analogy is nonsense. Newsmen decide what the news will be, how it will be presented, and how it will be interpreted. As David Brinkley explained, "News is what I say it is. It's something worth knowing by my standards." [8] Newsmen have the power to create some national issues and ignore others; elevate obscure men to national prominence; reward politicians they favor and punish those they disfavor. The best description of the newsmaking power of television is found in a book significantly entitled *News from Nowhere* by Edward Jay Epstein, who explains:

> The mirror analogy further tends to neglect the component of "will," or decisions made in advance to cover or not to cover certain types of events. A mirror makes no decisions, it simply reflects what occurs in front of it; television coverage can, however, be controlled by predecisions or "policy." . . .
>
> Policy can determine not only whether or not a subject is seen on television but also how it is depicted. . . .
>
> Intervention by the producer or assistant producers in decisions on how to play the news is the rule rather than the exception.[9]

The principal source of distortion in the news is caused by the need for drama, action, and confrontation, to hold audience attention. NBC news executive producer Reven Frank advised his producers in a memorandum: "The highest power of television journalism is not in the transmission of information but in the transmission of experience—joy, sorrow, shock, fear—these are the stuff of news." [10]

Ninety percent of the national news that reaches the American public arrives from ABC, NBC, and CBS.[11] Local television stations do not have the resources to produce their own national news, and consequently largely restrict themselves to local news coverage. The three networks "feed" approximately 600 local affiliated stations, with "The Evening News." These stations generally videotape these programs for rebroadcast later in the evening, usually in truncated form, on the local news program. Moreover, the networks also *own* key television stations in the nation's largest cities. While the Federal Communications Com-

[7] Ibid.

[8] *TV Guide*, April 11, 1964.

[9] Op. Cit., pp. 16–17.

[10] Ibid., p. 39.

[11] See Lewis H. Lapham, "The Temptation of a Sacred Cow," *Harpers Magazine* (August 1973), pp. 43–54.

mission limits station ownership by the networks to no more than seven stations, these network-owned stations are concentrated in the largest "market" cities. The twelve largest "market" cities contain 38 percent of all "TV households" in the nation, and these cities have network-owned stations.[12]

The nation's 1,748 daily newspapers get most of their national news from the Associated Press (AP) and United Press International (UPI) wire services, although the larger newspapers and newspaper chains also disseminate their own national news. Radio stations also rely heavily on AP and UPI. One large radio station admitted to filling its newscasts "90 percent with verbatim items from UPI teletype."[13] Of course, local newspapers can "rewrite" national news stories to fit their own editorial slant, and they usually write their own headlines on the national news. But the news itself is generated from an extremely small cadre of people at the top of the media industry.

Concentration is increasing in local newspaper ownership, as more and more local papers are being taken over by the major newspaper chains. Ten newspaper chains account for one-third of the total newspaper circulation in the United States. These chains, in order of their total daily circulation, are: Tribune Company, Newhouse, Scripps-Howard, Knight Newspapers, Hearst Corporation, Gannett Newspapers, Times Mirror Company, Dow Jones, Ridder, and Cox Enterprises.[14]

Our operational definition of leaders in positions of power in the mass media include the presidents and directors of

Columbia Broadcasting System, Inc. (CBS television)
American Broadcasting Company (ABC television)
National Broadcasting Company (NBC television)
New York Times Company (*New York Times*)
Washington Post Company (*Washington Post, Newsweek Magazine*)
Time, Inc. (*Time, Life, Sports Illustrated, Fortune* magazines)
Associated Press
United Press International
Newhouse (*Denver Post, Cleveland Plain Dealer,* etc.)
Hearst Corporation (Los Angeles, San Francisco, Baltimore, Boston, Albany, Seattle, San Antonio, etc.)
Scripps-Howard

[12] Ben H. Bagdikian, *The Information Machines* (New York: Harper & Row, 1971), pp. 171–72.

[13] Edwin Emery, *The Press in America* (Englewood Cliffs, N.J.: Prentice-Hall, Inc., 1972), p. 481.

[14] Raymond B. Nixon, "Nation's Dailies in Group Ownership," *Editor & Publisher,* July 17, 1971, pp. 7, 32.

Tribune Company (*Chicago Tribune, New York Daily News, Orlando Sentinal,* etc.)
Field Enterprises (*Chicago Sun-Times, Chicago Daily News,* etc.)
Dow Jones (*Wall Street Journal*)
Times Mirror (*Los Angeles Times,* etc.)
Ridder
Knight Newspapers, Inc. (*Detroit Free Press, Miami Herald, Philadelphia Inquirer,* etc.)
Cox

There are 213 presidents and directors of these institutions.

The Newsmakers

Who are the men who govern the flow of information to the nation? Let us examine a few brief sketches of those in the top leadership positions in the major media institutions.

William S. Paley. Chairman of the board, Columbia Broadcasting System Inc. Attended Western Military Academy, University of Pennsylvania. Began work in father's cigar company, but in 1928 at age 27 purchased CBS for $400,000. Recruited Edward R. Murrow to develop news policy for CBS, and supported Murrow's successful efforts to make television news an independent political force in America. Paley actively opposed creation of Federal Communications Commission; and over the years helped to prevent its intrusion into network broadcasting. Established the first regular schedule of television broadcasting in the U.S. in 1941. A trustee of the Museum of Modern Art, Columbia University, Resources for the Future, Inc., Bedford-Stuyvesant Development Corp. Past chairman of the United Jewish Appeal.

Roy E. Larson. Chairman of the board of Time, Inc., publishers of *Time, Life, Fortune, Sports Illustrated.* Attended Boston Latin School, Harvard College. Was hired by classmate Henry Luce, owner of Time, Inc., in 1922 to handle financial matters; rose to president in 1939. Is a trustee of Committee for Economic Development, Ford Foundation, New York Public Library, and a former trustee of Harvard University.

Arthur Ochs Sulzberger. Publisher and president, *New York Times.* Son of the *Times* board chairman and grandson of the newspaper's founder. Attended Loomis school and Columbia University. A corporal in World War II, but assigned as headquarters aide to General Douglas MacArthur. Began as a reporter with the *Times* in 1953 and became president in 1963. A director of the New York Times Co., the Chattanooga Publishing Co., the Spruce Falls Power and Paper Co. of Toronto, and the Gaspesia Pulp and Paper Co. of Canada. A trustee of the Boy Scouts of America, American Association of Indian Affairs, Columbia University, and the Metropolitan Museum of Art.

Julian Goodman. President, NBC. Attended public schools in Glasgow, Kentucky, and Western Kentucky University. Began as a newswriter for NBC in 1945; moved up to become Washington news manager in 1950. Recruited Chet Huntley and David Brinkley and pioneered in television coverage of national party conventions. Produced the Nixon-Kennedy TV debates in 1960, and became president of NBC in 1966. Helped to inaugurate the "news special" and the "documentary"; is a leading exponent of the notion that television should pay "more attention to analysis and interpretation."

Robert W. Sarnoff. President of RCA (Radio Corporation of America). Former president and director of NBC. Son of David Sarnoff, chairman of Board of RCA (which owns NBC). Attended Phillips Andover Academy and Harvard. Served in the Navy in World War II as communications officer for the Chief of Naval Operations, joined NBC in 1948, and became president in 1955. Regards his own documentary *Victory at Sea* as most personally satisfying undertaking. Is also director of Manufacturer's Hanover Trust, and Random House, Inc., and a trustee of John F. Kennedy Library, Boston University, Franklin and Marshall College, Roper Public Opinion Research Center, and Williams College.

Leonard H. Goldenson. President, ABC. Attended Harvard College and Harvard Law School. Began as an attorney for Paramount Pictures in Hollywood and became president of Paramount Pictures and United Paramount Theatres. In 1953, merged Paramount and ABC and became president of ABC. Also invested in Walt Disney Productions, started the popular *Mickey Mouse Club* TV shows. Hired top ABC news commentators himself. Is a director of United Cerebral Palsy Association, John F. Kennedy Library, Lincoln Center for Performing Arts, Will Rogers Memorial Hospital, and United Jewish Appeal.

Frank Stanton. President CBS. Attended public schools in Dayton, Ohio, then Ohio Wesleyan University; Ph.D. in psychology, Ohio State University, 1935. Sent his dissertation on radio listening behavior to CBS and won a job in its research department. Later worked with Paul F. Lazarfeld of Columbia to develop better methods of rating program audiences. In 1946, William S. Paley asked Stanton, then 38, to become CBS president. Paley and Stanton together established CBS as the largest advertising and communications corporation in the world. Stanton introduced diversification in CBS; invested in a Broadway show, *My Fair Lady,* and earned $100 million. Later purchased the New York Yankees. Is a leading opponent of the "equal-time" rule of the FCC requiring stations to give equal time to political candidates. A chairman of the RAND Corp., and trustee of Rockefeller Foundation, Center for Advanced Study of the Behavioral Sciences, Lincoln Center for the Performing Arts, and Stanford Research Institute.

Hedley Donovan. Editor-in-chief, Time, Inc. University of Minnesota, Rhodes scholar, Oxford. Began as reporter for *Washington Post,* and later *Fortune Magazine.* Became Time, Inc. editor-in-chief, 1964. Trustee of New York University, Carnegie Foundation. Member of Council of Foreign Relations.

Other top corporate directors of the media include Robert Lovett, CBS (former secretary of defense, senior partner of Wall Street investment firm of Brown Brothers, Harriman & Co., a director of North American Rockwell, Union Pacific Railroad, Carnegie Foundation and M.I.T.); Frank Pace, *Time* (former secretary of the Army, a director of Fidelity Life Insurance, Colgate-Palmolive, Continental Oil). Pace has also been named chairman of board of the Corporation for Public Broadcasting designed to use federal funds to produce shows for public TV stations. Also John W. Gardner, who serves on the Time, Inc. board; he was former secretary of Health, Education and Welfare and now heads Washington's heaviest spending lobby group, the liberal-oriented Common Cause.

Katherine Graham: The Most Powerful Woman in America

Katherine Graham, the owner and publisher of the *Washington Post* and *Newsweek Magazine,* was probably the most powerful woman in America even *before* Watergate. But certainly her leadership of the *Post,* which did more than any other publication to force the resignation of the president of the United States, established Ms. Graham as one of the most powerful figures in Washington. The *Washington Post* is the capital's most influential newspaper, and it vies with the *New York Times* as the world's most influential newspaper. These are the papers read by all segments of the nation's elite; and both papers feed stories to the television networks and wire services.

Ms. Graham inherited her position from her father and husband, but since 1963, when she became president of the *Washington Post* Company, she has demonstrated her own capacity to manage great institutional power. She is the daughter of a wealthy New York banker, Eugene Meyer. Like many elites, her education was in the fashionable private preparatory schools; she also attended Vassar College and the University of Chicago. In 1933 her father bought the *Washington Post* for less than one million dollars. Katherine Meyer worked summers on her father's paper, and then took a job as a reporter with the *San Francisco News.* After one year as a reporter, she joined the editorial staff of the *Washington Post.* "Father was very strong. There was a great deal of emphasis on not behaving rich and a lot of emphasis on having to *do* something. It never occurred to me that I didn't have to work." [15]

In 1940, she married Philip L. Graham, a Harvard Law School graduate with a clerkship under Supreme Court Justice Felix Frankfurter. After service in World War II, Philip Graham was made publisher

[15] *Current Biography* (1971), p. 170.

of the *Washington Post* by his father-in-law. Meyer later sold the paper to the Grahams for one dollar. The Washington Post Company proceeded to purchase other competitive papers in the nation's capital; it also bought *Newsweek* magazine from the Vincent Astor Foundation, as well as some television stations (including Washington's WTOP-TV) and several pulp and paper companies.

In 1963, Philip Graham committed suicide, and Katherine Graham took control of the *Washington Post–Newsweek* enterprises. By the early 1970s the *Washington Post* was challenging the *New York Times* as the nation's most powerful newspaper.

Both the *Washington Post* and the *New York Times* published the *Pentagon Papers,* stolen from the files of the Defense and State Departments by Daniel Ellsberg, and led the fight against the Vietnam War. But it was the *Washington Post* that developed the Watergate story and brought about Richard Nixon's humiliation and resignation.

Ms. Graham is a director of Bowaters Mersey Paper Company, the John F. Kennedy School of Government of Harvard University, and a member of the Committee for Economic Development. She is a trustee of George Washington University, the American Assembly, the University of Chicago, and St. Alban's School.

Liberal Bias in the News

When TV newscasters insist that they are impartial, objective, and unbiased, they may sincerely believe that they are, because in the world in which they live—the New York–Washington world of newsmen, writers, intellectuals, artists—the established liberal point of view has been so uniformly voiced. TV news executives can be genuinely shocked and affronted when they are charged with slanting the news toward the prevailing established liberal values.

Network entertainment programming, newscasts, and news specials are designed to communicate established liberal values to the masses. These are the values of the elite; they include a concern for liberal reform, a public-regarding attitude, an interest in problems confronting the poor and blacks, a desire to educate the ignorant and cure the sick, and a willingness to employ governmental power to accomplish these ends.

Admittedly, there are some restraints on television communication of elite values—the most important of which is the need to capture and retain the attention of the audience. Television must entertain. To capture the attention of jaded audiences, news must be selected which in cludes emotional rhetoric, shocking incidents, dramatic conflict, overdrawn stereotypes. Race, sex, violence, and corruption in government are favorite topics because of popular interest. More complex problems—inflation, government spending, foreign policy—must be simplified and dramatized or ignored. To dramatize an issue, the newsmakers must find or create a dramatic incident; film it; transport, process, and edit the film; and write a script for the introduction, the "voice-over," and the "recapitulation." All this means that "news" must be created well in advance of scheduled broadcasting.

But television has made some serious tactical mistakes in its (conscious or unconscious) advancement of liberal values. For example, for several years the national networks decided that incidents of violence, disruption, and civil disorder in American cities were to be treated as "news." Generally the media chiefs believed that the civil rights movement had to be carried to Northern black ghettos, that urban conditions had to be improved, that ghetto blacks deserved greater public attention to their plight. Televised riots and disorders dramatized black discontent, and "voice-overs" generally gave legitimacy to such discontent by citing various social evils as causes of the riots—poverty, racism, poor housing, police brutality. The purpose was to pave the way for mass acceptance of liberal public-regarding programs and policies in the nation's cities.

But the strategy backfired. Whites saw the visual image of black violence, and ignored the social message attached to it by the commentators. Images of black violence remained in their minds, while words of explanation were ignored. White mass hostilities and prejudices were actually *reinforced* by the urban violence shown on the media. The liberal network executives had created exactly what they did *not* want: a strong "law and order" movement and a surge of support for George C. Wallace as a presidential candidate.[16]

> For a long time there were two basic issues in national politics: foreign policy, a traditional advantage to the Republicans, and economics, a plus for the Democrats. Now there is a third: Law and Order—shorthand for street crime, race, protest tactics, and "revolution." It has been forty years since American politics generated an issue so intense that it could change partisan loyalties for vast numbers of citizens. Law and Order may be such an issue. Where did it come from?
>
> We suggest that the essential midwives in the birth of this issue are Mssrs. Cronkite, Brinkley, and their bretheren—television newsmen who,

[16] A study of bias during an election was made by journalist Edith Efron, in a book bluntly entitled *The News Twisters* (Los Angeles: Nash Publishing Co., 1971). Efron carefully counted words spoken for and against the 1968 presidential candidates—Nixon, Humphrey, and Wallace—in the nightly news broadcasts of ABC, CBS, and NBC. She also counted words revealing a friendly or unfriendly disposition of the networks toward particular groups.

we hasten to add, are probably as strongly revolted by the appearance of Law and Order as any group in America.[17]

There is far *less* diversity of news presented on television than one finds in the press. There are only three national television network corporations. But there are thousands of newspapers and hundreds of magazines throughout the land for Americans to choose from. Newspapers and magazines present a fairly wide spectrum of views because they represent a wider variety of such things as geographical area, communication policies, and above all, more diversified groups deciding their news presentation. Conventionally "liberal" and "conservative" news can be found in such publications as *The New York Times* versus *The Chicago Tribune; Time Magazine* versus *U.S. News and World Report; The Washington Post* versus *The Wall Street Journal; The New Republic* versus *The National Review; The Village Voice* versus *Barron's Weekly.* But television is so important in mass socialization that diversity of views is avoided, and a single Eastern, liberal "establishment" interpretation is presented over all three networks.

In an especially candid interview with *Playboy* magazine, Walter Cronkite commented on both the power and the bias of the television networks: [18]

> *Playboy:* A great deal of economic and social power is concentrated in the networks. CBS, for example, does research and development in military and space technology, owns two publishing houses, and has phonograph-record, record club, and film communications divisions.
>
> *Cronkite:* That's right. We're big. And we're powerful enough to thumb our nose at threats and intimidation from Government. I hope it stays that way.
>
> *Playboy:* Implicit in the Administration's attempts to force the networks to "balance" the news is a conviction that most newscasters are biased against conservatism. Is there some truth in the view that television newsmen tend to be left of center?
>
> *Cronkite:* Well, certainly liberal, and possibly left of center as well. I would have to accept that . . . But I don't think there are many who are *far* left. I think a little left of center probably is correct.

The federal government has made only a very feeble attempt to insure pluralism in television coverage of public affairs. The Federal

[17] Byron Shafer and Richard Larson, "Did TV Create the Social Issue?" *Columbia Journalism Review* (September/October 1972), p. 10. Also see Richard Scammon and Ben Wattenberg, *The Real Majority* (New York: Coward, McCann, Georghegen, 1970), p. 162.

[18] "Playboy Interview: Walter Cronkite," *Playboy* (June, 1973), pp. 68–90.

Communications Commission has developed a "Fairness Doctrine" that requires licensed stations that broadcast public affairs messages to provide equal airtime to present "all sides of controversial issues." The Fairness Doctrine does not restrict reporting or editorializing on television in any way, but it tries to guarantee access to airings of views not shared by the stations. But the Doctrine has proven impossible to enforce in newscasts, and no station has ever lost its license for violation of the Fairness Doctrine. Yet it is bitterly opposed by the broadcasting corporations. Their argument is that the First Amendment gives them the right to be biased, just as it protects the right of individuals or newspapers to be biased.

How Newsmakers Create News

In general, newsmakers are more liberal in their views than other segments of the American establishment. (We will compare the liberalism of various segments of the nation's elite in Chapter 9). But how are these views expressed on the tube itself? The primary source of bias is in the selection of topics to be presented as "news." Topics selected weeks in advance for coverage reflect, or often create, as we have seen, current liberal issues: concern for poor and blacks, women's liberation, opposition to defense spending and the CIA, ecology, migrant farm labor, tax loopholes, Indian rights,[19] and for nearly two years, Watergate. The Chappaquiddick incident involving Senator Edward M. Kennedy was given one or two weeks coverage, but barely mentioned thereafter, despite a closed judicial inquiry, many available witnesses to the pre-accident party, and an unexplained increase in the wealth of the non-complaining Kopechne family.

But there are other techniques of creating bias in the news:

Investing anonymous "high Washington sources" who express the newscasters' own opinions, or using phrases such as "observers point out . . ." and "experts believe . . ." to express their opinions.

Suppressing information that might clash with a liberal interpretation of the news. Thus Eldridge Cleaver's criminal conviction as a rapist was never mentioned, and he was presented as "a noted black nationalist."

Presenting glamorous, articulate spokesmen for the liberal side of an argument and "balancing" it with ugly, harsh, offensive spokesmen for the other side.

[19] The 1972 Wounded Knee incident was planned in advance by television producers and Indian leaders and then presented on cue as television "news." See Terri Schultz, "Bamboozle Me Not at Wounded Knee," *Harper's Magazine* (June 1973), pp. 46–56.

Winding up coverage of a controversy by a "summary" or "recapitulation" which directs humor, sarcasm, or satire at the other side.

"Mind-reading," in which newscasters glibly describe the motives and aspirations of large numbers of people—students, blacks, suburbanites, or whatever—and express the causes of society's discontents and other social and political ideologies.

Outright falsification is less frequent, but it does occur. One of the most impressive "news specials" ever produced by CBS was "Hunger in America"—a 1968 production presumably designed to increase support for the food stamp program and the fading war on poverty. The film began showing a dying baby, pitifully thin and malformed, and being given resuscitation in a hospital. The narrator, Charles Kuralt, said: "Hunger is easy to recognize when it looks like this. The baby is dying of starvation. He was an American. Now he is dead."[20] This image couldn't help having a tremendous impact on the viewer, who naturally assumed the baby died of starvation or malnutrition. But a subsequent congressional investigation disclosed that the dying baby was a three-month premature infant weighing less than three pounds at birth, whose parents were neither poor nor starving. In defending the falsification, CBS President Richard Salant said that he *believed* that babies were dying in America of starvation, and even though CBS could not find any to televise, a starving baby *would* look like the one pictured.[21]

Selective Perception: "All in the Family"

But the viewer's psychological mechanism of "selective perception" defends him against some portion of television bias. Indeed, one of the reasons why political scientists give little attention to the political impact of television newscasting is their belief in the theory of selective perception. This is the notion that viewers mentally screen out information, statements, or images with which they disagree, and see only what they

[20] Quotation from Epstein, *News from Nowhere*, p. 21.

[21] CBS President Richard Salant was also obliged to come to the defense of another "documentary," *The Selling of the Pentagon*, in which film was pasted and clipped during the interviews with Pentagon officials to make them *appear* to have made damaging statements. CBS also reported that there were 30,000 officers in the Pentagon, when there were only 5000. Salant justified the exaggeration by saying that 5000 was still too many. For a defense of *The Selling of the Pentagon*, see former CBS president Fred W. Friendly, "The Unselling of *The Selling of the Pentagon*," *Harper's Magazine* (June 1971), pp. 30–37.

want to see on the tube. The proponents of this theory argue that television rarely produces attitudinal or behavioral changes in viewers.[22] If this theory is true, newsmakers exercise little real power. But many of these studies have directed their inquiries to political *campaigns* and not to *issues* and *policies*. Many have ignored the *visual* impact of television. Only recently have a small number of political scientists come to grips with the real power of the mass media. Political scientists Gary Wamsley and Richard Pride cite Spiro Agnew's attack on TV—"No medium has a more powerful influence over public opinion. Nowhere in our system are there fewer checks on vast power." [23]

But there is just enough evidence of selective perception, and enough evidence of network executive blunders, to keep alive the notion that television cannot completely control public opinion. Consider the example of the enormously popular CBS television show *All In The Family*. Producer Norman Lear and the leadership of CBS believed that the crude, bumbling, working-class, conservative, superpatriotic, racist Archie Bunker would be an effective weapon against prejudice. Bigotry would be made to appear ridiculous; Archie would always end up suffering some defeat because of his bigotry; and the masses would be instructed in liberal reformist values. But evidence soon developed that many viewers applauded Archie's bigotry, believing he was "telling it like it is." [24] They missed the satire altogether. Sixty percent of the viewers liked or admired the bigoted Archie more than his liberal son-in-law, Mike. Vidmar and Rokeach's study indicated that highly prejudiced people enjoy and watch the show *more* than low-prejudice people; and few people believed that Archie was being "made fun of." When these trends in public opinion became apparent, the show was sharply attacked by the *New York Times*.[25] But by that time *All In The Family* had become the number one rated show on television. CBS opti-

[22] See Herbert Simon and Frederick Stern, "The Effect of Television upon Voting Turnout in Iowa in the 1952 Election," *American Political Science Review*, 49 (1955), 470–77; J. Blumler and T. McQuail, *Television in Politics* (Chicago: University of Chicago Press, 1969); Harold Mendelsohn and Irving Crespi, *Polls, Television and the New Politics* (Scranton: Chandler, 1970).

[23] Gary L. Wamsley and Richard A. Pride, "Television Network News: Rethinking the Iceberg Problem," *Western Political Quarterly*, 25 (September 1972), 434–50.

[24] See Neil Vidmar and Milton Rokeach, "Archie Bunker's Bigotry: A Study in Selective Perception and Exposure," *Journal of Communication* (Winter 1974), pp. 36–47.

[25] L. Z. Hobson, "As I Listened to Archie say 'Hebe,'" *New York Times*, September 12, 1972.

mistically predicted that eventually the humor of the program would help break down bigotry.[26] But it seems clear that the network vastly underestimated "selective perception."

Summary

The people who control the flow of information in America are among the most powerful in the nation. Television network broadcasting is the first form of truly *mass* communication; it carries a visual image with emotional content as well as information. Television news reaches virtually everyone, and for most Americans it is the major source of information about the world.

Control of the television media is highly concentrated. Three private corporations (CBS, NBC, and ABC) determine what the people will see and hear about the world; they feed the 600 local TV stations with 90 percent of the news and entertainment that is broadcast. Most of the nation's 1,748 daily newspapers receive their news from the AP and/or UPI wire services. The ten largest newspaper chains account for one-third of the total newspaper circulation in the country.

Those at the top of the mass media include both inheritors and individuals who worked their way up the management ladder. They include the heads of CBS, NBC, and ABC; AP and UPI; *New York Times; Washington Post–Newsweek;* Time, Inc.; and the ten largest newspaper chains.

Television programming is uniformly liberal in its news presentations—conveying the established elite values of those in positions of power. Bias is introduced primarily in the selection of topics to be treated as "news," but there are other ways in which liberal values are incorporated into newsmaking. While claiming to present merely a "mirror of society," newsmakers credit themselves with the success of the civil rights movement, ending the Vietnam War, exposing Watergate, and ousting two presidents from office.

The major counterbalance to the power of the media is the "selective perception" of the mass viewing audience. Viewers often mentally screen out information or images they do not want to see. Network executives have blundered in creating issues they did not want by underestimating selective perception, as in the case of the law and order movement stemming from media coverage of urban riots.

[26] Norman Lear, "As I Read How Laura Saw Archie," *New York Times*, October 10, 1971.

Five THE CIVIC ESTABLISHMENT

In a complex, industrial society, there are many specialized institutions and organizations that exercise power. In addition to economic organizations (corporations, banks, insurance companies, and utilities), governmental and military bureaucracies, television networks and news services, there are other less visible institutions which also provide bases of power in American society. An operational definition of a national elite must include individuals who occupy positions of power in influential law firms, major philanthropic foundations, recognized national civic and cultural organizations, and prestigious private universities. We shall refer to these institutions collectively as "the civic establishment."

The identification of a "civic establishment" involves many subjective judgments. We will try to defend these judgments, but we recognize that equally valid defenses of alternative judgments might be made in many cases.

The Superlawyers

As modern societies grow in scale and complexity, the need for rules and regulations increases geometrically, and so does the power of people whose profession it is to understand those rules and regulations. As early as 1832, deTocqueville felt that the legal profession in this country would become the "new aristocracy" of the Republic. C. Wright Mills asserts that lawyers are indeed a key segment of the nation's aristocracy of power:

> The inner core of the power elite also includes men of the higher legal and financial type from the great law factories and investment firms who are professional go-betweens of economic, political, and military affairs, and who thus act to unify the power elite.[1]

The predominance of lawyers among political elites has already been noted. Within the corporate elite—presidents and directors of the nation's largest industries, banks, utilities, and insurance companies—over 15 percent are lawyers. But neither the politician-lawyer nor the businessman-lawyer really stands at the top of the legal profession. The "superlawyers" are the senior partners of the nation's largest and most highly esteemed New York and Washington law firms. These are the firms that represent clients such as General Motors, AT&T, duPont, CBS, and American Airlines,[2] not only in the courts, but perhaps more importantly, before federal regulatory agencies. Of course, the nation's largest corporate and financial institutions have their own legal departments; but attorneys in these departments, known as "house counsels," usually handle routine matters. When the stakes are high, the great corporations turn to the "superlawyers."

Sociologist Erwin O. Smigel argues persuasively that the largest New York and Washington law firms are emerging as the dominant force in the legal profession:

> As our society has grown increasingly complex, the legal tools for social control have indeed increased beyond the possible total comprehension of a single individual. And the lawyers, like the scientists, have increasingly, although on a much smaller scale, met the problem of specialization within large law firms.[3]

Identification of the "top" New York and Washington law firms is necessarily a subjective task. Professional "ethics" prevent firms from listing their clients; so we cannot be certain what firms actually represent the nation's largest corporations. The listing in Table 5-1 was compiled

[1] C. Wright Mills, *The Power Elite* (New York: Oxford, 1956), p. 289.

[2] Quoted as clients of Covington and Burling by Joseph C. Goulden, *The Superlawyers* (New York: Dell Publishing Co., 1971), p. 27.

[3] Erwin O. Smigel, *The Wall Street Lawyer* (New York: Free Press, 1964), p. 9.

Table 5-1. The Top Law Firms

Wall Street	Washington
Shearman & Sterling	Arnold & Porter
Cravath, Swaine & Moore	Covington & Burling
White & Case	Arent, Fox, Kintner, Plotkin & Kahn
Dewey, Ballantine, Bushby, Palmer & Wood	Wilmer, Cutler & Pickering
Simpson Thacher & Bartlett	Clifford, Warnke, Glass, McIlwain & Finney
Davis Polk, & Wardwell	
Milbank, Tweed, Hadley & McCloy	
Cahill Gordon & Reindel	
Sullivan & Cromwell	
Chadbourne, Parke, Whiteside & Wolff	
Breed, Abbott & Morgan	
Winthrop, Stimson, Putnam & Roberts	
Cadwalader, Wickersham & Taft	
Wilkie Farr & Gallagher	
Donovan Leisure Newton & Irvine	
Lord, Day & Lord	
Dwight, Royall, Harris, Koegel & Caskey	
Mudge Rose Guthrie & Alexander	
Kelley Drye & Warren	
Cleary, Gottlieb, Steen & Hamilton	

from a variety of sources; it is our best estimate of the nation's "top" law firms.

We have identified 176 senior partners of these firms—these men are our "superlawyers." The names of the firms themselves do not always identify the "senior partners." Firms often retain the names of deceased founders, and most large firms have so many senior partners (20 or 30 is not uncommon) that it would be impossible to put all their names in the title of the firm. Some firms change names upon the resignation of partners, so it is sometimes difficult to maintain the identity of the firm over time.[4]

The great law firms are, of course, "the spokesmen for big business." But it would be naive to believe that they oppose government regulation, consumer laws, anti-trust laws, labor laws, or corporate tax legislation.

[4] For example, Mudge Stern Baldwin & Todd placed the name of Richard M. Nixon at the head of the firm during his Wall Street years, and later added John Mitchell's name to the firm. The result was "Nixon Mudge Rose Guthrie Alexander & Mitchell." When Nixon became president and Mitchell became attorney general, the firm went back to Mudge Rose Guthrie & Alexander. Despite the legal difficulties of its former partners, the firm remains one of the most powerful on Wall Street. Likewise, when one of Arnold, Fortas & Porter's clients, Lyndon Johnson, became president of the United States, and named his personal attorney Abraham Fortas to the Supreme Court (and then later tried unsuccessfully to make him chief justice), the Fortas name was removed from the firm. The firm is now Arnold & Porter—but it is still one of the most powerful in Washington.

On the contrary, the top law firms gain in power and influence as interaction between business and government multiplies. New laws mean new business for lawyers.

The superlawyers are philosophically liberal and public-regarding. Even the founder of one of Washington's most conservative and dignified firms, Judge J. Harry Covington of Covington and Burling, confided before his death: "I disagreed with the New Deal strongly. But it was a great benefit to lawyers because so many businessmen all over the country began squealing about what was happening and had to have lawyers. So when you ask me about bureaucracy, I say 'Oh, I'm for it. How would I eat otherwise?' "[5]

The senior partners of the nation's top law firms generally feel an obligation to public service. According to superlawyer Arthur Dean, the experience of serving in such a firm provides "an exceptional opportunity to acquire a liberal education in modern government and society. Such partnerships are likely in the future as they have in the past, to prepare and offer for public service men exceptionally qualified to serve." The arrogance of such an assertion has too much basis in fact to be dismissed as mere self-congratulation.

Earlier we identified several superlawyers among the "serious men" who have been called upon for governmental leadership:

John Foster Dulles, secretary of state (Sullivan & Cromwell)

Dean Acheson, secretary of state (Covington & Burling)

Clark Clifford, secretary of defense (Clifford, Warnke, Glass, McIlwain & Finney)

In an even earlier era, the New York Wall Street law firms supplied presidential candidates:

John W. Davis, Democratic Party nominee for president of the United States, 1928 (Davis, Polk, Wardwell, Sunderland & Kiendl)[6]

Wendell Willkie, Republican Party nominee for president of the United States, 1940 (Willkie, Farr, Gallagher, Walton & Fitzgibbon)

Thomas E. Dewey, Republican Party nominee for president of the United States, 1944 and 1948 (Dewey, Ballantine, Bushby, Palmer & Wood)

Equally important are the top lawyers who are called upon to represent the United States itself in periods of crisis where matters are too serious to be left to State Department bureaucrats.

[5] Quoted in Goulden, *The Superlawyers,* p. 36.

[6] Davis unsuccessfully argued the case for racial segregation on behalf of the Board of Education of Topeka, Kansas, in the famous case of *Brown v. Board of Education* (1954); opposing counsel for Brown, of course, was Supreme Court Justice Thurgood Marshall.

Cyrus R. Vance. U.S. negotiator at Paris Peace Conference on Vietnam. Senior partner, Simpson, Thacher & Bartlett. Member of board of directors of Pan-American World Airways, American Life Insurance Co., IBM, Council on Foreign Affairs, American Red Cross, University of Chicago, and the Rockefeller Foundation. Was formerly secretary of the Army and under secretary of defense.

John J. McCloy. Special adviser to the president on disarmament, 1961–1963. Chairman of the Coordinating Committee on the Cuban Crisis, 1962. Member of the president's commission on the assassination of President Kennedy. U.S. High Commissioner for Germany, 1949–1952. President of the World Bank, 1947–1949. Partner in Milbank, Tweed, Hadley & McCloy. Member of the board of directors of Allied Chemical Corp., AT&T, Chase Manhattan Bank, Metropolitan Life Insurance Co., Westinghouse Electric, E. R. Squibb and Sons. Member of the board of trustees of the Ford Foundation, Council on Foreign Relations, and Amherst College.

Arthur H. Dean. Chairman of the U.S. Delegation on Nuclear Test Ban Treaty. Chief U.S. negotiator of the Korean Armistice Agreement. Partner, Sullivan and Cromwell. Member of the board of directors of American Metal Climax, American Bank Note Co., National Union Electric Corp., El Paso Natural Gas Co., Crown Zellerbach Corp., Lazard Fund, Inc., and Bank of New York. Member of the board of trustees of New York Hospital, Cornell Medical Center, Cornell Medical College, Cornell University, Carnegie Foundation, and Council on Foreign Relations.

The typical path to the top of the legal profession starts with a Harvard or Yale Law School degree, clerkship with a Supreme Court justice, and then several years as an attorney with the Justice Department or a federal regulatory commission. Young government lawyers who are *successful* at defeating a top firm in a case are *more* likely to be offered lucrative junior partnerships than those who lose to big firms. Poorly paid but talented younger government lawyers are systematically recruited by the top firms.

Clark Clifford: Washington Superlawyer

Flavor the style of the nation's top Washington lawyer, Clark Clifford:

> There is one point I wish to make clear. This firm has no influence of any kind in Washington. If you want to employ someone who has influence, you will have to go somewhere else. . . . What we do have is a record of working with the various departments and agencies of the government, and we have their respect and confidence, and that we consider to be a valuable asset.[7]

[7] Quoted in Goulden, *The Superlawyers,* p. 78.

Clifford's "valuable assets" bring him such clients as Standard Oil of California, American Broadcasting Company, Hughes Tool Co. (Howard Hughes), Time-Life, Inc., General Electric, Penn Central Railroad, duPont Corporation, Phillips Petroleum, W. R. Grace Shipping, El Paso Natural Gas, TWA, and so forth. A former personal client was John F. Kennedy. The Clifford firm is Clifford, Warnke, Glass, McIlwain & Finney. (Paul Warnke himself is a former assistant secretary of defense and a man of considerable influence in Washington.)

Clifford was the son of an auditor for the Missouri-Pacific Railroad. He attended Washington University of St. Louis Law School, graduating in 1928. He promptly established a successful law practice in St. Louis, and included in his contacts Missouri Senators Harry S. Truman and Stuart Symington. Clifford enlisted in the Navy in World War II, but when Truman became president, he was called to the White House as counsel to the president. Clifford's title never changed, but he soon became a dominant figure on Truman's staff. He supervised foreign and domestic policy in the White House, as well as Truman's successful 1948 presidential campaign. In 1950, he left the White House, after five years of service, to open his own Washington firm. The decision to leave was fortunate, since the White House staff was shortly thereafter shaken by scandal.

Bureaucrats had become accustomed to answering Clifford's phone calls when they came from the White House, so they answered them when he called from his firm. His first big clients were Phillips Petroleum, Pennsylvania Railroad, Standard Oil of California, and Howard Hughes. Even during the Republican years under President Dwight Eisenhower, Clifford prospered; his close friend Senator Stuart Symington was chairman of the Senate Armed Forces Committee. McDonnell-Douglas Aircraft became a Clifford client. After duPont had lost its complex ten-year anti-trust case and was ordered to sell its ownership of General Motors, it called upon Clifford in desperation. (Covington & Burling had unsuccessfully represented duPont). If duPont were forced to sell its stock in GM immediately, the price of GM stock would plummet and income from the sale would be heavily taxed. Clifford obtained passage of a special congressional act allowing distribution of the GM stock to duPont stockholders as a capital gain and a tax saving to duPont of one-half billion dollars (and a tax loss to the U.S. Treasury of an equal amount). Clifford's modest legal fee—$1 million.

When President Kennedy prepared to take over the reins of government from his predecessor Dwight Eisenhower, he sent his personal attorney Clark Clifford to arrange the transition. He also sent Clifford to investigate the Bay of Pigs disaster and reorganize the CIA and Defense intelligence operations. Later he sent Clifford to the headquarters of U.S.

Steel to force a rollback of steel prices by threatening tax audits, contract cancellations, and FBI investigations. But Clifford did not accept any formal government appointment under Kennedy; by then his annual earnings regularly exceeded $1 million per year.

When the Vietnam War controversy had shattered the Johnson Administration and Robert McNamara was forced to resign as secretary of defense, Johnson persuaded his friend Clark Clifford to take over the Defense Department. Clifford reluctantly accepted the position of secretary of defense, reversed the policy of escalation in Vietnam, and began America's slow and painful withdrawal. Thus, the policy of military disengagement from Southeast Asia had already been started under Clifford when the Nixon Administration came to Washington.

The Foundations

The power of the nation's major foundations rests in their influence over major *new* directions in research and creativity in the social sciences, arts, and humanities. Actually the foundations spend far less for research and development than does the federal bureaucracy. But the major research components of federal bureaucracy—the National Science Foundation, Atomic Energy Commission, U.S. Public Health Service, the National Institute of Education—are generally conservative in their support of social research. These government agencies frequently avoid sensitive, controversial issues or major social innovations. It is the nation's large foundations that have played the major role in directing and supporting innovations in the scientific, intellectual, and cultural life of the nation.

Most foundations consider themselves to be in the forefront of national policy-making. "The foundations' best role," said Dr. Douglas D. Bond of the W. T. Grant Foundation, "is to identify, support, and bring to fruition certain ideas that government may later implement . . . Government is beset by crises of a social and political nature that divert it and its money from the nurturing of new ideas and new discoveries. It is the foundation's task to remain steady in its aim and to sacrifice immediate goals for the more distant." [8]

The foundations channel corporate and personal wealth into the policy-making process, providing both financial support and direction over university research and the activities of the policy-planning groups. Foundations are tax-free: contributions to foundations may be deducted

[8] "Medicine's Philanthropic Support," *Medical World News,* December 8, 1972, p. 65.

from federal corporate and individual income taxes, *and* the foundations themselves are not subject to federal income taxation.

Foundations can be created by corporations or individuals. These corporations or individuals can name themselves and their friends as directors or trustees of the foundations they create. Large blocks of corporate stock or large amounts of personal wealth can be donated as tax-exempt contributions to the foundations. The foundations can receive interest, dividends, profit shares, and capital gains from these assets without paying any taxes on them. The directors or trustees, of course, are not allowed to use foundation income or assets for their personal expenses, as they would their own taxable income. But otherwise they have great latitude in directing the use of foundation monies—to underwrite research, investigate social problems, create or assist universities, establish "think tanks," endow museums, theaters, operas, symphonies, etc.

According to the *Foundation Directory*, there are 6,803 foundations large enough to deserve recognition and listing; these are the foundations with at least $200,000 in assets and $10,000 in yearly distributions. (There are tens of thousands of other smaller foundations and trusts, some established as tax dodges by affluent citizens and therefore not having any appreciable effect on public policy except to reduce tax collections.) In 1970 these foundations controlled $200 billion in assets.

But as in other sectors of society, these foundation assets are concentrated in a small number of large foundations. The *Foundation Directory* reports: "One of the outstanding facts concerning assets is the degree of their concentration in a small number of large organizations." [9] The top twelve foundations control nearly 40 percent of all foundation assets (see Table 5-2). There are a total of 121 directors of these twelve leading foundations.

There are other less well-known, yet powerful foundations that do not spread their wealth widely but concentrate it in one enterprise. For example, the Danforth Foundation concentrates on higher education, and the Stone Foundation (established by the same Clement Stone who was Richard Nixon's major financial backer) concentrates on promoting religion in public life. Moreover, many prominent families establish multiple foundations. For example, if the assets of the Rockefeller Foundation, the Rockefeller Brothers Fund, and other Rockefeller-controlled foundations were combined, they would rank number one rather than number three in Table 5-2.

[9] *The Foundation Directory*, 3rd ed. (New York: Russell Sage Foundation, 1967), p. 16.

Table 5-2. The Foundations

Rank	Foundation	Assets B$	Source
1	Ford Foundation	2.9	Ford Motor Co.
2	Lilly Foundation	.8	Eli Lilly
3	Rockefeller Foundation	.8	Rockefellers, Standard Oil
4	Duke Endowment	.5	Duke
5	Kresge Foundation	.4	Kresge
6	Kellogg Foundation	.4	Kellogg
7	Mott Foundation	.4	Mott, General Motors
8	Pew Mutual Trust	.4	Pews, Sun Oil Co.
9	Hartford Foundation	.3	A&P Stores
10	Alfred P. Sloan Foundation	.3	Sloan, General Motors
11	Carnegie Corporation	.3	Carnegie, United States Steel
12	Mellon	.2	Mellons, Gulf, Alcoa
		7.7	

Source: ***Foundation Directory*** (New York: Russell Stye Foundation, 1967).

Some foundations play a more influential role in national policy-making because they concentrate their attention on broad social problems as opposed to medical research, oceanography, music, the arts, etc.—for example, poverty, health care, welfare reform, and foreign affairs.

The Rockefeller Foundation. A glance at the members of the *Rockefeller Foundation* board of directors confirms its ties to other top institutions.

John D. Rockefeller III. Oldest son of John D. Rockefeller II. Chairman of the Rockefeller Foundation, United Negro College Fund, Lincoln Center for the Performing Arts, and the Population Council.

Thomas J. Watson. Former chairman of the board of IBM. Director of Bankers Trust and a trustee of Cal Tech, Brown University, Boy Scouts of America, and the Institute for Advanced Study at Princeton.

Douglas Dillon. Former secretary of the treasury and under secretary of state, and a director of Chase Manhattan.

Frank Stanton. President, Columbia Broadcasting System.

Cyrus Vance. Director of Chase Manhattan.

W. Barry Wood. Dean of School of Medicine, Johns Hopkins University.

Arthur A. Houghton. Chairman of the board of Corning Glass.

Barry Bingham. Publisher of the *Louisville Courier-Journal* and *Louisville Times.*

John S. Dickey. President of Dartmouth College.

Theodore Hesburgh. President of Notre Dame.

Robert S. Goheen. President of Princeton.

Robert H. Ebert. Dean of Harvard Medical School.

Clark Kerr. President of Columbia University.

William Moyers. Former presidential press secretary under Lyndon B. Johnson, publisher of *Newsday.*

Robert V. Roosa. Partner, Brown Brothers, Harriman & Co., Investment firm.

Robert Seitz. President of Rockefeller University. Former president of the National Academy of Sciences.

The Ford Foundation. The president of the Ford Foundation is McGeorge Bundy, former dean of Harvard's College of Arts and Sciences, and special assistant to the president for national security affairs under both Presidents Kennedy and Johnson. But the driving force behind the foundation is Henry Ford II himself. His brother Benson Ford also serves on the board. The board is closely tied to the Brookings Institution: Kermit Gordon, the president of the Brookings Institution (former Council of Economic Advisors member and director of the Bureau of the Budget in the Kennedy-Johnson Administration), sits on the Ford Foundation Board. So also do:

Walter A. Hass. President of Levi Strauss & Co. and a director of Bank of America.

Edward H. Land. Former president and chairman of the board of the Polaroid Corp.

John H. Loudon. Former chairman of the board of Shell Oil Co.

Robert S. McNamara. Former president of Ford Motor Co., secretary of defense, and president of the World Bank.

Alexander Heard. President of Vanderbilt University.

Joseph Irwin Miller. Chairman of Irwin-Union Bank & Trust and a director of AT&T, Purity Stores, Equitable Life Insurance, Chemical Bank of New York.

Julius A. Stratton. Former president of M.I.T. A director of Westinghouse Electric and Standard Oil (Exxon).

The Carnegie Foundation. For many years the president of the Carnegie Foundation was John W. Gardiner, who went on to be secretary of Health, Education and Welfare under President Lyndon B. Johnson, and now uses his top connections to solicit support for the nation's heaviest spending congressional lobby—*Common Cause.*

The Carnegie Corporation board includes such men at the top as:

Walter B. Wriston. Chairman of the board, First City Bank of New York.

Charles M. Spofford. Senior Partner, Davis, Polk, Wardwell, Sunderland, and Kiendl.

Harding F. Bancroft. Executive vice-president of the *New York Times.*

Louis W. Cabot (of the original Boston Cabots who discovered America). Chairman of the board of the Cabot Corp.

David A. Shepard. Executive vice-president Standard Oil Co. of New Jersey, and chairman of the board of trustees of the RAND Corp.

The Cultural Organizations

The identification of the nation's leading civic and cultural institutions requires qualitative judgments about the prestige and influence of a variety of organizations. Six cultural organizations were selected:

Metropolitan Museum of Art
Museum of Modern Art
Lincoln Center for the Performing Arts
Smithsonian Institution
National Gallery of Art
John F. Kennedy Center for the Performing Arts

It is difficult to measure the power of particular institutions in the world of art, music, and theater. Certainly reasonable men may differ with our judgments and add or subtract from this listing.

The Metropolitan Museum of Art. This organization in New York City is the largest art museum in the United States, with a collection of nearly one-half million *objets d'art.* Decisions of the Metropolitan museum regarding exhibitions, collections, showings, and art objects have tremendous impact on what is or is not to be considered valued art in America. These decisions are the formal responsibility of the governing board. This board includes names such as:

Arthur A. Houghton. President and chairman of the board of Corning Glass.

C. Douglas Dillon. Former secretary of treasury, under secretary of state, and a director of Chase Manhattan.

Mrs. McGeorge Bundy. Wife of the former presidential assistant for national security affairs under Kennedy and Johnson. Former president of the Ford Foundation.

Arthur Ochs Sulzburger. Publisher and president of the *New York Times.*

Nelson A. Rockefeller. Vice-President of the United States.

Henry S. Morgan. Son of J. P. Morgan, who founded U.S. Steel Corp. and International Harvester and became one of the world's wealthiest men in the 1920s through his control of Morgan Guaranty Bank.

The Museum of Modern Art. This museum in New York City is the leading institution in the nation devoted to collecting and exhibiting contemporary art. It houses not only painting and sculpture, but also films, prints, and photography. Its loan exhibitions circulate art works throughout the world. The determination of what is to be considered "art" in the world of modern art is extremely subjective. The directors of the Museum of Modern Art, then, have great authority in determining what is or is not to be viewed as art. Its directors include such illustrious names as:

David Rockefeller. Chairman of the board of Chase Manhattan.

John Hay Whitney. Centimillionaire, former publisher of *New York Herald Tribune* and ambassador to Great Britain.

William S. Paley. Chairman of the board of CBS.

Mrs. C. Douglas Dillon. Wife of Douglas Dillon.

Mrs. Edsel B. Ford. Widow of Edsel B. Ford (son of Henry Ford) and mother of Henry Ford II.

Mrs. John D. Rockefeller III. Wife of oldest of four sons of John D. Rockefeller, Jr.

The Lincoln Center for the Performing Arts. The Lincoln Center in New York City is a major influence in the nation's serious theater, ballet, and music. The Lincoln Center houses the Metropolitan Opera, the New York Philharmonic, and the Juilliard School of Music. It also supports the Lincoln Repertory Company (theater), the New York State Theater (ballet), and the Library-Museum for Performing Arts. These component parts exercise some independence, but the Lincoln Center's board of directors has considerable formal responsibility over all of these activities. The chairman of the board of Lincoln Center is John D. Rockefeller III, the oldest of the Rockefeller brothers.

The *Metropolitan Opera,* which opened in 1883, is the nation's most influential institution in the field of serious operatic music. Decisions regarding productions influence greatly what is, or is not, to be considered serious opera in America and indeed the world. Such decisions are the formal responsibility of a board that includes such luminaries as the following:

Mrs. August Belmont. A daughter of the Saltonstalls of Massachusetts.

William Rockefeller. A cousin of the Rockefeller brothers. A senior partner of Shearman and Sterling, a top Wall Street law firm.

The Smithsonian Institution. The Smithsonian Institution in Washington supports a wide variety of scientific publications, collections, and exhibitions. It also exercises nominal control over the National

Gallery of Art, the John F. Kennedy Center for Performing Arts, and the Museum of Natural History, although these component organizations have their own boards of directors. The Smithsonian itself is directed by a board consisting of the vice-president of the United States, the chief justice of the Supreme Court, three U.S. Senators, three U.S. Representatives, and six "private citizens."

Its "private citizens" turn out to be people such as:

Crawford Greenewalt. Former chairman of the board of E. I. duPont de Nemours, and a trustee of the duPont's Christiana Securities Corp. and Morgan Guaranty Trust Co.

Thomas J. Watson, Jr. Chairman of the board of IBM.

William A. M. Burden. A descendant of the Vanderbilts of New York City. Investor in and director of Allied Chemicals, CBS, Lockheed Aircraft, Manufacturers Hanover Trust, and American Metal Climax. Also served as ambassador to Belgium.

Carl P. Haskins. President of the Carnegie Foundation and a trustee of the Council on Foreign Relations, RAND Corp.

James Edwin Webb. Former director of the U.S. Bureau of the Budget and under secretary of state. Former director of the National Aeronautics and Space Administration. A director of Kerr McGee Oil Corp. and Sperry Rand, and trustee of the Committee for Economic Development.

The National Gallery of Art. This art institution in Washington was begun in 1937 when Andrew W. Mellon made the original donation of his art collection together with $15 million to build the gallery itself. Since then it has accepted other collections from wealthy philanthropists and exercises considerable influence in the art world. Its directors include:

Paul Mellon. A son of Andrew W. and a director of Mellon National Bank and Trust and the Mellon Foundation.

John Hay Whitney. Centimillionaire, former publisher of *New York Herald Tribune* and ambassador to Great Britain.

Stoddard M. Stevens. Senior partner, Sullivan and Cromwell, top Wall Street law firm.

The John F. Kennedy Center for the Performing Arts. The Kennedy Center in Washington, which was begun in 1964, also has a considerable influence in the arts in America. Its board is largely "political" in origin, including:

Edward M. Kennedy. U.S. senator from Massachusetts.

Mrs. Michael J. Mansfield. Wife of U.S. Senate Majority Leader Mike Mansfield.

Mrs. J. W. Marriott. Wife of president of Marriott Motor Hotels, himself a heavy financial contributor to political candidates.

Jacqueline Kennedy Onassis. The former Mrs. John F. Kennedy.

Charles H. Percy. U.S. senator from Illinois.

Elliott M. Richardson. Former secretary of H.E.W., secretary of defense, and attorney general.

Arthur Schlesinger, Jr. Former special assistant to President John F. Kennedy.

The Civic Associations

Our judgments about power and influence in the civic arena are necessarily qualitative, as they were for cultural organizations. Six civic associations have been selected as being particularly representative of this category of the "public interest" elite.

Council on Foreign Relations
Committee on Economic Development
Brookings Institution
American Assembly
American Red Cross
National Association of Manufacturers

We shall focus particular attention on the political power of the nation's leading policy planning organizations—the Council on Foreign Relations, the Committee on Economic Development, and the Brookings Institution—both in this chapter and later in Chapter 9. These organizations are central coordinating mechanisms in national policy-making. They bring together people in top positions from the corporate world, the universities, the law firms, and the government, to develop explicit policies and programs for submission to Congress, the president, and the nation.

The Council on Foreign Relations. The most influential policy-planning group in foreign affairs is the Council on Foreign Relations. It was founded in 1921 and supported by grants from the Rockefeller and Carnegie Foundations and later the Ford Foundation. Its early directors were internationally minded Wall Street corporation leaders such as Elihu Root (who was secretary of state); John W. Davis (1928 Democratic presidential nominee); and Paul Cravath (founder of the famous law firm of Cravath, Swaine & Moore).

The CFR is designed to build consensus among elites on foreign policy questions. Its commissions make investigations concerning foreign policy, and set major directions of official U.S. policy. This council largely determines when reassessments of U.S. foreign or military policy are desired. Its studies are usually made with the financial support of foundations. The history of the CFR accomplishments are dazzling: it developed the Kellogg Peace Pact in the 1920s, stiffened U.S. opposition to Japanese Pacific expansion in the 1930s, designed major portions of the United Nations' charter, and devised the "containment" policy to halt Soviet expansion in Europe after World War II. It also laid the groundwork for the NATO agreement and devised the Marshall Plan for European recovery.

CFR publishes the journal *Foreign Affairs,* considered throughout the world the unofficial mouthpiece of U.S. foreign policy. Few important initiatives in U.S. policy are not first outlined in articles in this publication. It was in *Foreign Affairs* in 1947 that George F. Kennan, chief of the Policy Planning Staff of the State Department, writing under the pseudonym of "X", first announced U.S. intentions of "containing" Communist expansion in the world.

Recognizing that U.S. corporations make foreign poicy, as well as the U.S. government, the CFR provides "corporation services" for large fees; these sources include consultation, information, and the right to nominate "promising" young executives to attend its semi-annual seminars. Its corporate members include Chase Manhattan, General Motors, Ford Motors, Continental Can, Gulf Oil, General Electric, and other giant corporations—particularly those with overseas interests. The CFR limits itself to 700 individual resident members (New York and Washington) and 700 nonresident members. There are few individuals in top positions in American institutions with an interest in foreign affairs who are *not* CFR members. The CFR's list of former members include every person of influence in foreign affairs from Elihu Root, Henry Stimson, John Foster Dulles, Dean Acheson, Robert Lovett, George F. Kennan, Averell Harriman, and Dean Rusk, to Henry Kissinger.

In the early 1970s, its board of directors included these names.

David Rockefeller. Chairman of board, Chase Manhattan.

John J. McCloy. Senior partner, Milbank, Tweed, Hadley, & McCloy.

Gabriel Hauge. President Manufacturers Hanover Trust Co., former editor of *Business Week.*

Thomas K. Finletter. Former secretary of the Air Force and U.S. ambassador to NATO.

Phillip D. Reed. Former chairman of the board, General Electric Co.

Najeeb E. Halaby. President, Pan American World Airlines.

Cyrus Vance. Chairman of the board of Dillian Bead & Co. Director of Chase Manhattan.

Alfred C. Neal. President of the Committee on Economic Development.

Hedley Donovan. Editor in Chief, *Time* Inc.

Grayson Kirk. President of Columbia University.

Henry M. Wriston. President of Brown University. Chairman of the American Assembly.

William P. Bundy. Senior partner Covington & Burling. Former Deputy Director CIA. Assistant secretary of defense. Brother McGeorge Bundy was special assistant to President Johnson for National Security Affairs, and president of the Ford Foundation.

Arthur H. Dean. Senior partner, Sullivan and Cromwell. Chief U.S. Negotiation Korean Armistice, and Nuclear Test Ban Treaty.

Political scientist Lester Milbraith observes that the influence of CFR throughout the government is so pervasive that it is difficult to distinguish CFR from government programs: "The Council on Foreign Relations, while not financed by government, works so closely with it that it is difficult to distinguish Council actions stimulated by government from autonomous actions.[10]

The popular journalist and observer of presidential elections, Theodore H. White, reported of the Council:

> Its roster of members has for a generation under Republican and Democratic administrations alike, been the chief recruiting ground for cabinet level officials in Washington. Among the first eighty-two names on a list prepared for John F. Kennedy for staffing his State Department, at least sixty-three were members of the Council. When, finally, he made his appointments, both his Secretary of State (Rusk, Democrat) and Treasury (Dillon, Republican) were chosen from Council members; so were seven assistant and undersecretaries of State, four senior members of Defense, . . . as well as two members of the White House Staff (Schlesinger, Democrat; Bundy, Republican).[11]

Council on Economic Development. There are several private policy-planning groups that are influential in domestic affairs. None, however, is as influential in *domestic* policy-making as the CFR is in *foreign* policy-making. Yet the CED is a central organization for developing elite consensus, researching national problems, and directing national policy.

The CED was created in 1942 as an outgrowth of the realization that business would be required to work closer with government in World War II war production and in avoiding economic depression after the war. The CED was initially composed of businessmen who

[10] Lester Milbraith, "Interest Groups in Foreign Policy," in James N. Rosenau, ed., *Domestic Sources of Foreign Policy* (New York: Free Press, 1967), p. 247; also cited in Domhoff, *The Higher Circles* (New York: Vintage Books, 1971), p. 114.

[11] Theodore H. White, *The Making of the President, 1964* (New York: Atheneum, 1965), pp. 67–68; also cited in Domhoff, *The Higher Circles,* p. 118.

viewed the New Deal as an essential reform to save the capitalist system and their place in it. Early CED members were considered more progressive and far-sighted than the more conservative and less influential businessmen in the National Association of Manufacturers (NAM). As business gradually moved away from the discredited "public be damned" attitudes of the nineteenth-century robber barons, and assumed a new liberal public-regarding, social consciousness, a new organization was required to reflect these views. The once-powerful NAM became a discredited voice of conservatism and the CED became the spokesman of top corporate enterprise.

The CED's founder was Paul Hoffman. (Hoffman had been chairman of the board of Studebaker-Packard Corporation; a U.S. Delegate to the United Nations; a trustee of the Ford Foundation, the University of Chicago, and Kenyon College; a director of New York Life Insurance Co., Time, Inc., Encyclopedia Britannica, the Automotive Safety Foundation; and chairman of the Fund for the Republic.) He served as chairman of CED from 1942 to 1948. Another key figure in the formation of the CED was William Benton. (Former U.S. Senator from Connecticut; former assistant secretary of state; chairman of the board of Encyclopedia Britannica; a trustee of the University of Chicago, University of Bridgeport, Brandeis University, Kennedy Library, and the American Assembly; and a member of CFR.) Benton served as vice-chairman of CED under Hoffman. The early membership of CED was drawn heavily from the Business Advisory Council of the Department of Commerce, which President Roosevelt had established during the Depression to bring businessmen into his administration. The CED also brought in Robert Calkins, who was dean of the School of Business at Columbia from the academic world; later Calkins went on to become president of the Brookings Institution.

The CED grew in influence when one of its original trustees, Thomas B. McCabe, chairman of the board of Scott Paper Company, was appointed by President Truman to be chairman of the board of the Federal Reserve System, which directs U.S. monetary policy. McCabe served as FRS chairman from 1948 to 1951, and later became a governor of the New York Stock Exchange.

The first important accomplishment of the CED was the Employment Act of 1946 creating the Council of Economic Advisers and officially committing the U.S. government to fiscal and monetary policies devised to avoid depression, maintain full employment, and minimize inflation. At this time the CED was heavily interlocked with an organization called the National Planning Association. This latter group did the actual lobbying for the Act. The NPA was then headed by Charles E. Wilson, president of GE. (This Wilson was then referred to as "Electric Charlie" to distinguish him from Charles E. Wilson, president of General Motors and later Secretary of Defense, who was called "Engine Charlie.")

The CED does not restrict itself exclusively to fiscal and monetary policy. It works closely with CFR on foreign policy questions, particularly those involving international trade. There are many interlocks betwen CFR and CED members: Elliot V. Bell, of McGraw-Hill, has been both a CED and CFR trustee, and so has Phillip H. Reed, former chairman of the board of GE.

The trustees of the CED today represent a range of business, financial, governmental, and intellectual talent. William Benton and Thomas B. McCabe remain on the board together with such men as the following:

Emilio G. Callado. Executive vice-president of Exxon.

John A. Perkins. Former president of the University of Delaware, former under secretary of HEW, and president of Dun & Bradstreet.

Jevis J. Babb. Former president and chairman of the board of Lever Bros.

Frederick S. Beebe. A director of Washington Post–Newsweek Co.

Joseph L. Black. Chairman and chief executive officer, Inland Steel Company.

Robert C. Cosgrove. President, Jolly Green Giant Co.

Marion B. Folsom. Former president Eastman Kodak Co. and former secretary of HEW.

John M. Fox. President of United Fruit Co., former president of Minute Maid Corp., Director of the Federal Reserve Bank of Boston.

Richard C. Gerstenberg. Executive vice-president, General Motors Corp.

Ellison L. Hazard. Chairman of the board, Continental Can Co. A director of Kennecott Copper and Goodyear Tire & Rubber.

H. J. Heinz II. Chairman of the board of H. J. Heinz Co. A director of Mellon National Bank & Trust, a trustee of Carnegie Institute of Technology.

Robert J. Kleberg, Jr. President, King Ranch, Inc.

Ralph Lazarus. President, Federated Department Stores, Inc. A director of Chase Manhattan Bank, Scott Paper Co., General Electric.

Robert B. Semple. President, Wyandotte Chemical Corp. A director of Michigan Consolidated Gas Co., National Bank of Detroit, Chrysler Corp.

Theodore O. Yntema. Former vice-president, Ford Motor Co.

The Brookings Institution. In 1966, on the fiftieth anniversary of the Brookings Institution, President Lyndon B. Johnson praised the work of this organization:

In field after field, reports and studies that emerged from Brookings did

> bring about substantial changes in law and practice. It was often the case of concentrated brain power applied to national problems where ignorance, confusion, vested interests, or apathy had ruled before. Sometimes the Brookings study won the day; sometimes it only opened the way for other ideas and policies; but always it changed the temperature and cosmos of Washington.[12]

Today the Brookings Institution is the dominant policy-planning group for American domestic policy. Since the 1960s, it has overshadowed the CED, the American Assembly, the Twentieth Century Fund, and all other policy-planning groups. Brookings has been extremely influential in planning the war on poverty, welfare reform, revision of the nation's health-care system, and tax reform.

The Brookings Institution began as a modest component of the progressive movement of the early twentieth century. A wealthy St. Louis merchant, Robert Brookings, established an Institute of Government Research in 1916 to promote "good government," fight "bossism," assist in municipal reform, and press for economy and efficiency in government. It worked closely with the National Civic Federation and other reformist, progressive organizations of that era. Brookings himself was appointed to the War Production Board by President Woodrow Wilson.

The original trustees of Brookings included Frederic H. Delano (wealthy banker and railroad executive, a member of the first Federal Reserve Board, and an uncle of President Franklin Delano Roosevelt); James F. Curtis (banker and assistant secretary of the treasury under President Taft); Arthur T. Hadley (president of Yale University); Herbert Hoover (then a self-made millionaire engineer and later secretary of commerce and president of the United States); and Felix Frankfurter (Harvard law professor, later to become Supreme Court Justice.)

The first major policy decision of the Brookings Institution was the establishment of an annual federal budget. Before 1921 the Congress considered appropriations requests individually as they came from various departments and agencies. But the Brookings Institution proposed, and the Congress passed, the Budget and Accounting Act of 1921, which created for the first time an integrated federal budget prepared in the executive office of the president and presented to the Congress in a single budget message. This notable achievement was consistent with the early interests of the Brookings trustees in improving economy and efficiency in government.

In 1927, with another large gift from Robert Brookings as well as donations from Carnegie, Rockefeller, and Eastman (Kodak), the Brook-

12 U.S. 90th Congress, House of Representatives, Committee on Government Operations, *The Use of Social Research in Federal Domestic Programs* (Washington, D.C.: Government Printing Office, 1967), p. 178.

itution assumed its present name. It also added Wall Street Dean Acheson to its trustees; he remained a trustee until his ap- nt as secretary of state in 1947. For many years the full-time president and executive officer of Brookings was Robert D. Calkins, former dean of the School of Business at Columbia, and former CED director.

The Brookings Institution directors today are as impressive a group of top elites as are assembled anywhere. They include many individuals already described elsewhere in this volume: such as David M. Kennedy, Douglas Dillon, and the ubiquitous Elliot V. Bell, who sits on the board of the Council on Foreign Relations, the Committee on Economic Development, *and* the Brookings Institution!

But Brookings also lists other heavily interlocked directors:

Eugene R. Black. Former president, Chase Manhattan Bank.

Luther G. Holbrook. Former president T. Mellon & Sons and trustee of the Mellon Foundation.

John E. Lockwood. Senior partner, Milbank, Tweed, Hadley and McCloy.

Arjay Miller. Former president Ford Motor Co.

Herbert P. Patterson. President, Chase Manhattan Bank.

Edward W. Carter. President of Broadway Hale Stores. A director of AT&T, Southern California Edison, Del Monte Corp., Western Bank Corp.

Dillon Anderson. Houston attorney, former assistant to the president for national security affairs (Eisenhower Administration). A director of Westinghouse Electric Corp.

If the names are growing repetitious by now, it is for good reason. The same individuals who occupy top posts in the leading corporate, governmental, and mass media institutions are frequently the same individuals who direct the leading foundations, civic associations, and cultural organizations. In the next few pages, we shall see many of their names again, when we examine the trustees of the nation's leading universities. The purpose of "naming names," even when they become repetitive, is to suggest frequent interlocking of top elites in different institutional sectors. Later in Chapter 6, we will examine interlocking in greater detail.

The Universities

The growth of public higher education since World War II—the creation of vast state university, state college, and community college systems in every state in the nation—has diminished the influence of the prestigious private universities. There are now over 2500 separate institutions of higher education in America enrolling over 9 million students; about half of all high school graduates go on to higher education. Only about a quarter of these students are enrolled in *private* colleges and universities. Moreover, some leading public universities (University of California at Berkeley, University of Wisconsin, University of Michigan, etc.) are consistently ranked with the well-known *private* universities in assessments of the quality of higher education. Thus, the leading private universities in the nation no longer exercise the dominant influence over higher education that they exercised a few decades ago.

Nonetheless, among private colleges and universities it is possible to identify those few top institutions which control over half of the resources available to *private* higher education. The twelve universities listed in Table 5-3 control 54 percent of all private endowment funds in higher education; this was the formal basis for their selection. Moreover, they are consistently ranked among the "best" educational institutions in the nation. Finally, as we will see, a disproportionate number of the nation's top leaders attended one or another of these insitutions.

The presidents and trustees of these twelve institutions, then, can exercise significant influence over American higher education and thus American life. They are included in our formal definition of the nation's top institutional leadership. A brief look at some of the people at the top of higher-education institutions tells us a great deal about the educational elite group. Note their similarities in positions held now and in the past, and their close ties with other fields, notably business, culture, politics, and public interest. We will list some names of

Table 5-3. The Top Privately Endowed Colleges and Universities

Rank		Endowment (in billion $s)	Cumulative (in percent)
1	Harvard	1,013	18.5
2	Yale	358	25.0
3	Chicago	275	30.0
4	Stanford	223	34.1
5	Columbia	201	37.7
6	Massachusetts Institute of Technology	184	41.1
7	Cornell	163	44.0
8	Northwestern	135	46.5
9	Princeton	134	48.9
10	Johns Hopkins	112	51.0
11	Pennsylvania	95	52.7
12	Dartmouth	91	54.4
		2,984	

Number of Institutions = 107
Total Private Endowments Funds, U.S. = 5,488

trustees for the nation's top three private universities—Harvard, Yale and the University of Chicago.

Harvard University

Osborn Elliott. Editor of *Newsweek* and a director of Washington Post Co.

C. Douglas Dillon. Former secretary of the treasury, and a director of defense.

C. Douglas Dillon. Former Secretary of the Treasury, and a director of Chase Manhattan.

Gardiner Cowles. Chairman of board of Cowles Publication (largest U.S. newspaper chain).

Francis Keppel. Former U.S. commissioner of education and assistant secretary of HEW.

Robert C. Seamoris, Jr. Former secretary of the Air Force, and deputy director of NASA.

Louis W. Cabot. Chairman of the board of the Cabot Corporation.

Yale University

John Hay Whitney. Centimillionaire, former publisher of *New York Herald Tribune* and ambassador to Great Britain.

William McChesney Martin. Former chairman of the Federal Reserve Board, former governor of New York Stock Exchange.

William P. Bundy. Senior partner, Covington and Burling. Former assistant secretary of state for the Far East; former assistant secretary of defense.

William W. Scranton. Former governor of Pennsylvania.

Cyrus R. Vance. Senior partner, Simpson, Thachter & Bartlett, former secretary of the Army.

Arthur K. Watson. Chairman of board of IBM.

University of Chicago

David Rockefeller. Chairman of board Chase Manhattan.

Cyrus S. Eaton. Former director Republic Steel Corp., Inland Steel Corp., Kingstown Sheet & Tube, Sherman-Williams Co.

Albert Pick, Jr. President of Albert Pick Hotels.

Robert O. Anderson. Chairman of the board Atlantic Richfield Co.; a director of Smith, Kline, & French (pharmaceuticals).

Katherine Graham. Publisher *Washington Post, Newsweek.*

Robert S. Ingersoll. Chairman of board, Borg-Warner Corp.

David M. Kennedy. Former secretary of the treasury; chairman of the board of Continental Illinois National Bank & Trust.

John D. Rockefeller IV. Son of John D. Rockefeller III. Former Appalachian area poverty worker, and later secretary of state for West Virginia. President of W. Virginia Wesleyan College.

Charles H. Percy. U.S. Senator from Illinois.

We have already acknowledged the growing importance in higher education of the nation's leading *state* universities. Is there any reason to believe that their rise to prominence since World War II has distributed power in education more widely and opened positions of authority to men whose elite credentials are not necessarily as impressive as the ones we have seen again and again in our lists of top leaders. Our answer is a very qualified "yes": state boards of regents even for the nation's most renowned state universities are composed of many men who would probably *not* otherwise be among the top institutional elites according to our definition in Chapter 1. Many of these regents hold directorships in smaller corporations (ranked below the top hundred), smaller banks (ranked below the top fifty), and smaller communications, transportation and utility companies (ranked below the top thirty-three); they frequently have held state rather than national political office; their legal, civic, cultural, and foundation affiiliations are with institutions of state rather than national prestige and power.

Nonetheless, it is interesting to see, for example, who controls the University of California's multi-campus, billion-dollar educational enterprise. Four of the twenty-four regents are elected state officials—the governor, lieutenant governor, state assembly speaker, and superintendent of education. The other twenty appointed regents, serving sixteen-year appointments, sit on a total of sixty corporate boards. According to David N. Smith, these corporations include Western Bank Corporation, Croker-Citizens National Bank, United California Bank, AT&T, Pacific Telephone and Telegraph, Broadway Hale Stores (including Neiman Marcus), Western Airlines, Pacific Lighting Corporation, Southern California Edison, Pacific Mutual Life Insurance, Northern Pacific Railway, Lockheed Aircraft, and the Los Angeles Rams and California Angels.[13] Catherine Hearst (wife of publisher Randolph Hearst and mother of Patty Hearst), is a regent as well as Norton Simon, whose firm Norton Simon, Inc., is the 120th largest industrial corporation in the nation.

University presidents, particularly the presidents of the nation's top institutions, are frequently called upon to serve as trustees or directors of other institutions and to serve in high government posts. Most university presidents today have come up through the ranks of academic administration, suggesting that universities themselves may offer channels for upward mobility into the nation's elite. We must keep in mind, however, that presidents are hired and fired by the trustees, not the students or faculty.

[13] David N. Smith, *Who Rules the Universities* (New York: Monthly Review Press, 1974), pp. 30–33.

The Intellectual Elite

The intellectual "community" is not sufficiently organized or institutionalized to provide its leadership with formal control over any significant portion of society's resources. Indeed, "intellectuals" do not even have much control over universities, the institutions that house the largest group of the nation's intellectuals. Some intellectuals may have "influence" in America because men at the top of large institutions read their books and listen to their lectures and are persuaded by them. But intellectuals themselves (within this categorization) have no direct control over the institutional structure of society, *unless they are recruited into top institutional positions.* Our formal definition of elites as individuals in positions of control over institutional resources, then, means that we can only count as "intellectual elites" those who have been recruited to high institutional positions—particularly in government, the foundations, and the civic and cultural organizations. The prototype of the intellectual in power, of course, is Henry Kissinger.

Historian Richard Hofstadter divided intellectuals in a fashion that reflects our own notion about treating intellectuals in power separately from those not in power. Hofstadter expressed the hope that "the intellectual community will not become hopelessly polarized into two parts, one part the technicians concerned with power and accepting the terms of power put to them, and the other of willfully alienated intellectuals more concerned with maintaining their own sense of purity than with making their ideas effective." [14]

Actually, it is difficult to define precisely who is an intellectual. Seymour Martin Lipset defines intellectuals as:

> all of those who create, distribute, and apply culture, that is, the symbolic world of man, including art, science, and religion. Within this group there are two main levels: the hard core of creators of culture—scholars, artists, philosophers, authors, some editors and some journalists; and the distributors—performers in the various arts, most teachers, and most reporters.[15]

Such a broad definition includes millions of individuals with a wide range of institutional affiliations.

Perhaps the most systematic attempt to identify an intellectual

[14] Richard Hofstadter, *Anti-Intellectualism in American Life* (New York: Knopf, 1963), p. 429.

[15] Seymour Martin Lipset, *Political Man* (New York: Doubleday, 1960), p. 310.

elite is found in the work of Charles Kadusin and his associates at Columbia University.[16] According to Kadusin, "An elite intellectual may be defined roughly as one who is an expert in dealing with general ideas on questions of values and esthetics and who communicates his judgments on these matters to a fairly general audience." (Note that Kadusin excludes many specialists, particularly in the physical and biological sciences, who deal with specific scientific questions and communicate to a very specialized audience; this may be the greatest weakness in his definition.) To operationalize this definition, Kadusin employed a reputational approach to select twenty leading intellectual journals of general interest, excluding specialized or technical ones. A sample of professors, writers, and editors selected the following publications:

New York Review of Books
New Republic
Commentary
New York Times Book Review
New Yorker
Saturday Review
Partisan Review
Harpers
The Nation
Atlantic
Daedalus
Ramparts
Yale Review
Dissent
American Scholar
Hudson Review
Village Voice
The Progressive
Foreign Affairs
The Public Interest

It turns out that nearly 8000 persons had contributed articles to these intellectual journals in a four-year period. A second sample was then asked to identify those intellectuals "who influenced them on cultural or social-political issues, or who they believed had high prestige in the intellectual community." The result was the listing on Table 5-4.

We can now make some observations about the nation's intellectual elite. A few have occupied high places in government—Galbraith, Moynihan, Schlesinger, Gardner. But most have remained on the sidelines—perhaps exercising "influence" from time to time, but not "power" in terms of institutional authority. About half of America's intellectuals are Jewish (less than 3 percent of the nation's total population is Jewish). One-third are under 50 years old; one-third is between 50 and 60; and one-third is over 60. Their median income in 1969 was only $35,000, considerably less than the other elites identified in this book. There are very few women among the nation's *top* intellectuals, and only one black—Bayard Rustin.

16 Charles Kadushin, Julie Hover, and Monique Richy, "How and Where to Find an Intellectual Elite in the United States," *Public Opinion Quarterly*, 35 (Spring 1971), 1-18; see also Charles Kadushin, "Who Are the Elite Intellectuals?" *The Public Interest* (Summer 1972), pp. 109-25.

Table 5-4. The Most Prestigious Contemporary American Intellectuals

Ranks 1 to 10 (2 tied for 10th place)	
Daniel Bell	Norman Mailer
Noam Chomsky	Robert Silvers
John Kenneth Galbraith	Susan Sontag
Irving Howe	Lionel Trilling
Dwight MacDonald	Edmund Wilson
Mary McCarthy	
Ranks 11 to 20	
Hannah Arendt	Herbert Marcuse
Saul Bellow	Daniel Patrick Moynihan
Paul Goodman	Norman Podhoretz
Richard Hofstadter	David Riesman
Irving Kristol	Arthur Schlesinger, Jr.
Ranks 21 to 25 (numerous ties)	
W. H. Auden	Pauline Kael
Norman O. Brown	Alfred Kazin
Theodore Draper	Murray Kempton
Jason Epstein	George Lichtheim
Leslie Fiedler	Walter Lippmann
Edgar Friedenberg	Marshall McLuhan
John Gardner	Hans Morgenthau
Eugene Genovese	I. F. Stone
Richard Goodwin	C. Vann Woodward
Michael Harrington	
Ranks 26 and 27 (numerous ties)	
Edward Banfield	Willie Morris
Isaiah Berlin	Lewis Mumford
Barbara Epstein	Reinhold Niebuhr
R. Buckminster Fuller	Robert Nisbet
Nathan Glazer	Phillip Rahv
Elizabeth Hardwick	James Reston
Robert Heilbroner	Harold Rosenberg
Sidney Hook	Philip Roth
Ada Louise Huxtable	Richard Rovere
George F. Kennan	Bayard Rustin
Christopher Lasch	Franz Schurman
Seymour Martin Lipset	John Simon
Robert Lowell	George Steiner
Robert K. Merton	Diana Trilling
Barrington Moore	James Q. Wilson

Source: Charles Kadushin, "Who Are the Elite Intellectuals?" *The Public Interest,* Number 29 (Fall 1972), p. 123. Copyright © 1972 by National Affairs, Inc.

The American intellectual elite is far more liberal than any other segment of the nation's elite. Richard Hofstadter writes:

> If there is anything that could be called an intellectual establishment in America, this establishment has been, though not profoundly radical

(which would be unbecoming in an establishment), on the left side of center.[17]

Kadusin confirms this judgment; his intellectuals are left-liberal and generally critical of the government and the economic system. But only about 20 percent could be classified as "radical"—that is, convinced that the overthrow of capitalism is essential to improvement in the quality of life in America. Kadusin found that the few elite intellectuals who rose from working-class backgrounds are somewhat more *conservative* than the majority of intellectuals who came from middle, upper-middle, and upper-class families. But he adds, "The elite intellectuals have so long been involved in the culture of intellectuals that their past backgrounds have become almost irrelevant." [18]

Summary

Using the term "civic establishment," we refer collectively to the nation's top law firms, its major foundations, its national cultural institutions, influential civic organizations, and powerful universities. At the top of the legal profession, the senior partners of the nation's largest and best-known New York and Washington law firms exercise great power as legal representatives of the nation's largest corporations. These "super-lawyers" generally reflect the same liberal and public-regarding views that prevail among other segments of the nation's elites. Superlawyers are frequently called upon for governmental leadership, particularly when high-level, delicate negotiations are required. Many superlawyers have been educated at "Ivy League" law schools and serve apprenticeships in governmental agencies before entering law firms.

The power of the nation's large foundations rests in their ability to channel corporate and personal wealth into the policy-making process. They do this by providing financial support and direction over university research and the activities of policy-oriented, civic associations. There is great concentration of foundation assets: twelve of the nation's 6,803 foundations control 40 percent of all foundation assets. There is also a great deal of overlapping among the directorates of the leading foundations and corporate and financial institutions, the mass media, universities, policy-planning groups, and government.

A small number of cultural organizations exercise great power over

17 Hofstadter, *Anti-Intellectualism.*

18 Ibid., p. 120.

the nation's art, music, theater, and ballet. A brief glance at the directors of these institutions confirms that they are the same group of people identified earlier as influential in business, finance, government, and the mass media.

The civic associations, particularly the leading policy-planning groups—the Council on Foreign Relations, Committee on Economic Development, and the Brookings Institution—play key roles in national policy-making. They bring together men at the top of various institutional sectors of society to formulate recommendations on major policy innovations. More will be said about the important role of policy-planning groups in Chapter 9. But we have noted here that the directors of these groups are top leaders in industry, finance, government, the mass media, law, and the universities.

There may not be as much concentration of power in higher education as in other sectors of American life. The development of state universities since World War II has diminished the influence of the private, Ivy League-type universities. However, among *private* universities, only twelve institutions control over half of all private endowment funds. A glance at the trustees of three of these institutions—Harvard, Yale, and Chicago—suggests heavy overlapping of those in power in corporations, government, the mass media, the foundations, etc. The intellectual "community" does not exercise any formal control over any significant portion of the nation's resources. Only when an intellectual is recruited to high position, as in the case of Henry Kissinger, can he be said to have power.

PART 3

The Structure of Institutional Elites

Six

INTERLOCKING AND SPECIALIZATION AT THE TOP

Convergence or Specialization at the Top?

Is there a convergence of power at the "top" of the institutional structure in America, with a single group of individuals, recruited primarily from industry and finance, who occupy top positions in corporations, education, government, foundations, civic and cultural affairs, and the military? Or are there separate institutional structures, with elites in each sector of society having little or no overlap in authority and many separate channels of recruitment? In short, is the structure of power in America a pyramid or a polyarchy?

Social scientists have differed over this important question, and at least two varieties of leadership models can be identified in the literature on power.[1] A *hierarchical model* implies that a relatively small group

1 This literature is voluminous, and any characterization of positions results in some oversimplification. For good summary statements of positions, see the works of Mills, Hunter, Berle, Kolko, and Dahl, cited elsewhere in chapter notes. See also Arnold M. Rose, *The Power Structure* (New York: Oxford University Press, 1967); Suzanne Keller, *Beyond the Ruling Class* (New York: Random House, 1963); G. William

of individuals exercises authority in a wide variety of institutions—forming what has been called a "power elite." In contrast, a *polyarchical model* implies that different groups of individuals exercise power in different sectors of society, and acquire power in separate ways.

The hierarchical model is derived from the familiar "elitist" literature on power. Mills argues that "the leading men in each of the three domains of power—the warlords, the corporation chieftains, and the political directorate—tend to come together to form the power elite of America." [2] According to Mills, leadership in America constitutes "an intricate set of overlapping cliques." And Hunter, in his study *Top Leadership, U.S.A.*, concludes: "Out of several hundred persons named from all sources, between one hundred and two hundred were consistently chosen as top leaders and considered by all informants to be of national policy-making stature." [3] The notion of interlocking directorates has widespread currency in the power elite literature. Kolko writes that "interlocking directorates, whereby a director of one corporation also sits on the board of one or more other corporations, are a key device for concentrating corporate power. . . ." [4] The hierarchical model also implies that top leaders in all sectors of society—including government, education, civic and cultural affairs, and politics—are recruited primarily from business and finance.

In contrast, "pluralist" writers have implied a polyarchical leadership structure, with different sets of leaders in different sectors of society and little or no overlap, except perhaps by elected officials responsible to the general public. According to this view, leadership is exercised in large measure by "specialists" who limit their participation to a narrow range of societal decisions. These specialists are felt to be recruited through separate channels—they are not drawn exclusively from business and finance. Generally, writers on polyarchy have praised the dispersion of authority in American society. Dahl writes: "The theory and practice of American pluralism tends to assume, as I see it, that the existence of multiple centers of power, none of which is wholly sovereign, will help (may indeed be necessary) to tame power, to secure the consent

---

Domhoff, *Who Rules America?* (Englewood Cliffs, N.J.: Prentice-Hall, Inc., 1967); Nelson Polsby, *Community Power and Political Theory* (New Haven: Yale University Press, 1963); and David Ricci, *Community Power and Democratic Theory* (New York: Random House, 1971).

[2] C. Wright Mills, *The Power Elite* (New York: Oxford University Press, 1956), p. 9.

[3] Floyd Hunter, *Top Leadership, U.S.A.* (Chapel Hill: University of North Carolina Press, 1959), p. 176.

[4] Gabriel Kolko, *Wealth and Power in America* (New York: Frederick A. Praeger, 1962), p. 57.

of all, and to settle conflicts peacefully."[5] But despite the theoretical (and ideological) importance of the question of convergence versus specialization in the leadership structure, there has been very little *systematic* research on the concentration of authority or the extent of interlocking among top institutional elites.

"Interlockers" and "Specialists"

Earlier we identified over *five thousand* top institutional positions in twelve different sectors of society which we defined as the nation's elite (see Chapter 1). Individuals in these positions control half of the nation's industrial and financial assets and nearly half of all the assets of private foundations and universities; they control the television networks, the news services, and leading newspapers; they control the most prestigious civic and cultural organizations; and they direct the activities of the executive, legislative, and judicial branches of the national government.

These 5000 top positions were occupied by roughly 4000 individuals. In other words, there were fewer top individuals than top positions—indicating multiple holding of top positions by some individuals. Table 6-1 presents specific data on multiple top position-holding, which we shall call "interlocking."

Twenty percent of the individuals in top positions held more than one top position at a time. These are our "interlockers." Most of them

Table 6-1. Interlocking and Specialization in Top Institutional Positions

	Number Top Institutional Positions	Percent of Total Positions	Number of Individuals in Top Positions	Percent of Total Individuals
Total	5,416	100.0	4,101	100.0
Specialized	3,284	60.6	3,297	80.4
Interlocked	2,132	39.4	804	19.6
Number of Interlocks:				
Two	1,026	18.9	513	12.5
Three	552	10.2	184	4.5
Four	260	4.8	65	1.6
Five	105	1.9	21	0.5
Six	48	0.9	8	0.2
Seven or More	147	2.7	13	0.3

[5] Robert A. Dahl, *Pluralist Democracy in the United States* (Chicago: Rand McNally, 1967), p. 24.

held only two top positions, but some held six, seven, eight, or more! Eighty percent of the people at the top are "specialists"—individuals who hold only one top position. Many of these specialists hold other corporate directorships, governmental posts, or civic, cultural, or university positions, but not *top* positions as we have defined them. We will observe later that even our "specialists" fill a wide variety of lesser positions (directorships in corporations below the top hundred; positions on governmental boards and commissions; trusteeships of less well-known colleges and foundations; and directorships of less influential civic and cultural organizations) in addition to their top position. We will also observe that over a lifetime many of our specialists tend to hold a number of top positions, serially, rather than concurrently.

About 40 percent of all top *positions* are interlocked with other top positions. The reason that 40 percent of the top positions are interlocked, but only 20 percent of the top individuals hold more than one position, is that some individuals are "multiple interlockers"—they hold three or more positions.

The multiple interlockers turn out to be individuals of considerable stature, as the following listing in Table 6-2 indicates.[6]

These individuals comprised our top group of "multiple interlockers" in 1970—individuals occupying *six or more* top positions concurrently. By any criteria whatsoever, these individuals must be judged important figures in America. The fact that men of this caliber emerged at the top of our investigation of positional overlap lends some face validity to the assertion that interlocking is a source of authority and power in society. However, despite the impressive concentration of interlocking authority in this top group, it should be remembered that most of the universe of 4000 top position-holders were "specialists."

The Pattern of Interlocking

Let us turn now to an examination of the pattern of interlocking among the various sectors of society. The vast majority (84.6 percent) of top

[6] In addition to these *individuals,* it is important to know that several *family groups* whose members together hold a large number of authoritative positions also have positions of power in institutions. The Rockefeller family accounted for eighteen top positions in 1970. The duPonts accounted for eleven, the Houghtons for eight, and the Fords and Mellons for seven each. No *systematic* attempt was made to examine these or other family groupings. Interlocking here is treated only as an individual attribute. See Ferdinand Lundberg, *America's Sixty Families* (New York: Vanguard Press, 1937) and his *The Rich and The Super-Rich* (New York: Lyle Stuart, 1968) for an extended discussion of the importance of kinship ties and family groupings.

Table 6-2. Multiple Interlockers in Top Institutional Positions, 1970

Lloyd DeWitt Brace. Former chairman of the board and now a director of First National Boston Corp. Also a director of General Motors, AT&T, and John Hancock Life Insurance Co.

Ralph Manning Brown, Jr. Chairman of the board of New York Life Insurance Co. A director of Union Carbide, Morgan Guaranty Trust Co., Union Camp Corp., A & P, and Avon Products. Is also a trustee of the Sloan Foundation, Princeton University, and a director of the Metropolitan Museum of Art.

Arthur H. Dean. Senior partner, Sullivan & Cromwell; chairman of the U.S. delegation on Nuclear Test Ban Treaty, chief U.S. negotiator of the Korean Armistice Agreement; a director of American Metal Climax, American Bank Note Co., National Union Electric Corp., El Paso Natural Gas Company, Crown Zellerbach Corp., Campbell Soup Co., Northwest Production Corp., Lazard Fund, Inc., and the Bank of New York; a trustee of New York Hospital, Cornell Medical Center, Cornell Medical College, Cornell University, the Carnegie Foundation, and the Council on Foreign Relations.

Clarence Douglas Dillon. Chairman of the board of Dillon, Reed & Company and member of the New York Stock Exchange. He was formerly secretary of the treasury and undersecretary of state. He is presently a director of Chase Manhattan Bank, the Rockefeller Foundation, the Metropolitan Museum of Art, the Brookings Institution, the American Assembly, and he is a trustee of Harvard University. He is a large political contributor, and his wife is a trustee of the Museum of Modern Art.

Henry Ford II. Chairman and chief executive officer, Ford Motor Company. He is a director of General Foods Corporation and a trustee of the Ford Foundation. His brother, Benson Ford, is also a director of Ford Motor Company and the Ford Foundation, as well as a director of the American Safety Council and United Community Funds of America. Another brother, William Clay Ford, is president of the Detroit Lions Professional Football Club and a director of the Girl Scouts of America, Thomas A. Edison Foundation, and the Henry Ford hospital. These Fords are centimillionaires and heavy political contributors.

G. Keith Funston. Former president of the New York Stock Exchange. Chairman of the board of Olin Mathieson Corp., a director of Illinois Central Industries, Chemical Bank of New York, IBM, Metropolitan Life Insurance Co., Ford Motor Co., Republic Steel, and AVCO Corp. A trustee of Trinity College, and a director of the American Cancer Society. Was chairman of the War Production Board during World War II.

Thomas S. Gates. Chairman of the board and chief executive officer, Morgan Guaranty Trust Co. (J. P. Morgan, New York). He is a director of General Electric Co., Bethlehem Steel Corporation, Scott Paper Co., Campbell Soup Co., Insurance Co. of North America, Cities Service Co., Smith Kline and French (Pharmaceuticals). He is a trustee of the University of Pennsylvania. He has served as secretary of the navy and secretary of defense.

Harold Holmes Helm. Chairman of board of Chemical Bank of New York. A director of Equitable Life Insurance Co., McDonald-Douglas Aircraft, Uniroyal, Western Electric, Bethlehem Steel, Colgate-Palmolive, Woolworth Co., Cummins Engine Company, and Lord and Taylor. Also a trustee of Princeton University; a director of National Industrial Conference Board and Woodrow Wilson Foundation.

Amory Houghton. Chairman of the board of First National Bank of New York City (First National City Corporation); a director of Metropolitan Life Insurance Co., Dow Corning Corporation, Pittsburgh Corning Corporation, Boy Scouts of America, Eisenhower College. He is a former ambassador to France, and a trustee of the International Chamber of Commerce. He is a centimillionaire.

Arthur A. Houghton. President and chairman of the board of directors of Corning Glass Works; a director of Steuben Glass Company, Erie-Lackawanna Railroad Company, New York Life Insurance Company, and the United States Steel Corporation; a trustee of the Corning Museum of Glass, J. Pierpont Morgan Library, Philharmonic Symphony Society of New York, Fund for the Advancement of Education, Lincoln Center of Performing Arts, Cooper Union, Metropolitan Museum of Art, New York Public Library, Rockefeller Foundation, and Institute for Contemporary Art of Boston. He is a centimillionaire.

William McChesney Martin, Jr. Chairman of the Federal Reserve Board. He is a former chairman of the Export-Import Bank, governor of the New York Stock Exchange, and partner of A. G. Edwards & Sons. He is presently a director of IBM, Caterpillar Tractor, and General Foods. He is also a trustee of the American Red Cross, Johns Hopkins, and Yale University.

John Anton Mayer. Member of the board of Mellon National Bank and Trust Co. Also a director of Aluminum Co. of America, Bank of London, General Motors, Armco Steel, Monsanto, and is a trustee of the University of Pennsylvania and Carnegie Institute.

Richard King Mellon. Chairman of the board of Mellon National Bank and Trust Company; president, Mellon and Sons, director of the Aluminum Company of America, General Motors Corporation, Gulf Oil Corporation, Koppers Company, Pennsylvania Company, and the Pennsylvania Railroad. He is a centimillionaire. He is a lieutenant general in the Reserves, a trustee of the Carnegie Institute of Technology, the Mellon Institute, and the University of Pittsburgh.

Ellmore C. Patterson. President, J. P. Morgan & Co. He is a director of Atlantic Richfield Co., Canadian Life Assurance Co., International Nickel, Atcheson, Topeka and Santa Fe Railroad, Warner Patterson Co. He is a trustee of the Alfred P. Sloan Foundation, the Carnegie Endowment for International Peace, and the University of Chicago.

Richard S. Perkins. President and chairman of the board of Perkins-Elmer Corp. A director of Ford Motor Co., IT&T, New York Life Insurance Co., Consolidated Edison, Southern Pacific Railroad, Aetna Life Insurance Co., New England Telephone Co., U.S. Trust Co. of New York. A trustee of Metropolitan Museum of Art, American Museum of Natural History, and Pratt Institute.

David Rockefeller. Chairman and chief executive officer, Chase Manhattan Bank. He is a director or trustee of the Rockefeller Foundation, Museum of Modern Art, Harvard University, University of Chicago, Council on Foreign Relations. He is also a director of Chase International Investment Corporation, Morningside Heights, Inc., Rockefeller Center, Inc., Downtown Lower Manhattan Association. He is a centimillionaire and a heavy political contributor.

James Stillman Rockefeller. Former chairman and current director of First National City Bank of New York. A director of the International Banking Corp., National City Foundation, First New York Corp., First National City Trust Co., Mercantile Bank of Canada, National City Realty Corp., Kimberly-Clark Corp., Northern Pacific Railway Co., National Cash Register Co., Pan-American World Airways, and Monsanto Co.

Haakon Ingolf Romnes. Chairman and chief executive officer of American Telephone and Telegraph. He is a director of United Steel, Chemical Bank of New York, Colgate-Palmolive Co., Cities Service Oil Co., and Mutual Life Insurance Co. He is a trustee of M.I.T., the National Safety Council, and the Committee for Economic Development; he is also active in the United Negro College Fund, the Urban League, and the Salvation Army.

Robert V. Roosa. Partner, Brown Brothers, Harriman & Co. (investments). Is a director of American Express Co., Anaconda Copper Co., and Texaco. He is a trustee of the Rockefeller Foundation, The Rye County Day School, Council on Foreign Relations, and the National Bureau of Economic Research. He was formerly under-secretary of the treasury. He holds an earned Ph.D. from the University of Michigan.

Robert Baylor Semple. President of Wyandotte Chemical Corp. He is a director of Michigan Consolidated Gas Co., American Natural Gas Co., National Bank of Detroit, Atlantic Mutual Insurance Co., Centennial Insurance Co., and the Chrysler Corp. He is also on the board of the Committee on Economic Development, the National Industrial Conference Board, M.I.T., Harper Hospital, and is the president of the Detroit Symphony Orchestra.

Cyrus R. Vance. Senior partner of Simpson, Thacher & Bartlett. He is a director of Pan-American World Airways, Aetna Life Insurance Co., IBM, Council on Foreign Relations, the American Red Cross, the Rockefeller Foundation; and he is a trustee of the University of Chicago. He was the chief U.S. negotiator at the Paris Peace Talks on Vietnam under President Lyndon Johnson.

John Harris Ward. Chairman of the board and chief executive officer of Commonwealth Edison Co. Director of Nortrust Co., International Harvester, Union Carbide, New York Life Insurance Co., and the Urban League. Also a trustee of the University of Chicago and the Museum of Science and Industry.

Albert L. Williams. Chairman of the board of directors of the International Business Machines Corp. (IBM). He is a director of General Motors Corporation, Mobil Oil Corp., First National City Bank of New York, General Foods Corp. He is a trustee of the Alfred P. Sloan Foundation.

Leslie B. Worthington. Former president, United States Steel Corporation, and a current director. Also a director of Mellon National Bank and Trust Co., TRW, Inc., American Standard, Greyhound Corp., Westinghouse Air Brake Co., and the Pittsburgh Pirates. A trustee of the University of Illinois and the University of Pittsburgh.

---

governmental position-holders are "specialists"–individuals who occupy only one top position at a given time (see Table 6-3). Moreover, an examination of the pattern of interlocking reveals that governmental leadership is *not* interlocked with the corporate world. To the extent that governmental leadership is interlocked at all, it is interlocked with the public interest sector. High government officials and military officers do not hold top positions in anything other than civic and cultural and educational institutions. (The exception to this generalization in 1970 was William McChesney Martin, who served as chairman of the Federal Reserve Board at the same time that he was listed as a director of IBM, Caterpillar Tractor, and General Foods; Senator Richard B. Russell was counted as interlocked *within* government because he served as both president pro tem of the Senate and chairman of the Appropriations Committee.) If there is convergence between the corporate and governmental sectors of society, then, it is not by means of "interlocking directorates." Of course, convergence may result from patterns of *interaction* among specialized governmental and corporate elites, but the notion of formal interlocking directorates can be put to rest.

Interlocking *within* the *corporate* sector is widespread. Approximately 44 percent of all top corporate positions were interlocked with other top positions, most of which were in the corporate sphere. Yet a majority of top corporate elites were "specialists." The notion of interlocking directorates has widespread currency in the power elite literature. But our figures confirm those of the Temporary National Economic Committee, which reported in 1939 that within the top 200 corporations there were 3,511 directorships held by 2,500 persons, an overlap of less than one-third of all positions.[7] Of course, it must be noted that we are examining overlap among the *top* positions in all sectors of society. It is, after all, more likely that individuals with top positions in the lead-

[7] Temporary National Economic Committee, U.S. Senate, 76th Congress, *Investigation of Concentration of Economic Power* (Washington, D.C.: Government Printing Office, 1941).

Table 6-3. Specialization and Interlocking among Corporate, Governmental, and Public Interest Elites

	Corporate	Public Interest					Governmental	
	All	*Law*	*Found.*	*Educ.*	*Civic*	*Media*	*Domestic*	*Military*
Number of Positions	3,562	176	121	656	392	213	227	59
Positions "Interlocked"								
Number	1,560	26	64	216	168		44	0
Percent	43.8	14.8	52.9	32.9	42.9		80.6	0
Positions "Specialized"								
Number	2,002	150	57	440	224		183	59
Percent	56.2	84.2	47.1	67.1	57.1		19.4	100.0
Pattern of Interlocking:								
Percent of Interlocking with								
Corporate Positions	72.7			58.8			6.6	
Public Interest Positions	25.9			60.4			91.2	
Governmental Positions	0.2			4.7			2.2	
	100.0			100.0			100.0	

ing institutions would also hold positions in smaller, les organizations. But the figures shown in Table 6-3 deal or concurrent occupancy of multiple positions in top-ranked

Leadership in the *public interest* sector is only moderately interlocked. Nearly two-thirds of top elites in law, education, the foundations, the mass media, and civic and cultural affairs were "specialists." (These "specialists" may hold other positions in the corporate or governmental sectors, but not *top* positions, according to the definition set forth earlier.) Interlocking in the public interest sector was more common in the foundations, education, and civic and cultural associations, than in law. Interlocking in this sector was primarily with the corporate sector; few top public interest positions are interlocked with governmental positions.

Previous Institutional Experience of Men at the Top

Let us pursue the notion of "vertical" overlap a bit further. How many positions of authority in all types of institutions have top leaders *ever held* in a lifetime? We carefully reviewed the biographies of our top position-holders to see how many authoritative positions—president, director, trustee, etc.—were *ever held* by these men. The record of leadership of an average top official turned out to be truly impressive. The average corporate elite held 11.1 authoritative positions in his lifetime; the average public interest elite, 10.7; and the average governmental elite, 7.0 (see Table 6-4).

These are not merely previous posts, offices, or occupations, but top positions as presidents or directors of corporations, banks, or insurance companies; trustees or directors of colleges, universities, foundations, museums, civic and cultural organizations; partnerships in law firms or investment firms; and so forth. Of course, these positions are not all in *top-ranked* institutions. But it is clear that top leaders occupy a number of authoritative positions in their lifetime.

This impressive record of position-holding is found among leaders in all sectors of society. Table 6-4 shows the average number of authoritative positions ever held by top leaders in each sector of society. Leaders in government have held somewhat fewer top positions in their lifetime than leaders in the corporate world, but nonetheless their record of leadership experience is impressive. However, governmental leaders tended to gain their experience in *governmental* positions or *public interest* positions: over 80 percent of governmental leaders had held previous governmental posts and over half had held posts in the public interest sector. Only one-quarter of top governmental elites had previously held any top positions in the corporate world.

Table 6-4. Previous Experience of Corporate, Governmental, and Public Interest Elites

	Corporate	Public Interest					Governmental	
	All	*Law*	*Found.*	*Educ.*	*Civic*	*Media*	*Domestic*	*Military*
Average Number of Authoritative Positions Ever Held by Elites:								
Total	11.1	9.0	11.1	10.9	11.7	9.1	7.0	0.9
Corporate	6.2	2.4	5.2	3.6	4.4	2.0	1.0	0.3
Public Interest	3.9	5.3	4.2	5.6	4.7	5.1	2.9	0.4
Governmental	1.0	1.3	1.7	1.7	2.6	2.0	3.1	0.2
Percent of Elites Having Held Authoritative Positions in:								
Corporate	99.9			87.5			26.7	
Public Interest	82.5			92.0			62.0	
Governmental	39.6			48.5			83.5	

The tradition of public service is very much alive
institutional leaders in every sector. Both corporate and g
elites reported one or more public appointments during th
Nearly 40 percent of corporate elites held at least one government post at some time during their careers.

As we might expect, corporate directorships are common among top leaders in industry, communications, utilities, and banking. It is common for these individuals to have held four or more directorships in a lifetime. In contrast, top government officials have *not* held many corporate directorships. Their experience in authoritative positions is derived mainly from public service, and to a lesser extent from education, law, and civic organizations.

The Rockefeller Empire: Convergence at the Top

Our aggregate data indicates that a majority of the people at the top are specialists, that corporate and governmental elites are not interlocked, and that there appear to be multiple, differentiated structures of power in America. And earlier we suggested that most corporate, governmental, and public interest leaders were "up the organization" managerial elites, rather than "inheritors" who started at the top. All of these findings tend to undermine confidence in the hierarchical model, at least as it is represented in the traditional power elite literature.

Nonetheless, there are important concentrations of combined corporate, governmental, and social power in America. And these concentrations center about great, wealthy, entrepreneurial families—the Rockefellers, Mellons, duPonts, Fords, and the J. P. Morgan group. Doubtlessly the most important of these concentrations is the "Rockefeller Empire." Certainly no better illustration of convergence of power can be found than the Rockefeller network of industrial, financial, political, civic, and cultural institutions, headed by David Rockefeller of the Chase Manhattan Bank.

The Rockefeller family fortune was founded by John D. Rockefeller, originator of the Standard Oil Company. With his partners, H. M. Flagler and S. V. Harkness, Rockefeller created the company that controlled 90 percent of the nation's oil production by the 1880s. A series of anti-trust cases, culminating in the Supreme Court in *U.S. v. Standard Oil* (1911), resulted in the forced dissolution of the company into several separate corporations: Exxon, formerly Standard Oil of New Jersey (the nation's number-one-ranked industrial corporation in 1970), Standard Oil of California (ranked number 10), Standard Oil of Indiana (ranked number 13), Standard Oil of Ohio (ranked number 56), Atlantic Richfield (ranked number 16), Mobil Oil (ranked number 7), and the Marathon Oil Company (ranked number 79).[8] The best available evidence suggests that the Rockefeller family continues to hold large blocks of stock in each of these companies.[9] But the key to Rockefeller power today is no longer the oil industry, however impressive the holdings in this industry may be. The center of Rockefeller power is banking and finance.

The core financial institutions of the Rockefeller Empire consist of four large banks and three insurance companies. Three of the four banks are in New York—First National City Bank (the nation's number-two-ranked bank in 1970), Chase Manhattan (number three), and the Chemical Bank of New York (number seven); the out-of-town bank is the First National Bank of Chicago (number eleven). The three insurance companies are Metropolitan (the nation's number-two-ranked insurance company in 1970), Equitable (ranked number three), and New York Life (number four). These institutions *alone* control 12 percent of all banking assets in the nation, and 26 percent of all insurance assets. These Rockefeller financial institutions are tied together in a close pattern of interlocking directorates. This pattern is shown in Table 6-5, where each solid line represents multiple position-holding by family members.

The Rockefeller banks influence corporate decision-making in several ways—by giving or withholding loans to corporations, by placing representatives on corporate boards of directors, and by owning or controlling blocks of common stock of corporations. The Federal Reserve Board estimates that 90 percent of the lending of large banks is made to large corporations. These corporations are dependent upon bank loans for capital expansion. Often the banks dictate specific aspects of corporate policy as a condition of granting a loan (in the same fashion that federal agencies often dictate policies of state and local governments as a condition of receiving federal grants-in-aid). Frequently, banks will also require that corporations that borrow money must appoint bank officers or directors to the boards of the corporation. This gives the bank continuous oversight of the activities of the debtor corporation. Finally, the trust departments of major banks hold large blocks of common stock of industrial corporations on behalf of individuals, pension funds, and investment companies. Generally the banks vote the shares held in trust in corporate elections. The rules of the Securities

[8] See Table 2–1 for rankings.

[9] House of Representatives, Banking and Currency Committee, *Tax-Exempt Foundations* (Washington, DC.: Government Printing Office, 1968).

Table 6-5. Interlocking Directorates Among the Core Financial Institutions in the Rockefeller Group. (Numbers in parentheses link each director interlock to a particular individual listed below.)

A. Individual Interlocks*

1. Black, Eugene (CM) (E)
2. Eaton, Frederick (FNCB) (NYL)
3. Fitzhugh, Gilbert (CM) (M)
4. Funston, G. Keith (CB) (M)
5. Heineman, Ben (FNBC) (M)
6. Helm, Harold (CB) (E)
7. Houghton, Amory (FNCB) (M)
8. Jenkins, George P. (FNCB) (M)
9. Kappel, Frederick (CB) (M)
10. Keehn, Grant (CB) (E)
11. Long, Augustus (CB) (E)
12. Metcalf, Gordon (FNCB) (FNBC)
13. Miller, J. Irwin (CB) (E)
14. Oates, James (E) (FNBC)
15. Oates, James (E) (CM)
16. Oates, James (CM) (FNBC)
17. Paynter, Richard K. (CB) (NYL)
18. Perkins, Richard S. (FNCB) (NYL)
19. Renchard, William (CB) (NYL)
20. Saunders, Stuart (CM) (E)
21. Seiler, Lewis (CB) (E)
22. Sivage, Gerald (FNBC) (M)
23. Swearingen, John (CM) (FNBC)

B. Family Interlocks*

24. David Rockefeller (CM) – James Stillman Rockefeller (FNCB)
25. Hulbert S. Aldrich (CB) – Malcolm Aldrich (E)
26. Amory Houghton (FNCB) – Arthur K. Houghton, Jr. (NYL)
27. Amory Houghton, Jr. (FNCB) – Arthur K. Houghton, Jr. (NYL)
28. Amory Houghton (M) – Arthur K. Houghton, Jr. (NYL)

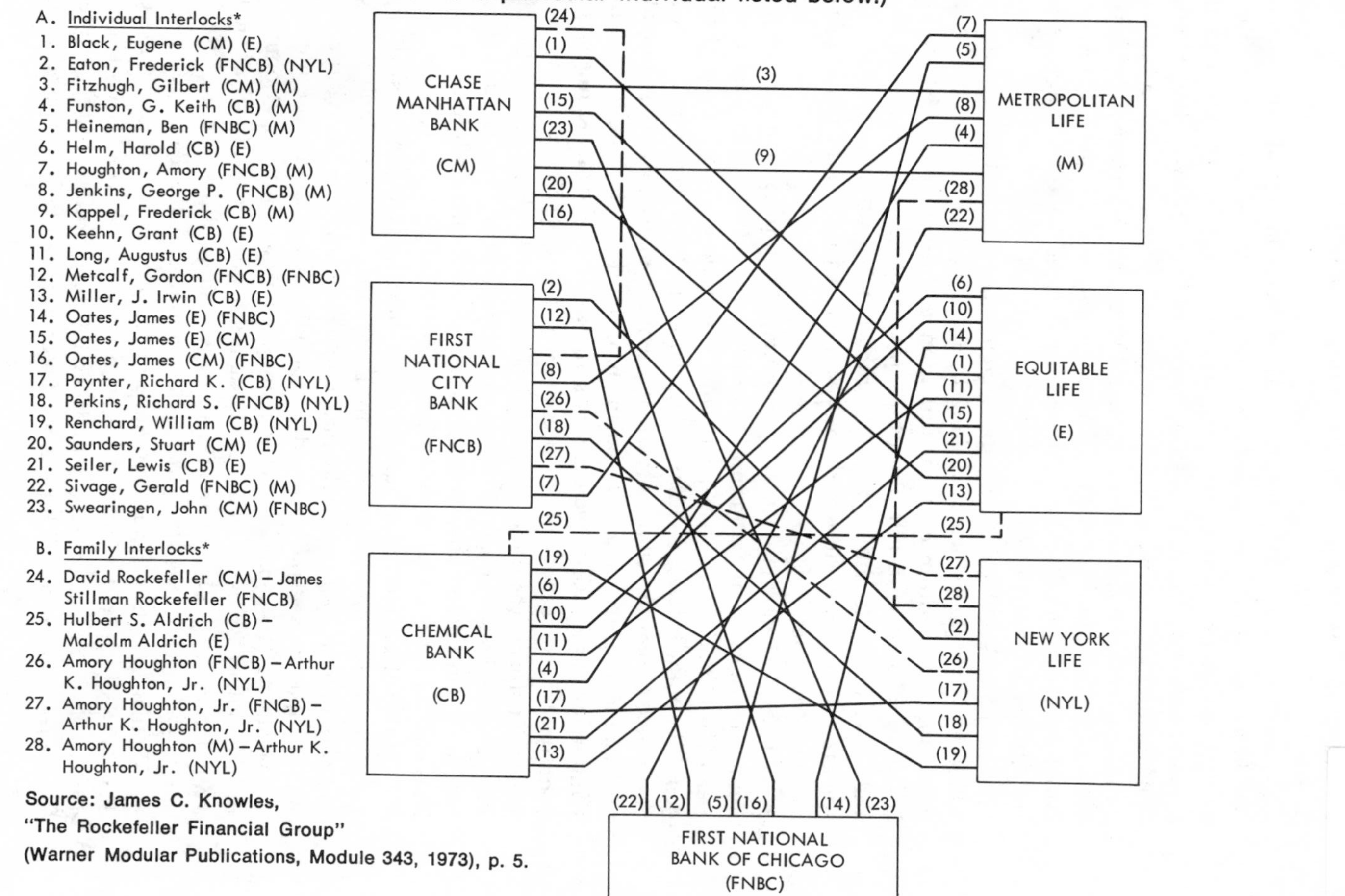

Source: James C. Knowles, "The Rockefeller Financial Group" (Warner Modular Publications, Module 343, 1973), p. 5.

and Exchange Commission presume that the ownership of 5 percent of a corporation's stock can give the holder a position of influence over its affairs.

Interlocking among the five core Rockefeller group institutions and large industrial corporations is extensive. Table 6-6 reveals interlocking of Chase Manhattan directors only; the list of interlocking corporations for all five institutions would have over 150 names. Consolidated Edison and Anaconda are generally regarded as Rockefeller-influenced, as well as Eastern Airlines, TWA, Pan American World Airlines, and Boeing. (The airlines, including Howard Hughes' TWA, fell into Rockefeller hands when they required large loans to purchase jet aircraft in the late 1950s.)

The Rockefeller interest in foreign affairs is particularly strong. The oil companies, which have long been the industrial core of Rockefeller holdings, require constant attention to foreign sources of supply. In addition, Rockefeller banks are deeply involved in overseas banking and investment activities. Chase Manhattan has over forty branches scattered throughout the world, and National City Bank boasts of offices in sixty countries.

The Rockefeller group has supplied the top foreign affairs personnel for the nation, including Secretaries of State John Foster Dulles, Dean Rusk, and Henry Kissinger. Dulles, secretary of state under President Eisenhower, was a senior partner in the Wall Street law firm of Sullivan & Cromwell, whose principal client for many years was Standard Oil Company. Dulles was also chairman of the trustees of the Rockefeller Foundation. Dean Rusk, secretary of state under Presidents Kennedy and Johnson, served seven years as president of the Rockefeller Foundation. Henry Kissinger was director of the Rockefeller Brothers Special Studies Project and personal adviser on foreign policy to Nelson Rockefeller before becoming special assistant for national security affairs and later secretary of state under President Richard Nixon.

Other Rockefeller group associates have played key roles in the nation's foreign involvements. John J. McCloy, a Chase Manhattan director, served as U.S. High Commissioner for Germany during the postwar occupation and later served as special adviser to the president on disarmament (1961–63) and chairman of the Coordinating Committee on the Cuban Crisis in 1962. Cyrus Vance, a director of the Rockefeller Foundation, as well as Pan American World Airlines, Aetna Life Insurance, and IBM, was the chief U.S. negotiator at the Paris peace talks on Vietnam. Arthur Dean, another senior partner in the Standard Oil firm of Sullivan & Cromwell, was chairman of the U.S. delegation on the Nuclear Test Ban Treaty and chief U.S. negotiator of the Korean Armistice Agreement. Thus, Rockefeller representatives played a key

Table 6-6. Chase Manhattan Influence in Industrial Corporations

Interlocking Directors with Chase Manhattan	Common Stock Ownership of over 5%[a]
Allegheny Ludlum Steel	Eastern Airlines
Youngstown Sheet & Tube	Pan American World Airlines
United States Steel	Western Airlines
Metropolitan Life	Safeway Stores
Equitable Life	Reynolds Metal
Travelers Insurance	J. C. Penney
American Machine	Northwest Airlines
Bucyrus-Erie	TWA
Otis Elevator	Ryder System
General Foods	Universal Oil
Chrysler Corporation	North Carolina Natural Gas
Standard Oil of Indiana	Armstrong Rubber
Standard Oil of New Jersey	Texas Instruments
New York Tire Co.	Beckman Instruments
Cummins Engine	Sperry Rand
Burlington Industries	Boeing
American Broadcasting Co.	Columbia Broadcasting System
R. J. Reynolds Tobacco	American Broadcasting System
Scott Paper	Aetna Life
International Paper	National Steel
United Aircraft	Addressograph
Singer Co.	Mobil Oil
ITT	
Goodyear Tire & Rubber	
Great Southwest Corp.	
Anaconda Copper	
American Smelting & Refining	
F. W. Woolworth	
Allied Stores	
Federated Department Stores	
R. H. Macy	
Penn Central	
Piedmont Aviation	
Wabash Railroad	
Celanese Corp.	
Colgate-Palmolive	
General Aniline & Film	
Consolidated Edison	
AT&T	

[a]Data on stock ownership from Report of House Banking Committee, Chairman Representative Wright Patman, reported in *New York Times,* August 9, 1968.

. major national and world events as the Vietnam and Korean ˏ agreements and the Cuban situation. It was David Rockefeller nimself who provided the major stimulus to the re-opening of U.S. relations with Communist China and the spectacular Nixon visit to China in 1972. Shortly after the president's visit, Chase Manhattan announced the opening of its own offices in Peking.

David Rockefeller: The View from Chase Manhattan

The single most powerful private citizen in America today is David Rockefeller, chairman of the board of Chase Manhattan Bank and director of the vast Rockefeller empire. The extent of that empire—from banking and insurance to oil, airlines, computers, steel, machinery, and utilities—and the extension of Rockefeller influence in government, international relations, education, law, foundations, and civic, cultural, and charitable affairs has already been described. Our interest for the moment is in the man who stands at the apex of financial and political power in America—"the only man for whom the presidency of the United States would be a step down."

David Rockefeller is the youngest of five sons of John D. Rockefeller, Jr., who was the only son of the founder of the Rockefeller empire, John D. Rockefeller. Despite the seniority of his brothers,[10] it was recognized that David was the serious and scholarly one. And it was to David that the family wisely entrusted most of its wealth; this is the really convincing evidence of his recognized leadership.

David was raised with his brothers at the Rockefeller's Pocantico Hills 3500-acre estate, east of Tarrytown, New York. He attended nearby Lincoln School. His early interest in art continues today. As a child, he traveled about to Rockefeller holdings—the Seal Harbor, Maine retreat, the Virgin Islands estate, the Venezuela ranch, the Grand Teton Mountains ranch—and collected beetles as a hobby. It soon became clear to David's father and grandfather that Nelson, Lawrence, and Winthrop were more interested in politics and pleasure than hard work, and that John D. III was content to pursue cultural interests. The elder Rockefellers wanted a businessman to care for the family fortune, and they were successful in motivating David in this direction.

[10] John D. III, chairman of the Rockefeller Foundation and the Lincoln Center for the Performing Arts; Nelson A., vice-president of the United States and four-term governor of New York; Lawrence, family dilettante in "venture capitalism"; and Winthrop, governor of Arkansas and cattle rancher.

David's undergraduate career at Harvard was undistinguished. But later he spent a year at the Harvard Graduate School of Business, and a year at the London School of Economics. He married Margaret "Peggy" McGrath, whose father was a senior partner in the esteemed Wall Street law firm of Cadwalader, Wickersham & Taft. He enrolled at the Rockefeller-funded University of Chicago and *earned* a Ph.D. in economics in 1940. He returned to New York for a short stint in public service as an unpaid assistant to Mayor Fiorello La Guardia. In 1942 he enlisted in the Army as a private, went through Officers Training School, and served in North Africa and Europe as an intelligence officer. He speaks French, Spanish, and German.

After the war he began his banking career in his uncle Winthrop W. Aldrich's bank, the Chase Manhattan. His first post was assistant manager of the foreign department; three years later he became vice-president and director of the bank's business in Latin America. When his uncle became ambassador to England in 1952, David became successively executive vice-president, vice-chairman of the board, and finally, president and chairman of the board.

Of course, David Rockefeller is active in civic and cultural affairs. He is, or has been, chairman of the Museum of Modern Art, president of the Board of Overseas Study of Harvard University, a director of the Council on Foreign Relations, a trustee of the Carnegie Endowment for International Peace, a trustee of the University of Chicago, a trustee of the John F. Kennedy Library, and so forth.

Above all, Rockefeller is an internationalist. His active intervention in American foreign policy has produced remarkable results. As has been mentioned, he was personally involved in Nixon's arrangement of détente with the USSR, the Strategic Arms Limitations Talks (SALT), and Nixon's spectacular trip to China. He is the key sponsor of the Council on Foreign Relations.

Under David Rockefeller's direction, Chase Manhattan has developed a reputation in the business world for "social responsibility"—which included the active recruitment and promotion of blacks, women, and other minorities; granting a large number of loans to minority-owned business enterprises; and active involvement in a variety of social projects. Indeed, this may be one reason that Chase Manhattan has fallen behind First National City Bank as the leading banking institution in New York. (Not only does First City Bank lead in assets but also in return on investment: in recent years Chase has shown 12.5 percent profit, compared to 15.1 percent for First City Bank.) Another reason for Chase's performance may be that David Rockefeller is so deeply involved in national and international affairs that he cannot devote full attention to banking matters.

Rockefeller himself believes that his own power, and the power of business and financial institutions is limited by public opinion.

> I don't believe a bank such as ours, for example, could long fly in the face of welfare consideration—welfare in the broader sense—without having major problems with Congress and with all kinds of groups in our society who would resent us and would do their best to take steps to force us to act differently.[11]

But Rockefeller's liberal concern for "doing good" is constrained by his institutional responsibilities in a capitalist system, and he recognizes this fact:

> I don't think one has to go to extremes. We don't feel that we can do everything for the community that we'd like to, nor do we feel it's wise to go all out 100 percent for the highest profits disregarding the best interests of the community. We have to find some kind of middle ground. We're very much bottom-line conscience,* but we also feel we have responsibilities to the community.[12]

David Rockefeller exercises great power, with *modesty,* of course, as one would expect of a man who has no reason to try to impress anyone. Indeed, he consistently understates his own power:

> I feel uncomfortable when you ask how I exert power. We accomplish things through cooperative action, which is quite different than exerting power in some mysterious and presumably evil way. I have no power in the sense that I can call anybody in the government and tell them what to do. Because of my position, I'm more apt to get through on the telephone than somebody else, but what happens to what I suggest depends on whether they feel this makes sense in terms of what they are already doing.[13]

David Rockefeller's own views on power tend to reinforce the importance of achieving consensus among separate groups of leaders. In commenting on the redevelopment of downtown New York City—Rockefeller Plaza and the World Trade Center—Rockefeller characteristically sees himself as a *catalyst* rather than as a *chieftain:*

> If you are interested in the analysis of power [says Rockefeller], I would think this is somewhat relevant: I'm not sure it is the power of an indi-

[11] "The Dilemma of Corporate Responsibility and Maximum Profits: An Interview with David Rockefeller," *Business and Society Review* (Spring 1974), p. 10.

* A businessman's phrase meaning concern with whether the last line on a quarterly or annual financial account shows a profit or loss.

[12] Ibid., p. 11.

[13] "Beyond Wealth, What?" *Forbes* (May 15, 1972), pp. 250–52.

vidual or even an institution, but more the power of cooperatio ideas. . . .

. . . We got the community and government working together i development of a plan that was of common interest to all parties involved. This isn't so much power; it is organization, coordination, cooperation. The reason we could do this is this group exists. The city couldn't have pulled this thing off by itself. Certainly neither could we. But working together, we could.

I didn't do this thing myself; this is a joint undertaking where I have been to some extent the catalyst in the sense of bringing others together, and I certainly served as chairman of the committee, but the strength of it is the unity and sense of cooperation.[14]

Of course, what Rockefeller is really saying is that when David Rockefeller is calling, people answer their phone; when he asks them to serve on a committee, they are flattered to be asked; when he suggests that they do something, they do it.

Summary

The question of hierarchy versus polyarchy in the elite structure is a familiar one in the literature on power in America. The "elitist" literature describes a convergence of power at the top, with a single group of leaders, recruited primarily from industry and finance, exercising power in many different sectors of society. The "pluralist" literature describes many separate structures of power in different sectors of society with little or no overlap in authority and many separate channels of recruitment.

Our findings do not all fit neatly into either the elitist or pluralist leadership models. The fact that roughly 4000 persons in 5000 positions exercise formal authority over institutions that control roughly half of the nation's resources is itself an indication of a great concentration of power. But despite institutional concentration of authority, there is considerable specialization among these 4000 leaders. Eighty percent of them have held only one "top" position. Only 20 percent were "interlockers"—holders of two or more top positions. However, because of "multiple interlockers," about 40 percent of all top positions were interlocked with another top position. Moreover, the top multiple interlockers (those people with seven or more top positions) turned out to be impressive figures in America, lending some support to the notion that interlocking itself is a source of power in society.

There is very little overlap among people at the top of the cor-

[14] Ibid., pp. 251–52.

porate, governmental, and military sectors of society. To the extent that high government officials are interlocked at all, it is with civic and cultural and educational institutions. It is *within* the corporate sector that interlocking is most prevalent. If there is a "coming together" of corporate, governmental, and military elites as C. Wright Mills contends, it does not appear to be by means of interlocking directorates.

The notion of hierarchy is strengthened, however, if we examine the record of leadership experience of top institutional elites *over a lifetime*. Most top leaders have held more than one top position in their career. However, governmental leaders tended to gain their leadership experience in governmental positions or in the law; only one-quarter of top governmental leaders have ever held high positions in the corporate world.

These aggregate figures suggest specialization rather than convergence at the top of the nation's institutional structure. However, we agree that there are special cases of concentrated corporate, governmental, and social power. These concentrations center about the great entrepreneurial families—Rockefellers, Mellons, duPonts, Fords. We believe the most important concentration of power in America today centers in the Rockefeller family group.

Seven

ELITE RECRUITMENT: GETTING TO THE TOP

A Ruling Class or an Open Leadership System?

Are there opportunities to rise to the top of the institutional structure of America for individuals from all classes, races, religions, and ethnic groups, through multiple career paths in different sectors of society? Or are opportunities for entry into top circles limited to white, Anglo-Saxon Protestant, upper- and upper-middle-class individuals whose careers are based primarily in industry and finance?

Social scientists have studied data on the social backgrounds of corporate and governmental leaders for many years. But there is still disagreement on the interpretation of the data. A "ruling class" school of thought stresses the fact that elites in America are drawn disproportionately from among wealthy, educated, "well-employed," socially prominent, "WASP" groups in society. These "ruling class" social scientists are impressed with the fact that leadership in industry, finance, government, education, the law, the mass media, and other institutional sectors are recruited primarily from society's upper social classes. Many of them have been educated at a few esteemed private prep schools and attended the "Ivy League" colleges and universities. They have joined the same private clubs, and their families have intermarried. Moreover, a disproportionate share of the top leadership in all sectors of society have made their career marks in industry and finance. "Ruling class" social scientists infer that these similarities contribute to cohesion and consensus among the institutional leaders in America.

In contrast, "pluralists" describe an open leadership system that enables a significant number of individuals from the middle and lower classes to rise to the top. High social background, or wealth, or WASP-ishness *itself* does not provide access to top leadership positions. Instead, top institutional posts go to individuals who possess outstanding skills of leadership, information, and knowledge, and the ability to communicate and organize. Admittedly, opportunities to acquire such qualities for top leadership are unequally distributed among classes. But lower-class origin, the "pluralists" believe, is not an insurmountable barrier to high position.

Classical elitist writers such as Mosca, acknowledge that some "circulation of elites" is essential for the stability of a political system. The availability of their opportunities to rise to the top siphons off potentially revolutionary leadership from lower classes; the elite system is strengthened when talented and ambitious individuals enter top positions. The fact that only a minority of top leaders are drawn from lower classes is not really important. It is the availability of *some* opportunity that encourages talented people to believe they can rise to the top and strengthens support for the system throughout all social classes.

Pluralist defenders of the American leadership system also argue that social background, educational experience, and social group membership are poor predictions of decision-making behavior. Individuals who are members of the social elite often differ over policy questions. These differences can be attributed to a variety of factors that are more influential than social background—for example, the nature of the top position occupied; the individual's perception of his own role; the institutional constraints placed upon him; systems of public accountability; interest-group pressures; public opinion; and so forth. Thus, pluralists argue that the class homogeneity among top leaders that is reported in many social background studies is meaningless, since the class background–decision-making behavior linkage is weak.

In contrast, the evidence of social-class influence on behavior is truly impressive. Social scientists have shown that social background affects whether or not you shoplift [1] or use LSD.[2] It has an important influence

[1] George Won and George Yamamoto, "Social Structure and Deviant Behavior: A Study of Shoplifting," *Sociology and Social Research*, 53, No. 1 (1968), 44–55.

[2] Reginald G. Smart and Dianne Fejer, "Illicit LSD Users: Their Social Backgrounds, Drug Use and Psychopathology," *Journal of Health and Social Behavior*, 10, No. 4 (1969), 297–308.

on whom you date and marry,[3] how happy your marriage is likely to be,[4] how you vote,[5] how many children you have[6] and how you go about raising them.[7] It largely determines your values,[8] how happy you are,[9] and how long you're likely to live.[10] It can even influence how large you think the circumference of a quarter is![11] In our opinion, it would be most unlikely that social-class membership could affect all these varied attitudes and behaviors and *not* affect decision-making behavior.

The recruitment of some non-upper-class individuals to elite positions may be essential to society, because these individuals bring new and different perspectives to societal problems. Sociologist Suzanne Keller speaks of "two irreconcilable tendencies in social life—the need for order and the need for change."

> If the social leadership becomes so conservative as to be immune to new ideas and social developments, the pressure for unfulfilled needs mounts until that leadership declines, resigns, or is violently displaced. If it is so receptive to the new as to neglect established traditions, social continuity is endangered.[12]

Thus, we would expect to find some recruitment of non-upper-class individuals to elite positions even in a very hierarchical society. The ques-

[3] A. B. Hollingshead, *Elmtown's Youth: The Impact of Social Classes on Adolescents* (New York: John Wiley & Sons, Inc., 1949).

[4] William J. Goode, "Marital Satisfaction and Instability: A Cross-Cultural Class Analysis of Divorce Rates," *International Social Science Journal,* 14, No. 3 (1962), 507–26.

[5] P. F. Lazarsfeld, B. Berelson, and H. Caudit, *The People's Choice* (New York: Columbia University Press, 1948). Also G. J. Selznick and Stephen Steinberg, "Social Class, Ideology, and Voting Preferences: An Analysis of the 1964 Presidential Election," in *Structural Social Inequality: A Reader In Comparative Social Stratification,* Celia S. Heller, ed. (New York: Macmillan, 1969).

[6] Dennis H. Wrong, "Trends in Class Fertility in Western Nations," *The Canadian Journal of Economics and Political Science,* 24, No. 2 (May 1958), 216–29.

[7] R. R. Sears, E. MacCoby, and H. Levin, *Patterns of Child Rearing* (New York: Harper and Row, 1957).

[8] Herbert H. Hyman, "The Value Systems of Different Classes: A Social Psychological Contribution to the Analysis of Stratification," in *Readings on Social Stratification,* Melvin M. Tumin, ed. (Englewood Cliffs, N.J.: Prentice-Hall, Inc., 1970), pp. 186–203.

[9] Alex Inkeles, "Class and Happiness," in Tumin, *Readings on Social Stratification,* pp. 180–86.

[10] I. M. Moriyama and L. Guralnick, "Occupational and Social Class Differences in Mortality," in Tumin, *Readings on Social Stratification,* pp. 170–78.

[11] J. S. Bruner and L. Postman, "Symbolic Value as an Organizing Factor in Perception," *Journal of Social Psychology,* 27 (1948), 203–8.

[12] Suzanne Keller, *Beyond the Ruling Class: Strategic Elites in Modern Society* (New York: Random House, 1968), p. 172.

tion remains *how much* opportunity exists in America for middle- and lower-class individuals to climb to the top.

Getting Ahead in the System

The American ideal is not a classless society, but rather a society in which individuals are free to get ahead on the basis of merit, talent, hard work, and good luck. Upward mobility is valued very highly in American culture. The nation is portrayed in its own literature as a "land of opportunity" where individuals can better themselves if they work at it.

And, indeed, there is a great deal of upward social mobility in America. Research on social mobility reveals that every major occupational category contains a majority of individuals whose fathers followed other occupations. The results of a typical study of social mobility are shown in Table 7-1. These figures suggest that very few sons have occupations with the same prestige as their fathers. Table 7-1 shows that

Table 7-1. Social Mobility: Occupational Mobility of Sons in Relation to Fathers by Educational Level

	Upward	Stable	Downward
Total	54%	11%	35%
College	69	17	14
High School	49	6	45
Some High School	52	12	36
Grade School	48	11	41

Source: Derived from Chicago Labor Mobility Sample figures reported by Otis Dudley Duncan and Robert W. Hodge, "Education and Occupational Mobility," *American Journal of Sociology,* 79 (May 1963), 629-44.

54 percent of sons have jobs with higher prestige than their fathers, while only 35 percent have jobs with lower prestige. There is more upward mobility than downward mobility in the American system. This circumstance is generally attributed to the nation's economic growth over generations—this growth is what permits upward mobility for successive generations of Americans.

Does this evidence of general social mobility tell us much about opportunities for getting to the *top*? Not really. There are several important reservations concerning this generally rosy picture of opportunity and mobility in America.

Most social mobility occurs within a very narrow range of occupations. Very few individuals ever start life at the very bottom of the social ladder and climb all the way to the top in their lifetime. Most upward mobility occurs step by step—from unskilled to skilled labor, from clerk to manager, from small businessman to professional, and so forth.

In summary, although there is a great deal of social mobility in America, we can expect a majority of the individuals at the top to be recruited from the upper social classes. Even those who have experienced considerable upward mobility are likely to have risen from middle- or upper-middle-class families rather than working-class families.

Social Origins of Men at the Top

What are the social-class origins of the men at the top? Determining this from biographical information is a subjective task—there are no hard and fast rules. G. William Domhoff suggests the following major indicators of "upper-class" origin:

1. Parents or wife's parents listed in the Social Register
2. Attendance at a private prestigious prep school
3. Membership in an upper-class club

Domhoff emphasizes the social-psychological, symbolic indicators of upper social class. Our own bias toward the institutional basis of power suggests additional indicators of "upper-class" origin:

4. Parent an officer or director of a major industrial corporation, bank, insurance company, or public utility
5. Parent a high government official or general in military service
6. Parent an attorney in a top law firm; a newspaper owner or director; or a president or trustee of a university, foundation, major civic or cultural association

Note that this is a very restricted definition of "upper class"—one that would include less than 1 percent of the total population of the United States.

"Upper-middle-class" origin is indicated by a person's private school education, or college or university attendance. Today about 21 percent of the nation's population is "upper-middle-class" by this definition. (An even smaller percentage of the general population was "upper middle class" at the time our elites were college age.) Lower-middle- or lower-class origin indicates the absence of any college or university education.[13] About 79 percent of the nation's population fits this definition of lower-middle and lower class. Our biographical information did not permit us to make any distinction between lower middle class and lower class.

The results of our investigations into the social backgrounds of our men are shown in Table 7-2. By our estimate, 30 percent of the

Table 7-2. Social Origins of the People at the Top

	Corporate	Public Interest					Governmental	
Social Origin	*All*	*Law*	*Found.*	*Educ.*	*Civic*	*Media*	*Domestic*	*Military*
Upper Class	30	35	42	25	40	30	25	10
Middle Class	59	53	52	66	53	59	61	70
Lower Class	3	2	0	1	0	3	5	15
Not Classified	8	9	6	8	7	8	9	5

corporate elite are "upper-class" in origin as we have defined it. Approximately 59 percent are "upper-middle-class"; 3 percent are lower-middle or lower-class; and 8 percent are not classifiable. Note that governmental elites were somewhat less "upper-class" in social origin than corporate elites. Military elites were distinctly not "upper-class" in origin. (Indeed, if we dropped the criterion of, parent a general, in our definition of upper class, none of our military elites would be "upper class.")

Combining all of our elites, and using the definitions of "upper class" and "upper middle class" suggested above, produces the recruitment picture shown in Figure 7-1.

Social Characteristics of Institutional Leaders

What do we know about the people who occupy authoritative positions in American society? There are a number of excellent studies of the social backgrounds of political decision-makers,[14] federal government executives,[15] military officers,[16] and corporate executives.[17] These studies

[13] U.S. Bureau of the Census, *Statistical Abstract of the United States, 1974* (Washington, D.C.: Government Printing Office, 1975), p. 116.

[14] Donald R. Matthews, *The Social Background of Political Decision-makers* (New York: Doubleday & Co., 1954).

[15] David T. Stanley, Dean E. Mann, and Jameson W. Doig, *Men Who Govern* (Washington: The Brookings Institution, 1967).

[16] Morris Janowitz, *The Professional Soldier* (New York: The Free Press, 1960).

[17] Lloyd Warner and James C. Abegglen, *Big Business Leaders in America* (New York: Harper and Row, 1955).

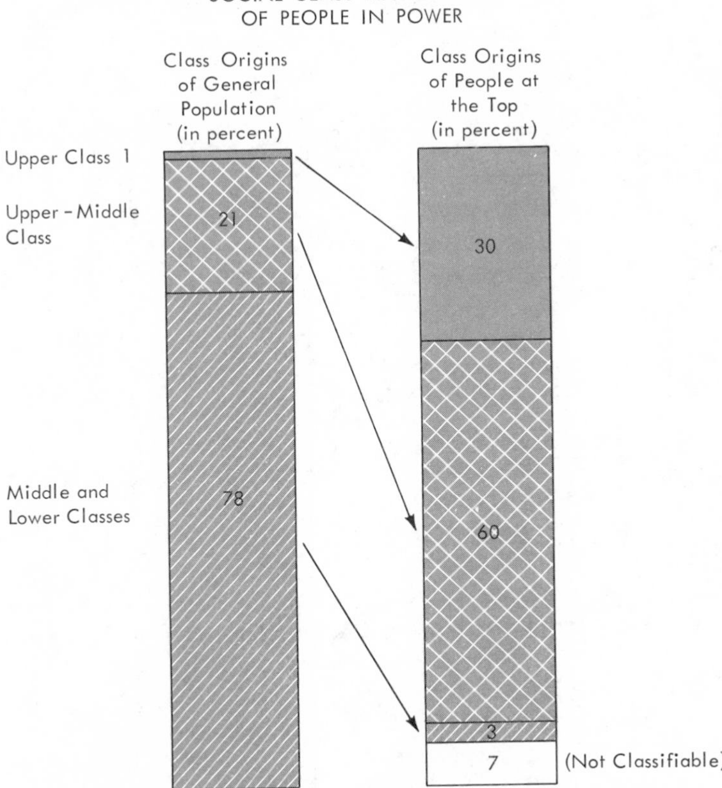

Figure 7-1. Social-Class Recruitment of People at the Top

consistently show that top institutional leaders are *atypical* of the American public. They are recruited from the well-educated, prestigiously employed, older, affluent, urban, white, Anglo-Saxon, upper and upper middle class male populations of the nation. We expected our top institutional elites to conform to the pattern, and we were not at all disappointed (see Table 7-3).

Age. The average age of all the corporate leaders identified in our study is 61. Leaders in foundations, law, education, and civic and cultural organizations are slightly older—average age 64. Top positions in the governmental sector are filled by slightly younger men.

Sex. The feminine sector of the population is seriously underrepresented at the top of America's institutional structure. Male dominance in top positions is nearly complete in the corporate world. The

Table 7-3. Social Characteristics of Corporate, Governmental, and Public Interest Elites

	Corporate	**Public Interest**					**Governmental**	
	All	*Law*	*Found.*	*Educ.*	*Civic*	*Media*	*Domestic*	*Military*
Average Age	61.0	65	64	66	64		58	56
Female Percentage	0.3	0	6.2	8.5	10.5	0.5	0.4	0
Schools								
Public	81.8	70.2	76.8	68.5	73.2	70.9	90.9	92.0
Private	7.0	8.8	7.1	13.2	8.8	12.8	3.0	3.0
Prestigious[a]	11.2	21.0	16.1	18.3	18.0	16.2	6.1	5.0
Colleges								
Public	31.8	10.5	24.6	4.0	17.5	36.5	35.5	30.0[c]
Private	13.3	5.6	6.7	0	16.5	15.7	21.0	2.0
Prestigious[b]	55.0	83.9	68.6	96.0	66.0	47.8	43.5	22.0
Education								
College Educated	90.1	100.0	88.0	96.5	90.2	85.5	88.3	96.0
Advanced Degree	49.2	100.0	62.0	62.5	55.8	56.5	70.5	38.0
Urban Percent	89.0	88.5	87.9	84.9	84.8		69.7	52.8

[a]Andover, Buckley, Cate, Catlin, Choate, Cranbrook, Country Day, Deerfield, Exeter, Episcopal, Gilman, Groton, Hill, Hotchkiss, Kingswood, Kent, Lakeside, Lawrenceville, Lincoln, Loomis, Middlesex, Milton, St. Andrew's, St. Christopher's, St. George's, St. Mark's, St. Paul's, Shattuck, Taft, Thatcher, Webb, Westminister, Woodbury Forest.

[b]Harvard, Yale, Chicago, Stanford, Columbia, M.I.T., Cornell, Northwestern, Princeton, Johns Hopkins, Pennsylvania, and Dartmouth.

[c]U.S. Military Academy (West Point) and U.S. Naval Academy (Annapolis) account for an additional 46.0 percent.

same is true in government; in 1970 only one woman served as secretary or under secretary or assistant secretary in any executive department; none served as chairperson of any standing committee of either the House or Senate; only two served as ranking minority committee members; none served as a member of the Supreme Court, the Council of Economic Advisers, or Federal Reserve Board. Only in civic and cultural affairs, education, and foundations are women found in significant numbers among the top position-holders.

Race. We were able to identify only two blacks in 5000 positions of authority in top-ranked institutions in 1970. Both were in government. One was Thurgood Marshall, associate justice of the Supreme Court, former solicitor general of the United States and former director of the Legal Defense and Educational Fund of the NAACP. The other was James Farmer, assistant secretary of HEW and former national director of the Congress of Racial Equality. We were unable to identify any blacks in top institutional positions in industry, banking, communications and utilities, insurance, law, etc., although it is possible that some may have escaped identification in our biographical search. Certainly it is justifiable to conclude that very few blacks are in any positions of authority in America.

However, the new movement toward "corporate responsibility" has resulted in some recent appointment of blacks to top corporate boards. In 1972 First National City Bank announced the appointment of Frank Thomas, president of the Bedford-Stuyvesant Restoration Corporation in New York, to its board of directors. Thomas is also a director of the Columbia Broadcasting System.

The first black four-star general in the armed forces of the United States was appointed in 1975—Air Force General Daniel "Chappie" James, Jr. General James, the highest ranking black man in American military history, graduated from Tuskegee Institute in Alabama and joined the Army Air Corps in 1943. He flew 101 combat missions in Korea and 87 in Vietnam. In his public statements he emphasizes the opportunities that have opened for blacks in recent years, particularly in the armed forces.

Education. Nearly all our top leaders are college-educated, and more than half held advanced degrees. Some 25.8 percent hold law degrees and 23.8 percent advanced academic or professional degrees. (These are earned degrees only; there are a host of honorary degrees that were not counted.) Governmental leaders were found to be somewhat more likely to hold advanced degrees than were corporate leaders.

A glance at the pre-collegiate education of our top elites reveals that about 18 percent of the corporate leaders and 10 percent of the governmental leaders attended private school. Perhaps the more surprising fact is that 11 percent of corporate leaders and 6 percent of the governmental leaders attended one of the thirty "name" prep schools in America. When these individuals were attending school, only 6 or 7 percent of the population of the nation attended private school at all. Needless to say, only an infinitesimal proportion of the population had the benefit of education at a prestigious "name" prep school. What is even more impressive is the fact that 55 percent of the corporate leaders and 44 percent of the governmental leaders are graduates of twelve heavily endowed "name" private universities—Harvard, Yale, Chicago, Stanford, Columbia, M.I.T., Cornell, Northwestern, Princeton, Johns Hopkins, Pennsylvania, and Dartmouth. Elites in America are notably "Ivy-League."

Urban. Most of our top leaders were urban dwellers. Governmental leaders (notably congressmen) are somewhat more likely to be drawn from rural areas than are leaders in business, and finance and law, but fewer than one-third of the key government posts in our study were found to be filled by individuals from rural areas.

These social background characteristics suggest again a slight tendency for corporate elites to be more "upper-class" in origin than government elites. There are somewhat lower proportions that attended private schools, and fewer "Ivy-Leaguers" among governmental leaders, than among corporate or public interest sector leaders. The study showed a slight tendency for governmental leaders to have had more advanced professional education. And more governmental leaders were seen to come from rural backgrounds.

Women at the Top

Women now comprise about 40 percent of the labor force.[18] But most of these women are secretaries (12 percent), cooks and household domestics (6 percent), clerks in stores (5 percent), bookkeepers (4 percent), teachers (4 percent), and waitresses (3 percent). Only 3 percent of the female labor force are listed as "managers and administrators." Men outnumber women in these jobs by more than five to one. Few women are in the ranks of top leadership in corporations, banks, governments, television networks, or Wall Street or Washington law firms.

[18] U.S. Bureau of the Census, *Statistical Abstract of the United States, 1974* (Washington, D.C.: Government Printing Office, 1975), pp. 354–55.

[19] Catherine Cleary, First Wisconsin Trust; Dorothy Chandler, Times Mirror Co.; Stella Russell, Norton Simon Co.; Ruth Handler, Mattel Toys (inventor of Barbie Dolls); Olive Ann Beech, Beech Aircraft (wife of company president and founder); Katherine Graham, *Washington Post* and *Newsweek;* Bernice Lavin, Alberto Culver (wife of company president and founder); Vera Neuman, Vera Co.; Tillie Lewis, Ogden Corp.; Mala Rubinstein, Helena Rubinstein, Inc. (niece of deceased founder); Rose Cook Sunall, Bluebird, Inc. See Wyndham Robertson, "The Highest Ranking Women in Big Business," *Fortune Magazine* (April 1973), pp. 81–89.

In 1972 *Fortune Magazine* surveyed the 1000 largest industrial corporations and the 300 largest nonindustrial businesses and acquired lists of names of officers and directors who earned $30,000 or more. Of some 6,500 names received, *only 11 were women!* [19] To add further to this portrait of male dominance, *Fortune*'s investigations of these women revealed that three were co-founders of corporations with their husbands, and four others inherited large blocks of stock in their corporations. Only two moved up the corporate hierarchy without family sponsorship.[20]

The few women at the top deserve closer observation. Our own list of top institutional leaders includes:

> *Katherine Graham.* Owner of the *Washington Post* and *Newsweek* magazine. (See Chapter 5, section on "Katherine Graham: The Most Powerful Woman in America.")
>
> *Catherine B. Cleary.* President and director of First Wisconsin Trust. Cleary is a single, up-the-organization manager; she received her B.A. from the University of Chicago in 1937 and a law degree from the University of Wisconsin. Her career centered on First Wisconsin Trust (ranked number 32 in the nation). She served as assistant treasurer of the United States in the Eisenhower administration. In recent years she has accepted directorships of General Motors, AT&T, Kraft Co., and Northwestern Mutual Life Insurance. She has appointed women to top posts at First Wisconsin, but she reportedly has little interest in "Women's Liberation." "We've gone beyond the point where we're looking for women just because they are women."
>
> *Patricia Roberts Harris.* Newly prominent black Washington attorney. Educated at Howard University (B.A. in 1945); received law degree from George Washington University in 1960. Was a delegate to the Democratic National Convention in 1964; appointed ambassador to Luxemburg (1965–67) by President Johnson. Served as Credentials Committee chairperson in the 1972 Democratic National Convention. In 1972 was discovered by the corporate world; is now a director of IBM, Chase Manhattan Bank, and Scott Paper Co. Her career success depended heavily on the civil rights movement of the 1960s and the Johnson Administration efforts to bring more blacks and women into government. Served on the NAACP Legal Defense Fund board of directors, National Citizens Committee on Community Relations, National Women's Committee on Civil Rights, and American Civil Liberties Union board of directors. Began her career as a YMCA director in Chicago, worked full time on the staff of the American Council for Human Rights and later Delta Sigma Theta, before returning to law school. After completing her law degree, served as a Justice Department attorney and then joined the Howard University Law School faculty.

Other women who have recently entered top corporate boardrooms include Chicago attorney Jewel Stradford LaFontant, a director of TWA and Jewell Co. grocery chain; Girl Scouts of America director Cecily Cannan Selby, who was appointed to the boards of Avon and RCA;

20 Catherine Cleary and Stella Russell.

Jayne Spain, a member of the U.S. Civil Service Commission and a director of Litton Industries; and Barnard College President Martha E. Peterson, who was named to the board of Metropolitan Life.[21] It is not clear, however, how much real influence over corporate affairs these new women will enjoy—whether they are token directors appointed for symbolic "window dressing" or not.

Women have failed to acquire any significant power in government. The nation regularly elects ten to fifteen women to Congress, out of 535 members. But so far these women have failed to acquire power positions in the Congress. Shirley Chisholm may attract public attention as an outspoken presidential aspirant and the nation's first black woman in Congress, but she wields little real power on Capitol Hill. Since the first woman entered Congress in 1917, Jeanette Rankin (R. Mont.), a total of only 75 women have served in the Congress. Moreover, many of these woman were elected to fill vacancies caused by the death of their husbands.[22] In 1975, President Ford appointed Carla A. Hills as secretary of housing and urban development. Ms. Hills is only the third female cabinet member in U.S. history. She is a Yale Law School graduate and former assistant attorney general.

Finally, it should be noted again that women frequently acquire top positions in civic and cultural associations and foundations through family connections, civic work, or philanthropy. Our own figures indicate that about 10 percent of the top posts in civic and cultural affairs are filled by women. Moreover, many women inherit great welath and presumably acquire influence, although not necessarily institutional power, through that wealth. Indeed, of the nation's 66 top personal wealthholders in 1970, ten were women. Among these women are Rockefellers, Mellons, duPonts, Fords, Dukes, and Whitneys.

Multiple Paths to the Top

How do people at the top get there? Certainly we cannot provide a complete picture of the recruitment process in all sectors of society. But we can learn whether the top leadership in government is recruited from the corporate world, or whether there are separate and distinct channels of recruitment.

Biographical information on individuals occupying positions of authority in top institutions in each sector of society reveals that there are multiple recruitment paths to top institutional positions. Table 7-4 shows the principal lifetime occupational activity of individuals at the

[21] *Time*, October 16, 1972.

[22] See Congressional Quarterly Editorial Research Report, *The Women's Movement* (Washington: Congressional Quarterly, Inc., 1973).

Table 7-4. Recruitment to Top Institutional Positions

Sector from Which Top Elites Were Recruited	**Corporate**	**Public Interest**					**Governmental**	
	All	*Law*	*Found.*	*Educ.*	*Civic*	*Media*	*Civilian*	*Military*
Corporate	89.1	1.3	49.5	52.9	50.3	23.5	16.6	0
Public Interest								
Law	7.8	96.1	11.5	18.8	16.1	17.4	56.1	0
Civic, Cul., Found.	0.0	0.0	0.0	0.0	0.0	0.0	0.0	0
Education	.6	0.0	23.0	14.2	10.0	0.0	9.2	0
Mass Media	.4	0.0	8.0	6.3	5.3	51.5	5.4	0
Government								
Civilian	1.0	2.6	6.0	6.8	11.4	2.3	16.7	0
Military	.7	0.0	0.0	0.0	0.0	0.0	0.0	100.0
Other								
(Labor, Religion, Art, Literature, etc.)	.2	6.2	2.0	5.9	6.2	4.3	6.9	0

top of each sector of society. (This categorizing of people by their principal activity in life depended largely on their own designation of principal occupation in *Who's Who*.)

As we might expect, the corporate sector supplies most of the occupants of top positions in the corporate sector (89.1 percent). The corporate sector also supplies a majority of the top leadership in civic and cultural organizations and foundations (50.3 percent), and a majority of the trustees of private and renowned educational institutions (52.9 percent). However, the corporate world provides only 16.6 percent of governmental elites, and only a small fraction of elites in mass media (23.5 percent) and the law (1.3 percent).

Top leaders in government are recruited primarily from the legal profession (56.1 percent); some have based their careers in government itself (16.7 percent) and education (10.6 percent). This finding is important. Government and law apparently provide independent channels of recruitment of high public office. High position in the corporate world is *not* a prerequisite to high public office.

The mass media provides another separate path to elite membership. A majority of presidents and directors of TV networks, wire services, and the influential press have been associated throughout their lives with the mass media. Of course, the nation's top lawyers also spent most of their lives in the legal profession; only a fraction identify primarily with their corporate roles (1.3 percent) or governmental roles (2.6 percent).

Educators supply only a small fraction of the top leadership of the nation. Of the top governmental leaders, only 9.2 percent were educators; and educators compose about 10 percent of the directors and trustees of civic and cultural associations and foundations. Indeed, educators do not even supply a majority of the membership of university boards of trustees; only 14.2 percent of our educational elites were drawn from the ranks of educators.

Life at the Top: Compensation, Leisure, Travel

"All societies offer rewards to men assuming leadership positions," writes Suzanne Keller.

> Some rewards are tangible material benefits such as money, land, cattle, or slaves, while others are intangible such as social honor and influence. . . .
>
> Rewards play a two-fold role in the recruitment of elites: they motivate

individuals to assume the responsibilities of elite positions; and they maintain the values of hierarchical social position.[23]

Institutional leaders receive compensation in many forms. Corporate executives usually receive a bonus based on company performance, in addition to their salary. Then there are stock options, low-interest loans, and deferred compensation paid out over future years to reduce the current tax bite. There are indirect forms of compensation too, the so-called perquisites or "perks," which may include personal aides and assistants, plush offices and equipment, paid club membership, expense accounts, and the use of company cars and planes.

In the early 1970s, top corporate executive salaries—*ex*clusive of investments, interests on stock holdings, capital gains, or "perks"—clustered around $250,000 per year. The highest-paid top executive was Harold S. Geneen, president of IT&T, who was paid over $800,000 in salary and bonuses in 1971. These salaries must finance an expensive lifestyle; most of this income is taxable; and it is doubtful that many "up-the-organization" managers can accumulate much wealth from their salaries and bonuses. Few of them become multimillionaires.

But "inheritors" generally receive much more compensation than the paltry $250,000 paid to corporate presidents. Their income is mainly from dividends, interest, and capital gains on investments, including the companies in which they own controlling blocks of stock. Dividends and interest (except for interest on state and municipal bonds) are taxable as income. But capital gains are not taxed unless the asset (stock, real estate, etc.) is sold and the profit realized in cash. Even then, capital gains are taxed at a lower rate than income (35 percent maximum, compared to 70 percent maximum tax on income). Hence one cannot expect to acquire any real wealth from salary incomes, even six-figure salary incomes, given current tax laws. The only way to acquire great wealth in America today is through capital gains.

The salaries of government leaders are considerably lower than those of corporate executives, although the "perks"—aides, offices, cars, planes, expense accounts, secretaries, etc.—are roughly equivalent. The president of the United States receives a salary of $200,000, plus $50,000 for expenses, plus $40,000 for travel and official entertainment. The White House office, including salaries, expenses, and travel of special assistants, aides, secretaries etc. runs $10 million or more per year. The vice-president receives $62,500 salary plus $19,000 for expenses. All Cabinet members receive $60,000 in salary. The chief justice of the Supreme

[23] Keller, *Beyond the Ruling Class,* pp. 183–84.

Court receives $62,000; other justices receive $60,000. Congressmen—both Senators and Representatives—receive $42,500 per year in salaries; but they are given another $200,000 or more to hire staff assistants and run their offices. (In 1975, Congress surreptitiously inserted an annual cost-of-living increase in their own salaries.) Committee chairmen have spent over $2 million per year running their committees.

A surveyed "self-portrait" of the chief executive by *Fortune* magazine, which included responses from half of the presidents of the nation's 500 largest corporations, reports many interesting tidbits about life at the top of the corporate world:

> Over 60 percent of these corporate executives own or rent second "get-away" homes.
>
> A surprisingly large number (48 percent) collect original works of art.
>
> The most popular leisure activity is golfing (56 percent), followed by boating, hunting, tennis, and running. Few attend theatres, go to movies, or watch TV (other than the news).
>
> A majority do not smoke, and contrary to popular impressions, most top executives live longer than the average American.[24]

Most people at the top are very well-traveled. Indeed, *Fortune* reports that four out of five travel outside the United States each year. Europe is the leading destination of this travel, but 20 percent travel to South America each year and 40 percent to Asia.

Social Clubs: Elites at Play

Institutional leaders are "joiners." The overwhelming majority of those who hold top positions in America belong to one or more social clubs. More importantly, nearly half of our people at the top belong to just a few very prestigious private clubs. Corporate directors, network moguls, cabinet members, foundation presidents, and superlawyers rub shoulders at such places as the Links and the Knickerbocker in New York, and the Metropolitan and the Burning Tree in Washington. These private clubs provide an opportunity for informal interaction among elites in different segments of society. The importance of these clubs in developing elite consensus and cohesion is the subject of a great deal of speculation. E. Digby Baltzell writes: "At the upper class level in America . . . the club [a private voluntary association] lies at the very core of the social orga-

[24] Robert S. Diamond, "Self-Portrait of the Chief Executive," *Fortune Magazine* (May 1970), pp. 181, 320–23.

nization of the access to power and authority."[25] Ferdinand Lundberg says: "The private clubs are the most 'in' thing about the . . . elite. These clubs constitute the societal control centers of the elite."[26]

Perhaps the most persuasive case for the importance of such private social clubs is set forth by sociologist G. William Domhoff:

> The Bohemian Grove [a luxury retreat on 2700 acres of giant redwoods maintained by the Bohemian Club of San Francisco], as well as other watering holes and social clubs, are relevant to the problem of class cohesiveness in two ways. First, the very fact that rich men from all over the country gather in such close circumstances as the Bohemian Grove is evidence of the existence of a socially cohesive upper class. It demonstrates that many of these men do know each other, that they have face-to-face communications, and that they are a social network. In this sense we are looking at [clubs] as a *result* of social processes that lead to class cohesion. But such institutions also can be viewed as facilitators of social ties. Once formed, these groups became another avenue by which the cohesiveness of the upper class is maintained.[27]

It is our judgment, however, that club membership is a result of top position-holding in the institutional structure of society rather than an important independent source of power. An individual is selected for club membership *after* he has acquired an important position in society; he seldom acquires position and power because of his club memberships. Personal interaction, consensus-building, and friendship networks all develop in the club milieu, but the clubs merely help facilitate processes that occur anyway. Nonetheless, the club memberships of men at the top are worthy of attention.

Corporate leaders are more likely to be members of private social clubs than are governmental leaders. Table 7-5 shows that over two-thirds of our corporate elites held private club memberships; a third of them held five or more memberships. In contrast, only one-third of top governmental leaders held such memberships, and even fewer military chiefs were club members. Doubtless this differential reflects the greater importance of social interaction in the corporate world (and perhaps the fact that businessmen can shift the exorbitant costs of such memberships to their corporations while government officials cannot). The fact that a majority of top governmental and military elites are *not* club members undercuts the importance attributed to club membership by many

[25] E. Digby Baltzell, *The Protestant Establishment* (New York: Random House, 1964), p. 354.

[26] Ferdinand Lundberg, *The Rich and the Super-Rich* (New York: Bantam Books, 1968), p. 339.

[27] G. William Domhoff, *The Bohemian Grove and Other Retreats* (New York: Harper and Row, 1974), p. 88.

Table 7-5. Club Memberships of Institutional Leaders

	Corporate	Public Interest					Governmental	
		Law	*Found.*	*Educ.*	*Civic*	*Media*	*Domestic*	*Military*
Club Memberships								
None	25	24	30	22	10	33	62	71
One to Four	45	45	38	50	48	41	30	22
Five or More	30	31	32	28	42	26	8	7
Exclusive Clubs*								
None	56	58	50	38	34	56	94	91
One or More	44	42	50	62	66	44	6	9

*Links (N.Y.), Century (N.Y.), Knickerbocker (N.Y.), Piping Rock (N.Y.), River (N.Y.), Metropolitan (D.C.), Pacific Union-Bohemian (S.F.), Brook (N.Y.), Burlington (S.F.), California (L.A.), Casino (Chi.), Chagrin Valley (Clev.), Chicago (Chi.), Denver (Den.), Detroit (Det.), Eagle Lake (Hous.), Everglades (Fla.), Hartford (Conn.), Hope (R.I.), Idlewild (Dallas), Maryland (Md.), Milwaukee (Mil.), Minneapolis (Minn.), New Haven Town (Conn.), Philadelphia (Phil.), Rittenhouse (Phil.), Racquet (St. L.), Rainier (Seattle), Richmond (Va.), Cuyamuca (San Diego), Charleston (S.C.), Rolling Rock (Pitts.), Saturn (Buf.), St. Louis (St. L.), Somerset (Bos.), Union (Clev.), Woodhill (Minn.).

"power elite" writers. If a majority of top governmental elites sip cocktails at the Metropolitan Club, it is difficult to argue that the real decision-making in Washington takes place in that club's lounge.

Nonetheless, the fact that nearly half of the top elites in the corporate, legal, educational, foundation, and mass media sectors of society, belong to one of *forty* selected clubs is impressive testimony to the prestige of these clubs.

Summary

The "elitist" literature on power stresses the disproportionate numbers of top leaders drawn from the upper and upper middle strata of society. But even classical elite theorists acknowledge the necessity of some opportunities for upward mobility in society, if only to maintain order and strengthen support for the political system. The "pluralist" literature on power describes a more open leadership system where individuals from all social backgrounds can rise to the top if they have the necessary skills, information, and talents. However, the "pluralists" acknowledge that opportunities to acquire such qualities are unequally distributed among classes in society. Pluralists also argue that social class is a poor predictor of decision-making behavior. We have not resolved this debate but perhaps we have added some more factual information about exactly how much opportunity exists for various social classes to reach the top.

Our definition of "upper-class" origin is very restrictive. It roughly parallels our notion of institutional leadership. This definition includes less than 1 percent of the population. Yet it is our estimate that 30 percent of the people at the top are "upper-class" in social origin—that is, their parents occupied positions at or near the top of the nation's institutional structure. Only about 3 percent of the men at the top in our study were lower-middle or lower-class in origin—lacking in a college education. The rest were upper-middle-class in origin.

On the whole, those at the top are well-educated, older, affluent, urban, WASP, and male. There were only two blacks among men at the top in 1970, both in government; although recently a few blacks have been appointed to top corporate boards. There are very few "women at the top" of the nation's institutional structure: only a handful on corporate boards and high governmental positions, and about 10 percent in civic and cultural associations and foundations.

There is a slight tendency for corporate elites to be more urban and "upper-class" than governmental elites. There are more private prep-school types and Ivy Leaguers in corporate board rooms than in government. Governmental leaders tend to have more advanced degrees, not only in law but also in academic and professional fields.

There are multiple recruitment paths to the top of the nation's institutional structure. The corporate world supplied a majority of the top leaders in the corporate sector itself, and in civic and cultural organizations, foundations, and universities. However, top governmental leaders are recruited primarily from the law, and to a lesser extent from government itself and education. The mass media, the law, and education all provide separate recruitment channels. In short, the corporate world, while an important recruitment channel, is not the exclusive road to the top.

Eight

CONFLICT AND CONSENSUS AMONG INSTITUTIONAL LEADERS

Conflict or Consensus Among Elites?

How much agreement exists among people at the top about the fundamental values and future directions of American society? Do America's top leaders agree on the *ends* of policies and programs and disagree merely on the *means* of achieving those ends? Or are there significant differences among American elites over the goals and purposes of our society?

Social scientists frequently give conflicting answers to these questions—not because of differences in the results of their research, but because of differences in the interpretation of these results. Although it is sometimes difficult to survey elite attitudes and opinions (individuals at the top do not have much time to spend with pollsters), nonetheless, social scientists have produced a number of good studies of the values of corporate executives, governmental officials, political party leaders, university intellectuals, and even newsmen.

Pluralists contend that these studies reveal significant conflicts between Democrats and Republicans, liberals and conservatives, corporate

..s and labor leaders, intellectuals and bankers, and other leadership groups, over a wide range of policy issues. They cite studies showing significant differences between various segments of the nation's elite over poverty programs and welfare reform proposals, government regulation of business and labor, specific energy proposals, tax reform and tax loopholes, alternative approaches to national health care, and the appropriate measures to deal with inflation and recession. In the middle years of the Vietnam War, the nation's leadership appeared divided between "hawks" and "doves." But early in the war there had been widespread support for the idea of containing Communist expansion in Asia, and after 1968 a new consensus emerged on the need to disengage, with only the speed of withdrawal at issue.

In contrast, elitists contend that despite these differences over *specific* policy questions, all segments of American leadership share a broader consensus about the *fundamental* values of private property, limited government, separation of church and state, individual liberty, and due process of law. Moreover, since the Roosevelt era, American elites have generally supported liberal, public-regarding, social welfare programs, including social security, fair labor standards, unemployment compensation, a graduated income tax, a federally aided welfare system, government regulation of public utilities, and countercyclical fiscal and monetary policies. Today, elite consensus also includes a commitment to equality of opportunity for women and blacks and a desire to end direct, lawful discrimination. Finally, elite consensus includes a desire to exercise influence in world affairs, to oppose the spread of Communism, to maintain a strong national defense, and to protect pro-Western governments from internal subversion and external aggression.

Both elitist and pluralist interpretations can be supported by available data. Most surveys conducted *within* the United States deliberately emphasize differences among elites by choosing public issues that are known to be sources of conflict. But there is indeed a fairly broad consensus among men at the top on fundamental values and future directions of American society—a consensus which we will label "the liberal establishment."

However, we will *not* contend that disagreement never occurs among men at the top. On the contrary, the mutiple bases of power in American society—industry, finance, law, government, mass media, etc.—insure that different segments of America's elite will view public issues from slightly different vantage points. The notion of consensus on societal goals and conflict over specific means of their achievement is clearly expressed by sociologist Suzanne Keller:

What is required for effective social life is moral accord among the stra-

> tegic elites: they must have some loyalties and goals in common. As societies become more differentiated, a considerable degree of cohesion and consensus is needed at the top.
>
> . . . The point need not be labored that doubt and conflicts are necessary: societies advance both as a result of achievements and as a result of disagreements and struggles over the ways to attain them. This is where power struggles play a major and indispensable role. Loyalty to common goals does not preclude conflict over how they are to be realized.[1]

Thus, we contend that disagreement occurs *within* a framework of consensus on fundamental values, that the range of disagreement among elites is relatively narrow, and that disagreement is generally confined to means rather than ends.

The Liberal Establishment

The prevailing philosophy of America's elite is liberal and public-regarding. By this we mean institutional leaders show a willingness to take the welfare of others into account as an aspect of their own sense of well-being; they exhibit a willingness to use governmental power to correct perceived wrongs done to others. This is a familiar philosophy—elite responsibility for the welfare of the poor and downtrodden, particularly blacks. Today's liberal elite believes that it can change people's lives through the exercise of governmental power: end discrimination, abolish poverty, eliminate slums, insure employment, uplift the poor, eliminate sickness, educate the masses, and instill dominant culture values in everyone. The prevailing impulse is to *do good* to perform public services, and to assist the poorest in society. This philosophy is not widely shared among America's masses, however.

Historically, upper-class values in America have been liberal, public-regarding, and service-oriented. Society's elites are confident that with sufficient effort, they can improve men's lives. They feel a strong obligation to improve not only themselves, but everyone else—whether they want to be improved or not.

Leadership for liberal reform has always come from America's upper social classes. This leadership is more likely to come from established "old families" rather than "new rich," self-made men. Before the Civil War, abolitionist leaders were "descended from old and socially dominant Northeastern families" and were clearly distinguished from the emerging "robber barons"—the new leaders of the Industrial Revolution.

1 Suzanne Keller, *Beyond the Ruling Class: Strategic Elites in Modern Society* (New York: Random House, 1963), p. 146.

Later, when the children and grandchildren of the robber barons inherited positions of power, they turned away from the Darwinist philosophy of their parents and toward the more public-regarding ideas of the New Deal. Liberalism was championed not by the working class, but by men like Franklin D. Roosevelt (Groton and Harvard), Adlai Stevenson (Choate School and Princeton), Averell Harriman (Groton and Yale), and John F. Kennedy (Choate School and Harvard).

This elite "character" defies simplistic Marxian interpretations of American politics; wealth, education, sophistication, and upper-class cultural values do *not* foster attitudes of exploitation, but rather of public service and do-goodism. Liberal elites are frequently paternalistic toward segments of the masses they define as "underprivileged," "culturally deprived," "disadvantaged," etc., but they are seldom hostile toward them.

Today's upper-class liberalism was shaped in the era of Franklin Delano Roosevelt. Roosevelt came to power as a descendant of two of America's oldest families, the Roosevelts and the Delanos, original Dutch patrician families of New York whose landed wealth predates the English capture of New Amsterdam. The Roosevelts and other patrician families whose wealth predates the industrial revolution, never fully accepted the Social Darwinism "public be damned," rugged individualism of the industrial capitalists. They were not schooled in the scrambling competition of the upwardly mobile, *nouveau riche,* but instead in the altruism and idealism of comfortable and secure wealth and assured social status. In describing FDR, historian Richard Hofstadter summarizes upper-class liberalism:

> At the beginning of his career he took to the patrician reform thought of the progressive era and accepted a social outlook that can best be summed up in the phrase "noblesse oblige." He had a penchant for public service, personal philanthropy, and harmless manifestos against dishonesty in government; he displayed a broad easy-going tolerance, a genuine liking for all sorts of people; he loved to exercise his charm in political and social situations.[2]

This liberal consensus is not strictly or necessarily humanitarian in origin. The values of welfare and reform are functional for the preservation of the American political and economic system. A radical criticism of the liberal establishment is that its paternalism toward the poor and the black is really self-serving; it is designed to end poverty and discrimination while preserving the free enterprise system and the existing class structure.

[2] Richard Hofstadter, *The American Political Tradition* (New York: Knopf, 1948), pp. 323–24.

What Big Business Thinks

The notion that America's established elites, particularly corporate and financial leaders, are generally liberal and public-regarding, challenges longstanding assumptions of many college teachers. Generations of students who have been taught that America's business leaders are hopeless reactionaries find it difficult to accept the idea of a *liberal* establishment. But let us examine some studies that contradict the ultra-conservative image of America's top corporate leaders.

First of all, top corporate leaders are interested in maintaining a stable world and a lasting peace. More importantly, they believe that the most important means to these goals are through international trade and technical cooperation, rather than military superiority. Few top corporate leaders could be characterized as "hawks" or Cold War anti-Communists. On the contrary, most favor improved relations with Communist nations, and a retrenchment of U.S. military commitments abroad.

Political scientists Bruce Russett and Betty Hanson of Yale University analyzed 600 questionnaires returned by 1000 presidents and vice-presidents of the nation's 500 largest corporations.[3] They asked these executives whether the threat of communism had increased or decreased or remained the same over the last ten years: only 15 percent perceived an increase, 27 percent saw the threat remaining the same, and 58 percent perceived a decrease. Perhaps more importantly, when asked how best to maintain world peace, these executives replied as follows:

Which one of these do you consider the most important approach to world peace?

Trade, technical cooperation, economic interdependence	61.5%
Military superiority of the U.S.	10.9
Efforts to achieve a balance of power	8.6
Narrowing the gap between rich and poor nations	7.8
Strengthening international institutions	6.2
Arms control	3.2
Collective security through alliances	1.8

Note that these businessmen have little confidence in political agreements and institutions—collective alliances, arms control, or the United Nations. But many believed that narrowing the gap between rich and poor was as important as achieving a balance of power or military superiority. Of course, most businessmen believed that the best approach to peace was through world trade and economic interdependence.

3 Bruce M. Russett and Betty C. Hanson, "How Corporate Executives See America's Role in the World," *Fortune Magazine* (May 1974), pp. 165–68.

Top corporate leaders are also interested in maintaining a stable and ordered domestic society:

Ranking of the most serious problems facing the U.S. today:

Domestic order and stability	37%
Social and racial disparities within the U.S.	20
World ecological problems: pollution and population pressures	18
National and socialist movements in less developed countries	15
Military and technological advances of China and Russia	9

Note that traditional Cold War concerns came last. Those at the top seek a stable domestic scene for planned economic development with little risk of disruption. They realize that social and racial disparities in the U.S. threaten their major goal and they are prepared to support efforts to reduce these disparities. It makes little difference whether this "liberalism" is ideological and humanitarian, or simply "enlightened self-interest." Ecological problems are ranked third by these top executives, which calls into question the popular portrait of businessmen as opponents of environmental protection efforts.

A separate study by *Fortune Magazine,* a survey of 270 presidents of the nation's 500 largest corporations, confirms the concern of top corporate leaders with protection of the environment. *Fortune* concluded: "It may come as quite a surprise that the elite of business leadership strongly desire the federal government to step in, set the standards, regulate all activities pertaining to the environment, and help finance the job with tax incentives." [4] *Fortune* asked two questions about federal regulation:

Would you like to see it [the government] step up its regulatory activities, maintain them at the present levels, or cut them back?

Step up regulatory activities	57%
Maintain	29
Cut back	8
Not sure	6

Do you favor a single national agency to establish standards on air and water pollution control, land use, etc., or should local standards prevail?

Single national standard	53%
Local standards	35
Not sure	12

[4] Robert S. Diamond, "What Business Thinks," *Fortune Magazine* (February 1970), pp. 118–19.

(Note that top corporate elites in this study indicated that they not only wanted *more* regulatory activity, but wanted it at the *federal* level.) This contrasts with popular notions that Big Business always opposes government regulation, and that when it is forced upon them prefers state and local regulation to federal law.

Corporate leaders reflect traditionally liberal positions on a wide range of issues. One study of the 1949 graduates of the Harvard Business School tested the ideas of these men on a broad spectrum of social, political, and economic issues.[5] (Not all of these individuals qualify as "people at the top" by our standards. But 23 percent were presidents or board chairmen of their companies by 1974, 45 percent were top corporate executives, and 16 percent were millionaires. Collectively, this single class of 621 Harvard business graduates employed yearly one million people and took in $40 billion of revenue in that year (1974). This is itself an interesting comment on the importance of prestigious educational background.)

What Corporate Leaders Think

	Favor Strongly	Favor Somewhat	Oppose	Uncertain
Free-enterprise system	87%	10%	1%	0.3%
Media censorship	2	12	80	4
Protective tariffs	5	33	55	5
Farm price supports	4	30	57	7
Equal pay for women	68	26	2	3
Legalized abortion	53	27	15	4
Trade with USSR & China	41	52	2	4
Socialized medicine	11	34	46	8
Negative income tax	10	31	32	23
Interracial marriages	6	25	46	22
Legalized marijuana	9	21	61	9

These men are hardly right-wing reactionaries. They support the free enterprise system and oppose press censorship by overwhelming margins. They support equal pay for women and legalized abortion by wide margins, as well as trade with Russia and China. They oppose protective tariffs and farm price supports. They are almost equally divided on two proposals generally associated with left-liberals—socialized medicine and a negative income tax. The only "conservative" positions supported by these men are opposition to interracial marriage and legalized marijuana.

5 Marilyn Wellemeger, "The Class the Dollars Fell On," *Fortune Magazine* (May 1974), pp. 226–30.

The Limits of Elite Consensus

We have already suggested the broad outlines of elite consensus on behalf of private enterprise, due process of law, liberal and public-regarding social welfare programs, equality of opportunity and a strong national defense posture. But let us examine more closely the nature and extent of elite *disagreement*.

Over 500 top elites in business, labor, government, the Democratic and Republican parties, and the mass media were interviewed in 1971 and 1972 by Columbia University's Bureau of Applied Social Research. These interviews defined the limits of agreement and disagreement on specific policy questions among these separate elite segments. Table 8-1 reveals the limits of consensus on selected key economic policy questions. At the left of the table are those questions suggesting "liberal consensus" on which all groups agreed to help the poor and use government power to stabilize the economy. Next are those questions which won agreement by every group of leaders except businessmen. Businessmen dissented on issues involving the environmental problem and its control and the causes, and remedies for poverty. At the right of the table are issues that reveal a "conservative" consensus on behalf of the private enterprise economy, unlimited opportunity to acquire wealth, and confidence in the opportunities provided the working class in the American system. Next are those questions which won disagreement from every group of leaders except labor union officials. Labor is cut off from other elites when it comes to government intervention into labor disputes (labor is opposed, while others favor such intervention) and labor's demand for a greater role in management of the plant.

In the middle are questions that actually divided elites along the lines suggested by pluralist political theory: Republican politicians and business leaders disagreed with Democratic politicians, labor leaders, government officials, and the mass media. It seems safe to say that only in this relatively narrow range of issues—the oil depletion allowances, federal versus state and local government control of social programs, inheritance taxes, and the proper range of income differences—are traditional notions of pluralist politics applicable.

Professor Alan Barton, director of the study, summarized his findings in part as follows:

> While there were sharp divisions on some economic policies, there were certain general actions favored by a majority of every one of the groups studied. These include some kind of action to help the poor, deficit spending in times of recession, wage-price controls against inflation, and federal

Table 8-1. Elite Consensus: Economic Policy Questions (Percent Giving Liberal Answers)

	Liberal Consensus				Bi-partisan Liberalism with Business Dissenting				Pluralist Division: Business and Repub. Disagree with Labor and Demo.				Bi-partisan Conservatism with Labor Dissenting					Conservative Consensus		
	DISAGREE: Too much done for poor	DISAGREE: Govt. spending should be cut in recession	Federal govt. should create jobs	Wage-price controls are needed	Tax polluting industries	DISAGREE: Environmental problem exaggerated	DISAGREE: Poverty mainly cultural	Increase political power of poor	End oil depletion allowance	DISAGREE: Local control of social programs	Reduce income differences	More effective inheritance tax	Welfare reform not generous enough	DISAGREE: Compulsory arbitration needed	Larger workers' role in management	Tax capital gains 50% or more	DISAGREE: Pricing system competitive	Limit job incomes	Take big corps. out of private ownership	Worker's son doesn't have a chance
Business Owners and Executives	75	73	59	69	45	41	48	36	32	43	20	21	15	30	12	13	11	4	3	8
Republican Politicians and Officials	84	78	70	62	57	60	62	60	35	34	38	24	11	26	16	20	15	3	3	6
Career Civil Servants	90	94	81	82	76	75	64	60	67	53	56	56	31	21	33	68	31	12	4	4
Mass Media Execs. % Professionals	93	76	91	82	84	84	66	69	80	69	56	46	54	22	48	36	40	30	9	11
Democrat Politicians	82	83	83	82	70	77	65	75	68	44	49	56	43	44	33	47	33	17	7	9
Labor Union Leaders	95	88	98	63	88	84	77	82	85	80	70	93	71	88	65	54	63	37	17	10
Total	86	81	77	74	68	66	62	59	57	50	45	45	35	34	33	33	29	16	7	7

Table reads: 75% of business owners and executives disagree with the statement that too much is done for the poor. 69% of business owners and executives favor wage and price controls, etc.

Source: Allen H. Barton, "The Limits of Consensus Among Leaders" Bureau of Applied Social Research, Columbia University, 1972.

Source: "Consensus and Conflict among American Leaders" by Allen H. Barton, *Public Opinion Quarterly,* v. 38 (Winter 1974-75), 507-30.

> job creation in the public sector for the unemployed. "Keynesian economics" and the welfare state in some form are now orthodoxy among American leaders; so also—since the Republican administration adopted them shortly after our interviewing began—were direct controls on wages and prices in periods of inflation. . . .
>
> Some issues sharply divided the businessmen from the labor and liberal interest-group leaders, with differences of over 50 percentage points on most: the Republicans come close to the business position on all of these issues, while Democrats tend toward the labor position. . . .
>
> Just as there are some things which "everyone" now favors, like Keynesian economics, controls, and the welfare state, there are some things which "everyone" opposes. Three such items rejected by large majorities in every group are: a top limit on incomes, taking big corporations out of private hands, and the belief that a worker's son doesn't have much chance to get ahead in our society. There are very few socialists among American leaders—only one out of every six labor leaders give even qualified support to socializing large corporations, and 90 percent of them subscribe to the Horatio Alger theory. . . .[6]

Factionalism Among Elites

Exactly how much competition and conflict exists among America's elites? Are American elites generally cohesive, with only traditional Democratic and Republican affiliations and conventionally liberal and conservative attachments dividing them? Or are there serious conflicts among elites—serious splits which threaten the national consensus and the stability of the system itself? Are political conflicts in America merely petty squabbles among ambitious individuals, competing interest groups, or competing institutions—all of which agree on the underlying "rules of the game"? Or is American leadership seriously divided—so much so that the very framework of the political system is being shaken?

The pluralist view is that competition is a driving force in the American political system. But the very purpose of the political system, according to pluralist political theory, is to manage this competition, to channel it through the institutional structure, to modify its intensity, to damage compromises and balance conflicting interests. In short, pluralism recognizes and encourages competition as a system of checks and balances within American society.

However, even pluralists realize that this competition must be kept

[6] Alan Barton, "The Limits of Consensus Among American Leaders," paper delivered at the Southwestern Social Science Association Meeting, April 1973.

within bounds—it must not be permitted to grow with an intensity that threatens the stability of the political system. Generally, pluralists contend that competition will be limited by several forces which act to maintain an "equilibrium" in the political system. First of all, there is supposed to be a large, nearly universal *latent group* in American society which supports the constitutional system and the prevailing rules of the game. This group is not always visible, but it can be activated to administer overwhelming rebuke to any faction that resorts to unfair means, violence, or terrorism. Secondly, *overlapping group membership* is also supposed to maintain the system in equilibrium: individuals who belong to any one group also belong to other groups, and this fact moderates the demands of groups who must avoid offending their members who have other group affiliations. Finally, pluralists offer the notion the *checking and balancing* resulting from competition itself is a stabilizing force. No single segment of society—no single group of powerful leaders—could ever command a majority. The power of each segment is checked by the power of competing segments—corporations by government, government by parties and civic groups, the mass media by government and advertisers, etc. These "countervailing" centers of power function to check the influence of any single segment of the nation's elite.

The elitist view is one of much greater cohesion and unity among various segments of the nation's leadership. Yet elitism does not imply a single monolithic or impenetrable body of power-holders. Elitism does not pretend that power in society does not shift over time, or that new elites cannot emerge to compete with old elites. Indeed, it is unlikely that there was ever a society in which various men and factions did not compete for power and pre-eminence. The notion of a "circulation of elites" insures that new elite numbers are continually being admitted to elite circles; these new elites bring slightly different interests and experiences to their roles than older established elites.

But elite theory contends that serious splits among elites—disagreements over the fundamental values and future directions of American society—are rare. Indeed, perhaps the only really serious split in the nation's elite led to the Civil War—the split between Southern planters, land-owners, exporters, and slave-owners; and Northern manufacturers, merchants, and immigrant employees, over whether the nation's future, particularly its western land, was to be devoted to a plantation, exporting, slave economy or a free, small-farmer, market economy for domestic manufactured goods. This conflict led to the nation's bloodiest war. However serious we believe our present internal conflicts to be, they do not match the passions which engulfed this nation over a century ago.

The New Rich: The Emergence of the Sunbelt Cowboys

Nonetheless, elite factionalism today is evident. A major source of this factionalism among America's elite is the division between the new-rich, Southern and Western COWBOYS and the established, Eastern, liberal YANKEES. This factional split transcends partisan squabbling among Democrats and Republicans, or traditional riffs between Congress and the president, or petty strife among organized interest groups. The conflict between COWBOYS and YANKEES derives from differences in their sources of wealth and the newness of the elite status of the COWBOYS.

Since World War II, new opportunities to acquire wealth and create new bases of power have developed as a result of technological change and adjustments in the economy. The major areas of opportunity have been:

1. Independent oil drilling operations
2. Aerospace industry
3. Computer technology, cameras, and copying machines
4. Real estate development, particularly in the "Sunbelt" from Southern California and Arizona through Texas to Florida
5. Discount drugs and merchandising, fast foods, and low cost insurance

Most of the "self-made men" among America's top wealth-holders have acquired their wealth in one or another of these endeavors: [7]

J. Paul Getty (oil)
Howard Hughes (Hughes Tool Co., real estate)
H. L. Hunt (oil)
Edwin H. Land (Polaroid)
R. E. (Bob) Smith (oil)
Leon Hess (Hess Oil and Chemical)
William R. Hewlett (Hewlett-Packard, aerospace & computers)
David Packard (Hewlett-Packard, aerospace & computers)
Chester Carlson (inventor of xerography)
Bob Hope (entertainment)
Peter Kiewit (construction)
J. S. McDonnell, Jr. (McDonnell-Douglas, aircraft)

[7] Arthur M. Louis, "America's Centi-Millionaires," *Fortune Magazine* (May 1968).

Even since this listing was compiled in the 1960s, new opportunities for acquiring great personal wealth have developed *in the 1970s* and added new names to America's list of centimillionaires. Below is a listing from *Fortune* magazine of individuals who have become centimillionaires since 1968: [8]

Leonard N. Stern (pet food and real estate, Hartz Mountain Corp.)
Ray A. Kroc (hamburgers, chairman of the McDonald's Corp.)
H. Ross Perot (computer services, founder of Electronic Data Systems, owner of duPont, Walston Inc., brokers)
Roy F. Carver (tire-retreading, chairman of Bandag, Inc.)
Leonard Davis (low-cost insurance, founder of Colonial Penn Group)
Milton J. Petrie (merchandising, founder of Petrie Stores Corp.)
Arthur G. Cohen (real estate, chairman of Arlen Realty & Development Corp.)
Jack M. Eckerd (drugs, founder of Jack Eckerd Corp.)
Leo Goodwin, Jr. (low-cost insurance, Government Employees Insurance Co.)
Henry S. McNeil (drugs, founder of McNeil Laboratories, now an affiliate of Johnson & Johnson)
Galen J. Roush (trucking, chairman of Roadway Express)
Curtis L. Carlson (trading stamps—Gold Bond, hotels, real estate)
Arthur S. Moss (low-cost insurance, founder of National Liberty Corp.)
John K. Hanson (motor homes, chairman of Winnebago Industries)
Alex Monogian (metal products, founder of Masco Corp.)

However, the personal wealth of the *new* rich is frequently unstable, compared, for example, to the established wealth of the Rockefellers, Fords, duPonts, or Mellons. Wealth that is institutionalized in giant corporations—corporations that form the basis of an industrialized economy such as autos, steel, oil, and chemicals—is likely to remain intact over generations with only minor fluctuations in value. But many of today's *new* rich have acquired their wealth in relatively new and unstable industries. Independent oil operations and the aerospace industry are highly fluctuating businesses. The computer industry has now stabilized and appears to be an integral part of a mature economy. But fortunes in real estate, drug stores, discount merchandising, and low-cost insurance can quickly disappear.[9]

8 Arthur M. Louis, "The New Rich of the Seventies," *Fortune Magazine* (September 1973).

9 Consider for example the case of H. Ross Perot, the only man ever to *lose* $1 billion in personal wealth. When he first publicly offered shares of his company Electronic Data Systems, shares sold for $16.50. Perot held 9 million shares himself, of a total value of over $150 million. In 1970, the value of EDS stock had risen to

The Predominance of Established Wealth

Despite the rise of many new men of wealth in America, established Eastern sources of wealth and power continue to dominate national life. Indeed, there is some evidence of a decline in the rate of new elite formation in the twentieth century. Most of America's great corporate families built their empires in the period between the Civil War and World War I. The Industrial Revolution propelled many new waves to the top of the national elite structure. This was a period of rapid industrial expansion, the growth of new sources of wealth, and corresponding changes in the elite structure. But today the nation's economy is mature; large corporate and governmental institutions control most of the nation's re-

Table 8-2. Social Origins of the Super-Rich 1900-1970

Social Origin	1900	1925	1950	1970
Upper Class	39%	56%	68%	82%
Middle Class	20	30	20	10
Lower Class	39	12	9	4
Not Classified	2	2	3	4

Sources: Estimates for 1900, 1925, and 1950 are from C. Wright Mills *The Power Elite* (New York: Oxford University Press, 1950), pp. 104-5. The percentages are derived from biographies of the 275 people who were and are known to historians, biographers, and journalists as the richest people living in the United States—the 90 richest of 1900, the 95 of 1925, and the 90 of 1950. Estimates for 1970 are from our own analysis of biographies of the nation's 66 richest Americans, *Fortune Magazine,* July 1968. At the top of the 1900 list is John D. Rockefeller; at the top of the 1925 list is Henry Ford; at the top in 1950 is H. L. Hunt; at the top in 1970 is J. Paul Getty.

sources; and opportunities for the accumulation of great personal wealth are more limited. Table 8-2 presents estimates by C. Wright Mills of the social backgrounds of the nation's richest men in 1900, 1925, and 1950; we have added our own estimates for 1970. Only 39 percent of the richest men in America came from the upper social class in 1900; but 68 percent of the richest men were born to wealth in 1950 and 82 percent in 1970. Mills estimates that 39 percent of the richest men in 1900 had struggled

---

$162 a share, making Perot's fortune worth close to $1.5 *billion*. But the stock crashed shortly thereafter to $29 a share, leaving Perot with a mere $270 million. Apparently these fluctuations fascinated Perot, so he purchased duPont, Walston, Inc., one of the largest brokerage firms on the New York Stock Exchange, perhaps to learn more about the stock market. But Perot failed as a broker, too; duPont, Walston collapsed and Perot disappeared from the list of "people at the top." See "The Man Who Lost a Billion," *Fortune Magazine* (September 1973).

up from the bottom compared to only 4 percent in 1970. We do not believe that *any* of today's 66 richest men rose from the bottom.

The Sunbelt Cowboys versus the Established Yankees

The Sunbelt COWBOYS are the new-money people who acquired their wealth in the post–World War II era of dramatic growth and expansion. Their wealth and power was generated in (1) independent oil and natural gas exploration and development; (2) aerospace and defense contracting; (3) discount merchandising and low-cost insurance; and (4) real estate operations in the population boom areas running from Southern California and Arizona, through Texas and the new South, to Florida. In contrast, the YANKEES are themselves second- and third-generation descendants of the great entrepreneurial families of the Industrial Revolution (the familiar Rockefellers, Fords, Mellons, duPonts, Kennedys, Harrimans, etc.). Other YANKEES have been recruited through established corporate institutions, Wall Street and Washington law firms, Eastern banking and investment firms, well-known foundations, and Ivy League universities.

The COWBOYS do not fully share in the liberal, public-regarding values of the dominant Eastern establishment. However, the COWBOYS do not exercise power that is proportional in any way to the overwhelming hegemony of the established YANKEES. The COWBOYS may have gained in influence in recent years. And much of the petty political fighting reported in today's press has its roots in COWBOY-YANKEE factionalism. But the liberal establishment remains dominant. And COWBOYS and YANKEES agree on the overriding importance of preserving political stability and a healthy free enterprise economy.

The COWBOYS are "self-made" men who acquired wealth and power in an intense competitive struggle that continues to shape their outlook on life. Their upward mobility, their individualism, and their competitive spirit shape their view of society and the way they perceive their new elite responsibilities. In contrast, the YANKEES either inherit great wealth or attach themselves to established institutions of great wealth, power, and prestige. The YANKEES are socialized, sometimes from earliest childhood, into the responsibilities of wealth and power. They are secure in their upper-class membership, highly principled in their relationships with others, and public-regarding in their exercise of elite responsibilities.

The COWBOYS are new to their position; they lack old-school ties, and they are not particularly concerned with the refinements of ethical conduct. The YANKEES frequently regard the COWBOYS with disdain—as uncouth and opportunistic gamblers and speculators, shady wheeler-dealers and influence-peddlers, and uncultured and selfish bores.

The COWBOYS are newly risen from the masses—many had very humble beginnings. But it is their experience in *rising* from the masses that shapes their philosophy, rather than their mass origins. The COWBOYS are *less* public-regarding and social-welfare-oriented than the YANKEES. They tend to think of solutions to social problems in individualistic terms—they place primary responsibility for solving life's problems on the individual himself. COWBOYS believe that they "made it" themselves through initiative and hard work, and they believe that anyone who wants more out of life can get it the same way they did. The COWBOYS do not feel guilty about poverty or discrimination—they do not believe that either they nor their ancestors had any responsibility for these conditions. Their wealth and position was not given to them—they earned it themselves and they have no apologies for what they have accomplished in life. They are supportive of the political and economic system that provided them the opportunity to rise to the top; they are very patriotic; sometimes vocally "anti-communist"; and moderate to conservative on most national policy issues.

An examination of the backgrounds of some of the new-rich, Sunbelt COWBOYS reveals their connections with the oil, defense, and real estate industries and illuminates some of our contentions about their general qualities.

Clint Murcheson (Murcheson Brothers Investments, Dallas, Texas). Attended public schools and Trinity College, Texas. A director of the First National Bank of Dallas, and Delhi-Australian Petroleum Co. Owner of the Dallas Cowboys, a professional football team. Owns substantial interest in Atlantic Life Insurance, Transcontinental Bus, Southeastern Michigan Gas, and Holt, Rinehart and Winston Publishers. A former director of the New York Central Railroad, which he purchased with partner Sid W. Richardson.

John B. Connally. Special adviser to former President Richard Nixon. Former secretary of treasury, secretary of Navy, governor of Texas, and administrative assistant to Lyndon B. Johnson. Wounded in the assassination fire that killed President John F. Kennedy. Attorney for oilman Sid W. Richardson.

Sid W. Richardson. Independent oil operator. Formerly a director of New York Central Railroad. Attended University of Texas.

Roy Ash. Did not attend undergraduate college. Director, Office of Management and Budget, under Nixon. Former president and director of Litton Industries. Director of Bank America, Global Marine, Inc., Pacific Mutual Life Insurance. A trustee of California Institute of Technology, Marymount College, Loyola University. Formerly chief financial officer of Hughes Aircraft.

Table 8-3. A Guide to Distinguishing Yankees from Cowboys

Eastern Establishment	Sunbelt Cowboys
	Universities
Harvard, Yale	University of Texas Air Force Academy
	Newspapers
New York Times *Washington Post*	*Chicago Tribune* *New York Daily News*
	Music
Leonard Bernstein	Lawrence Welk
	Books
David Halberstam, *The Best and The Brightest*	Kevin Phillips, *The Emerging Republican Majority*
	Religious Leaders
Sloan Coffin	Billy Graham
	Movies
Last Tango in Paris	*Patton*
	Magazines
Harpers, Newsweek	*Readers Digest, U.S. News & World Report*
	Food
Quiche Lorraine	Charcoal Steak
	Foundations
Brookings Institution Ford Foundation Rockefeller Foundation	W. Clement Stone Foundation Herman Kahn's Hudson Institute
	Intellectuals
Herbert Marcuse Arthur Schlesinger, Jr.	NONE
	Car
Porsche	Cadillac
	Entertainment
Concerts Tennis	Golf Football
	Actors
Warren Beatty	John Wayne
	Singers
Barbra Striesand	Johnny Cash

With apologies to Kevin Phillips' "Conservative Chic," *Harpers Magazine* (June, 1973) pp. 66-70; whose notions of "elite liberal" and "new majority" overlap with our own idea of Eastern YANKEES and Sunbelt COWBOYS.

H. L. Hunt. Achieved only a fifth-grade education. Owner of Hunt Oil Co., Dallas, Texas. Owner of Life Line Inc. (radio broadcasts). Son Lamar Hunt owns Kansas City Chiefs, a professional football team. A billionaire and heavy contributor to presidential campaign of Barry Goldwater.

Howard Hughes. Attended Rice University. Owner and president of Hughes Oil Co., Houston, Texas; Hughes Aircraft Co., Silver City, California. Extensive real estate holdings, Las Vegas, Nevada. Holder of world's land plane speed record, transcontinental speed record, and world flight record in 1930s. A billionaire recluse.

COWBOYS have risen to the top echelons of government in both the Democratic administration of President Lyndon B. Johnson and the Republican administration of Richard M. Nixon. Johnson and Nixon themselves were "self-made" men from the South and West, respectively. Both devoted many years of their lives to the task of convincing established Eastern elites of their trustworthiness—Johnson in the U.S. Senate as a leader in civil rights and poverty legislations, and Nixon as vice-president and Wall Street corporation lawyer. Yet many of the attacks on these two presidents arose from their closeness to the new-wealth components of America's elite, and the resulting distrust of them by influential segments of the Eastern liberal establishment.

YANKEE distrust of COWBOYS may have begun with the assassination of President John F. Kennedy in Dallas, and the rash of conspiracy theories linking the assassination to reactionary Texas oil interests. President Johnson acted decisively to discredit these rumors with the appointment of the Warren Commission, composed mainly of Eastern liberals, which concluded that Kennedy's death was the act of a lone gunman.

Until his death in 1974, H. L. Hunt was the richest man in America.[10] His formal education ended in the fifth grade, and he drifted from job to job as a cowboy, lumberjack, and farm hand. It is not clear how he got his first oil well, but the popular rumor is that he won it in a card game in Lake Village, Arkansas. It produced enough oil to give Hunt the capital to move to Tyler, Texas, and to buy into what was later to become one of the world's largest producing fields. Despite a lack of formal education, Hunt was described by associates as a man with a photographic memory for details of contracts, maps, oil leases, and production statistics. But Hunt himself attributed much of his success to

[10] J. Paul Getty, although an American citizen, lives in England. His wealth was also derived from independent oil operations but is now widely invested in other corporations. Getty claims that Hunt was the richest American because Hunt's money is largely independent of corporate control. According to Getty, "The corporations in which I own shares are rich enterprises, but *I* am not wealthy. They had the property. They control me. In terms of extraordinary, independent wealth, there is only one man—H. L. Hunt." "Portrait of a Super-Patriot," *The Nation,* February 24, 1964, pp. 182–94.

luck. He used both brains and luck to expand Hunt Oil Company into the world's largest independent "wildcat" oil operation; to buy thousands of acres of ranchland, timberland, and citrus groves; and to begin a food-processing business bearing his HLH trademark.

His son Lamar Hunt has followed in the father's footsteps in taking chances on new enterprises. Lamar Hunt was an original promotor of the American Football League and the owner of the Kansas City Chiefs. When the Chiefs lost $1 million in its first year of operation, a reporter asked H. L. Hunt whether it worried him to see his son lose this much supporting a football team: "Certainly it worries me," said the elder Hunt. "At that rate Lamar will be broke in 250 years."

Hunt's early poverty, lack of education, and rough life, however, did not create in him any great regard for liberals or do-gooders. Hunt was a patriotic defender of the free enterprise system, an opponent of government regulation, a fiery anti-communist. He was the major backer of General Douglas MacArthur's short-lived presidential campaign in 1952. Hunt regarded Eisenhower as a liberal who was soft on communism—"the most harmful president we have ever had." So he used his money to back the passage of the 22nd Amendment to the Constitution preventing presidents from serving more than two terms. Hunt also financed *Facts Forum,* an "educational" organization that disseminated his political philosophy through books, pamphlets, and "Life Line" radio broadcasts.

Cowboys, Yankees, and Watergate

The Watergate Affair and the subsequent movement to impeach President Nixon also involved COWBOY-YANKEE conflict. Early in the affair, the Eastern liberals were content merely to chastise the president; there was little open talk of impeachment. The president appointed a YANKEE, Elliot Richardson (Harvard Law, clerkship under Supreme Court Justice Felix Frankfurter, prestigious Boston law firm, prior to government service as secretary of HEW and secretary of defense), as attorney general to replace Richard Kleindienst (Arizona attorney and former assistant to Senator Barry Goldwater). Richardson appointed as special prosecutor, YANKEE Archibald Cox (Harvard Law Professor, U.S. solicitor general under Kennedy and Johnson) to conduct the Watergate investigation. But when President Nixon fired Cox over the use of taped presidential conversations, and Richardson resigned, the Eastern establishment turned against the president.

Eastern liberals in both parties charged that President Nixon had surrounded himself with Southern and Western, Sunbelt "wheeler-dealers" whose opportunism and lack of ethics created the milieu for Watergate. Liberals attacked the president's closeness to John Connally, and his personal friendships with Charles "Bebe" Rebozo (who started life as a gas station attendant, opened a successful tire recapping business, expanded into Florida real estate, and later established the Key Biscayne Bank) and Ralph Abplanalp (inventor of the spray valve used on aerosol cans, and co-owner of Nixon's Key Biscayne and San Clemente properties). Easterners decried the unwholesome influence of many White House staffers whose careers were tied to Southern and Western interests: H. R. "Bob" Haldeman (California public relations), John Erlichman (Seattle lawyer), Ronald Ziegler (California public relations), Herbert Klein (California press executive), and Frederick Dent (South Carolina textile millionaire).

The *New York Times,* voice of the Eastern establishment, published an article specifically blaming Watergate on the COWBOYS:

> The Nixonian bedfellows, the people whose creed the President expresses and whose interests he guards, are, to generalize, the economic sovereigns of America's Southern rim, the "sunbelt," that runs from Southern California, through Arizona and Texas down to the Florida Keys. . . . They are "self-made" men and women in the sense that they did not generally inherit great riches. . . . whether because of the newness of their position, their frontier heritage, or their lack of old school ties, they tend to be without particular concerns about the niceties of business ethics and morals, and therefore to be connected more than earlier money would have thought wise, with shady speculations, political influence-peddling, corrupt Nixons, and even organized crime. . . .
>
> Other scandals are sure to follow, for it seems obvious that the kind of milieu in which the President has chosen to immerse himself will continue to produce policies self-serving at best, shady at average, and downright illegal at worst. . . . the new-money wheeler-dealers seem to regard influence-peddling and back-scratching as the true stuff of the American dream.[11]

Of course, this charge overlooks the fact that former Attorney General John Mitchell, who as chairman of the Committee to Re-Elect the President was directly responsible for campaign tactics, possesses impeccable Eastern establishment credentials: senior partner, top Wall Street law firm of Mudge Rose Guthrie Alexander & Mitchell; and specialist in tax-free municipal bond investing (a favorite tax shelter for establishment fortunes).

[11] Kirkpatrick Sale, "The World Behind Watergate," *The New York Times Book Review,* May 3, 1973.

Summary

Elitist and pluralist scholars disagree over the extent and significance of conflict among national leaders. Pluralists observe disagreements over specific programs and policies; they contend that this competition is a significant aspect of democracy. Competition among elites makes policies and programs more responsive to mass demands, because competing elites will try to mobilize mass support for their views. Masses will have a voice in public policy by choosing among competing elites with different policy positions. Moreover, competitive elites will check and balance each other and help prevent abuses of power. In contrast, elitist scholars observe a fairly broad consensus among national leaders on behalf of fundamental values and national goals. Elitists contend that the range of disagreement among elites is relatively narrow and generally confined to means rather than ends.

It is our own judgment, based on our examination of available surveys of leadership opinion as well as public statements of top corporate and governmental executives, that consensus rather than competition characterizes elite opinion. Despite disagreements over specific policies and programs, most top leaders agree on the basic values and future directions of American society. This consensus we have labeled "the liberal establishment."

The established liberal values of the nation's leadership include a willingness to take the welfare of others into account as a part of one's own sense of moral well-being, and a willingness to use governmental power to correct the perceived wrongs done to others—particularly the poor and the black. Popular notions of corporate and financial leaders as exploitative, reactionary robber-barons are based on nineteenth-century stereotypes. The best available evidence indicates that top corporate leaders favor: improved relations with Communist nations, retrenchment of U.S. military commitments abroad, elimination of social and racial inequalities, increased efforts to protect the environment, and equal pay for women. They support the free enterprise system and believe in the profit motive, but they are generally willing to spend some portion of corporate profits for social programs.

Disagreement among various sectors of national leaders—businessmen, Democratic and Republican politicians, bureaucrats, mass media executives, and labor leaders—is confined to a relatively narrow set of issues—the oil depletion allowance, federal versus state-local control of social programs, inheritance taxes, and the proper range of income differences. There is widespread agreement on the essential components of welfare-state capitalism.

Nonetheless, there is evidence of elite factionalism. In recent years, the major faultline among the nation's leaders is the division between the new-rich Southern and Western COWBOYS and the established Eastern liberal YANKEES. The COWBOYS have acquired their wealth since World War II in independent oil operations, the aerospace and computer industries, Sunbelt real estate from California through Texas to Florida, and discount stores. These COWBOYS do not fully share the liberal values of the established YANKEES. The COWBOYS are self-made men of wealth and power—individualistic, highly competitive, and politically conservative. The YANKEES have enjoyed wealth for generations, or slowly climbed the rungs of the nation's largest corporations, law firms, banks, and foundations. They have acquired a sense of civic responsibility, and they look upon the COWBOYS as unprincipled gamblers, shady wheeler-dealers, and uncultured influence-peddlers.

The YANKEES continue to dominate positions of power in America. Two presidents—Johnson and Nixon—with close ties to Southern and Western, new-wealth COWBOYS, have been forced from office. In both cases opposition from Eastern establishment YANKEES, particularly those in the mass media, played an important role in their loss of power.

Nine

HOW INSTITUTIONAL LEADERS MAKE PUBLIC POLICY

Policy as Elite Preference or Group Interaction?

Are the major directions of public policy in America determined by a relatively small group of like-minded individuals interacting among themselves and reflecting their own values and preferences in policy-making? Or are the major directions of American policy a product of competition, bargaining, and compromise among a large number of diverse groups in society? Does public policy reflect the demands of "the people" as demonstrated in elections, opinion polls, and interest-group activity? Or are the views of "the people" easily influenced by communications flowing downward from elites? Are the "proximate policy-makers" —the president, Congress, and courts—truly representatives of their constituents' views in public policy. Or are these public officials relatively free from constituency pressure on most issues and more responsive to elitist views?

The "elitist" model of the policy process would portray policy as the preferences and values of the dominant elite. Public policy does not reflect demands of "the people" but rather the interests, sentiments, and values of the very few who participate in the policy-making process. Changes or innovations in public policy come about when elites redefine their own interests or modify their own values. Of course, elite policy need not be oppressive or exploitative of the masses. Elites may be very "public-regarding," and the welfare of the masses may be an important consideration in elite decision-making. But the important point of the model is that *elites* make policy, not masses. The elite model views the masses as largely passive, apathetic, and ill-informed about policy. Mass views are easily manipulated by the elite-dominated mass media. Communication between elites and masses flows downward. The "proximate policy-makers" knowingly or unknowingly respond primarily to the opinions of elites.

No serious scholar today claims that the masses make policy—that each individual can directly participate in all of the decisions that shape his life. The ideal of the New England town meeting where the citizenry convenes itself periodically as a legislature to make decisions for the whole community is irrelevant in a large, complex, industrial society. A pure democracy is a romantic fiction. All social scientists acknowledge that all societies, even democratic societies, are governed by elites.

But the "pluralist" model of policy process portrays policy as the product of competition, bargaining, and compromise among many diverse groups in society. Few individuals can directly participate in policy-making but they can join groups that will press their demands upon government. The interest group is viewed as the principal actor in the policy-making process—the essential bridge between the individual and his government. Public policy at any time reflects an equilibrium of the relative influence of interest groups. Political scientist Earl Latham describes public policy from the pluralist viewpoint as follows:

> What may be called public policy is actually the equilibrium reached in the group struggle at any given moment, and it represents a balance which the contending factions or groups constantly strive to tip in their favor. . . . The legislature referees the group struggle, ratifies the victories of the successful coalition, and records the terms of the surrenders, compromises, and conquests in the form of statutes.[1]

The individual can play an indirect role in policy-making by voting, joining interest groups, and working in political parties. Parties themselves are viewed as coalitions of groups: the Democratic Party a coalition of labor, ethnic groups, blacks, Catholics, central-city residents, black intellectuals, and Southerners; the Republican Party a coalition of

[1] Earl Latham, "The Group Basis of Politics," in Heinz Eulau, Samuel J. Eldersveld, and Morris Janowitz, eds., *Political Behavior* (New York: Free Press, 1956), p. 239.

middle-class white-collar workers, rural and small-town residents, suburbanites, and Protestants. Mass demands flow upward through interest groups, parties, and elections to the proximate policy-makers.

An Oligarchical Model of National Policy-Making

Any model of the policy-making process is an oversimplification. The very purpose of a model is to order and simplify our thinking about the complexities of the real world. Yet too much simplification can lead to inaccuracies in our thinking about reality. Some models are too simplistic to be helpful, others are too complex. A model is required that *simplifies,* yet at the same time *identifies* the really significant aspects of the policy process.

In our judgment, the typical portrayal of the *elitist* policy-making model as a pyramid, with the "elite" at the narrow pinnacle, a slightly wider group of public officials, legislators, party leaders, and interest groups underneath, and a broad base of "mass" at the bottom, is indeed an oversimplification. It fails to tell us *how* the elite goes about making national policy. If elite theory is to become a useful tool in systematic social science research, it must identify important actors in the policy-making process, postulate linkages between these actors, direct inquiry and research into these linkages, and suggest explanations for policy outcomes.

Let us try to set forth a model of the policy-making process derived from the literature on national elites—an "oligarchical model of the national policy-making process." Our model will be an abstraction from reality—not every major policy decision will conform to our model. But we think the processes described by the model will strike many knowledgeable readers as familiar, that the model indeed actually describes the way in which a great many national policies are decided, and that the model at least deserves consideration by students of the policy-making process.

Our "oligarchical model" of national public policy-making is presented in Figure 9-1. The model assumes that the initial resources for research, study, planning, and formulation of national policy are derived from corporate and personal wealth. This wealth is channeled into foundations, universities, and policy-planning groups in the form of endowments, grants, and contracts. Moreover, corporate presidents, directors, and top wealth-holders also sit on the governing boards of the foundations, universities, and policy-planning groups to oversee the spending of their funds. In short, corporate and personal wealth provides both the

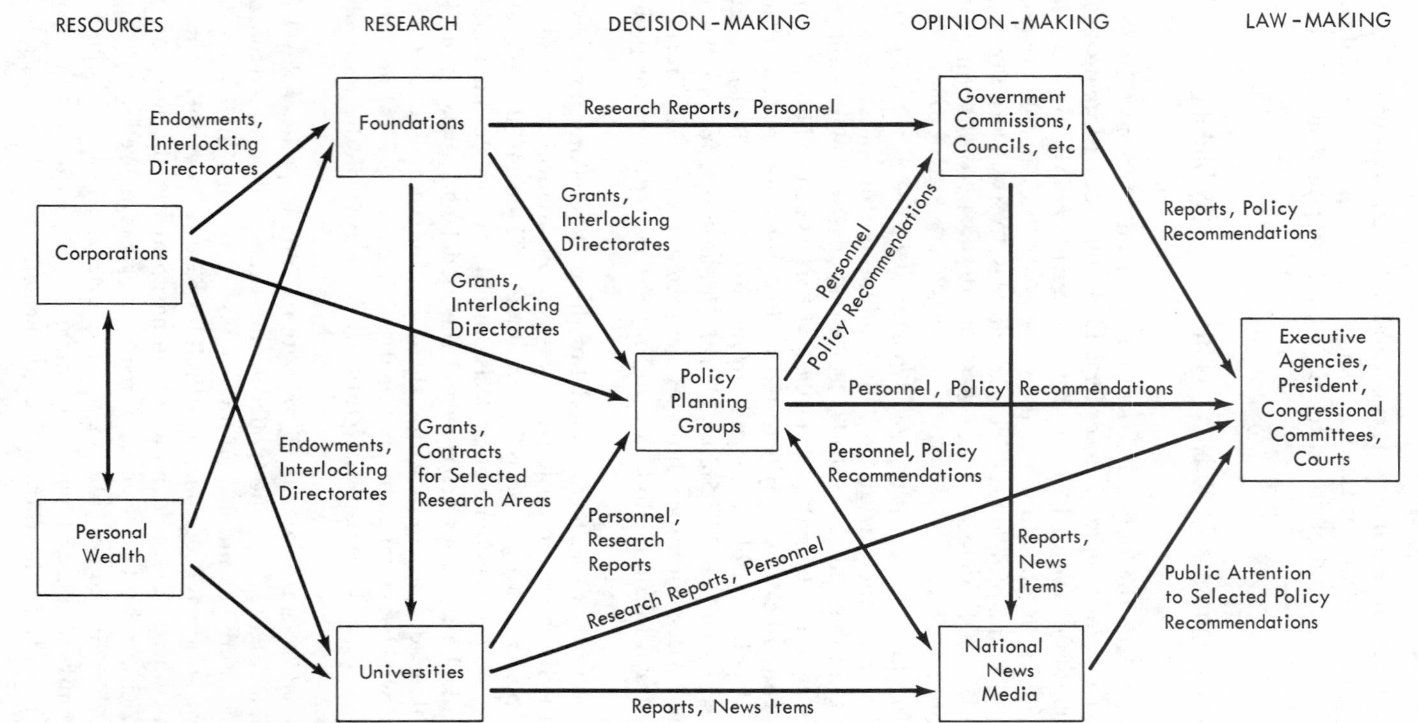

Figure 9-1. The Policy Process: The View from the Top

financial resources and the overall direction of policy research, planning, and development.

The foundations are the essential linkages between wealth and the intellectual community. The foundations determine broad policy objectives—strategic arms limitations, relations with the Soviet Union and China, defense strategies, urban renaissance, the quieting of racial violence in cities, population control, welfare reform, improved public health-care systems, and so forth. The foundations provide the initial "seed money" to analyze social problems, to determine national priorities, and to investigate new policy directions. At a later period in the policy-making process, massive government research funds will be spent to fill in the details in areas already explored in these initial studies.

Universities respond to the policy interests of the foundations, although of course they also try to convince foundations of new and promising policy directions. But research proposals originating from universities which do *not* fit the previously defined "emphasis" of foundation interests are usually lost in the shuffle of papers. While university intellectuals working independently occasionally have an impact on the policy-making process, on the whole, intellectuals respond to policy directions determined by the foundations, corporations, and government agencies that underwrite the costs of research.

The university intellectuals are deeply in debt to the foundations and policy-planning groups. Henry Kissinger might have remained an obscure professor of government if the Council on Foreign Relations and the Ford Foundation had not underwritten his *Nuclear Weapons and Foreign Policy*.[2] Many other intellectuals have been, and continue to be, supported in their work by the foundations.

At the same time the foundations direct and fund major university research, they also contribute financial support to the policy-planning groups. These groups may also be directly supported by corporations and wealthy individuals.

The policy-planning groups are central coordinating points in the entire elite policy-making process. They bring together people at the top of the corporate and financial institutions, the universities, the foundations, the mass media, the powerful law firms, the top intellectuals, and influential figures in the government. They review the relevant university- and foundation-supported research on topics of interest, and more importantly they try to reach a consensus about what action should be taken on national problems under study. Their goal is to develop *action recommendations*—explicit policies or programs designed to resolve or

[2] Henry A. Kissinger, *Nuclear Weapons and Foreign Policy* (New York: Harper & Row, 1957).

ameliorate national problems. At the same time, they endeavor to build consensus among corporate, financial, university, civic, intellectual, and government leaders around major policy directions.

Certain policy-planning groups—notably the Council on Foreign Relations, the Committee on Economic Development, and the Brookings Institution—are influential in a wide range of key policy areas. Other policy-planning groups—the Population Council, for example—specialize in a particularly important policy field. The well-known "think-tanks"—the RAND Corporation, the Stanford Research Institute, the Hudson Institute—are a combination of a research organization and a policy-planning group. Their research is more "action-oriented" than typical university research, but these organizations do not usually engage in consensus-building and policy implementation in the same fashion as the true policy-planning groups (CFR, CED, and Brookings, for example). Generally the "think tanks" submit their reports to foundations and policy-planning groups for further discussion before efforts at policy implementation begin.

Generally, corporate representatives—company presidents, directors, or other high officials—sit on the boards of trustees of the foundations, universities, and policy-planning groups. So also do individuals of great wealth whose families have contributed large amounts to these organizations. The personnel interlocking between corporation boards, university trustees, foundation boards, and policy-planning boards is extensive. (We have described interlocking among Rockefeller, Ford, and Carnegie foundations, and the Council on Foreign Relations, the Committee on Economic Development, and the Brookings Institution in Chapter 5.)

Policy recommendations of the key policy-planning groups are then distributed to the mass media, federal executive agencies, and the Congress. The mass media play a vital role in preparing public opinion for policy change. They also encourage political personalities to assume new policy stances by allocating valuable network broadcast time to those who will speak out in favor of new policy directions.

If policy recommendations call for *major* departures from current programs or policies, or if they are sufficiently innovative and therefore not widely understood, an additional consensus-building step may be utilized—that performed by the Presidential Commission. Presidential Commissions have become increasingly popular in recent years. The President's Advisory Commission on Civil Disorders, chaired by Governor Otto Kerner of Illinois, followed in the wake of the urban violence of the 1960s. The President's Commission on the Causes and Prevention of Violence, chaired by Milton S. Eisenhower, brother of the former president, considered the rising problems of political assassination and violence in society. The President's Commission on Campus Unrest, chaired by millionaire Republican Governor William Scranton of Pennsylvania, was the government's response to campus disturbances.

These Presidential Commissions are designed more for "window dressing" than actual policy development. The membership of such commissions usually includes a few individuals at the top, but also includes stereotyped representatives of labor, blacks, women, students, and other "political" appointments. The commissions may contract for university research or simply hear testimony from prominent persons before making their recommendations. But their recommendations are clearly predictable; they reflect sometimes word for word the previous reports of the established policy-planning groups. But they provide the news media additional material for distribution to the general public, and perhaps win the cooperation of the representatives of minority groups appointed to the commissions. More importantly, presidential commissions offer the public "symbolic reassurance" that the government and the nation's leadership is *concerned* about a particularly vexing problem. But presidential commissions have had a poor record in developing and implementing really innovative solutions to national problems.

A more fruitful path in policy development is for federal executive agencies to respond directly to policy recommendations from the policy-planning groups. Very often agencies do so initially by contracting with universities for supporting research in the same subject areas in which the foundations and policy-planning groups have already been working. This new research is not so much to discover new alternative policies, but rather (1) to confirm the need for change, and (2) to deal with the details of the new policy direction. The results of much of this research are already known before it is begun, since the same university intellectuals and "think-tank" members who were initially working on these policy areas under foundation and policy-planning group grants and contracts are now employed by federal agencies to continue their work. The initial "seed money" of the foundations and corporations is now supplanted by massive infusions of government research contracts and grants. Government agencies, aware of support from those at the top of the policy-planning groups, now feel free to support research in approved areas.

The White House staff, which usually maintains close contact with policy-planning groups, is contacted with increasing frequency by representatives of such groups, foundation heads, corporate representatives, and officials within the federal bureaucracy, when it is felt that the time has come for government action. Frequently before the results of government-sponsored research are available, federal executive agencies, with the assistance of policy-planning groups, will prepare legislation for the Congress to implement policy decisions. Particular versions of bills will pass between executive agencies, the White House, policy-planning groups, and the professional staffs of the congressional committees that will eventually consider the bills. The groundwork is laid for making policy into law. Soon the work of the people at the top will be reflected in the actions of the "proximate policy-makers."

The Role of the "Proximate Policy-Makers"

The activities of the "proximate policy-makers"—the president, the Congress, federal agencies, congressional committees, White House staff, and interest groups—in the policy-making process have been described in countless books and articles. The term "proximate policy-maker" is derived from political scientist Charles E. Lindbloom, who uses the term merely to distinguish between citizens and elected officials: "Except in small political systems that can be run by something like a New England town meeting, not all citizens can be the immediate, or *proximate,* makers of policy. They yield the immediate (or proximate) task of decision to a small minority." [3] In typically pluralist fashion, Lindbloom views the activities of the proximate policy-makers as the *whole* of the policy-making process. But our oligarchic model of public policy-making views the activities of the proximate policy-makers as only the *final phase* of a much more complex process. Ths is the open, public stage of policy-making, and it attracts the attention of the mass media and most political scientists. It is much easier to study than the private actions of corporations, foundations, universities, policy-planning groups, and mass media executives. Most "pluralists" concentrate their attention on this phase of public policy-making and conclude that it is simply a process of bargaining, competition, and compromise among governmental officials.

Undoubtedly bargaining, competition, persuasion, and compromises over policy issues continue throughout this final phase of the policy-making process—the law-making phase. This is particularly true in domestic policy-making; the president is much freer to pursue elite recommendations in foreign and military policy areas without extensive accommodation of congressional and interest-group pressures. And admittedly, many elite recommendations fail to win the approval of Congress or even of the president in the first year or two they are proposed. Conflict between the president and Congress, or between Democrats and Republicans, or liberals and conservatives, and so forth, may delay or

[3] Charles E. Lindbloom, *The Policy-Making Process* (Englewood Cliffs, N.J.: Prentice-Hall, Inc., 1968), p. 30.

alter somewhat the final actions of the "proximate policy-makers." Indeed, important policy changes—welfare reform, for example—can be postponed for years by bickering in the Congress. Other important policy innovations—national health care, for example—can be delayed by conflicting ambitions of a Republican president and a Democratic senator.

But the agenda for policy consideration has been set by other elites *before* the "proximate policy-makers" become actively involved in the policy-making process—the major directions of policy change have been determined, and the mass media have prepared the public for new policies and programs. The formal law-making process concerns itself with details of implementation: who gets the "political" credit, what agencies get control of the program, and exactly how much money will be spent. These are not unimportant questions, but they are raised and decided within the context of policy goals and directions that have already been determined. These decisions of the "proximate policy-makers" tend to center about the *means* rather than the *ends* of public policy.

Public Policy-Making: A Case Study—Population Control

Following World War II, American scientists became increasingly aware that the world's rapidly growing population would someday threaten the very existence of mankind. But before 1952, there was little elite awareness of population problems, and hence no government activity in the field. The only group in either the public or private sector actively concerned with population control was the Planned Parenthood Federation of America, which had been created by Margaret Sanger, a pioneer in America's feminist movement. Planned Parenthood provided birth control information materials to indigent females, but its attempts to promote birth control as public policy were unsuccessful. Indeed, the subject of birth cotnrol was a political taboo. As late as 1959, President Eisenhower said he "could not imagine anything more emphatically a subject that is *not* a proper political or governmental activity or function or responsibility" than family planning.

But more advanced segments of the nation's elite began to take notice of early scientific warnings about the world population explosion. Several Rockefeller Foundation study grants had produced disquieting facts and projections regarding population growth in the 1940s. In 1952, John D. Rockefeller III convened a Conference on Population Problems at Williamsburg, Virginia. Rockefeller invited thirty participants, most of whom were physical and social scientists from universities in the

United States, together with some federal officials, Rockefeller Foundation representatives, and staff members of the Planned Parenthood Federation. The Williamsburg Conference ended with a recommendation to establish a new body to formulate population policy for the nation. Given the political sensitivities surrounding the issue of birth control, the new body was to be a private rather than a public agency.

Accordingly, Rockefeller, buttressed by the scientific consensus expressed at the Williamsburg Conference, formed the Population Council. The Council was funded by generous grants from the Rockefeller Foundation and later the Ford Foundation. It quickly assumed a leadership role in the development of national population control policy. It supported population research, including an energetic program in contraceptive product development and family-planning programs. The Population Council gathered together an eminent group of medical and social scientists as its staff members and consultants. It mobilized the nation's universities through research grants, contracts, and fellowships from both the Population Council and the Rockefeller and Ford Foundations. Population study centers were established at Harvard, Johns Hopkins, Columbia, University of California at Berkeley, University of North Carolina, Michigan, and Tulane.

At the same time, efforts were begun to restructure public opinion regarding population control through the use of the mass media. Hugh Moore, chairman of the board of the Dixie Paper Cup Company, the St. Lawrence Seaway Development Corporation, and a director of the Planned Parenthood Federation (also a member of the Council on Foreign Relations, Harvard Club, Century Club), set out to remold public opinion. Moore published a pamphlet called "The Population Bomb" which has been described as an exaggerated but compelling document. A series of full-page newspaper advertisements appeared periodically in the *New York Times* and other leading newspapers warning of "the population bomb" and signed by prominent Americans from industry and finance and the professionals of the academic and intellectual community. Soon image-conscious scientists were turning out popular scare books about population growth: Paul Ehrlich produced his popular, best-selling *The Population Bomb*.[4]

Moore also created a permanent lobbying group in Washington—the Population Crisis Committee—headed by a well-known American banker and public servant, General William H. Draper, Jr. Draper was senior partner of a New York investment banking firm, a former chairman of the board of Combustion Engineering Corporation, and a former

[4] Paul Ehrlich, *The Population Bomb* (New York: Ballantine, 1964).

vice-president of Dillon, Reed, and Company, a New York investment firm headed by Douglas Dillon. He had also served as under secretary in the Army in the Truman Administration. The Population Crisis Committee itself was an impressive array of major corporate executives, retired ambassadors and generals, members of leading law firms, government officials, and prominent university figures.

While the Planned Parenthood Federation of America had historically led the way in the fight for population control, it was soon reduced to a supportive role after the entry into the field of these two elite-backed organizations—the Population Council and the Population Crisis Committee. The Federation became a national network for the dissemination of information and policy positions from national elites to the community level. It created hundreds of local affiliates, each characterized as a "junior-league-type" organization. Later, a somewhat more youth-oriented organization, Zero Population Growth was organized by publicist Paul Erhlich. ZPG was principally a campus-based organization composed of faculty and students in large universities. It had little influence and it declined when the ZPG fad evaporated from campuses.

While President Eisenhower publicly denounced government-supported birth control, he responded positively to elite advice that foreign aid to developing countries was being dissipated by rapid population growth. In 1959, Eisenhower created a committee to study military assistance and foreign aid programs in underdeveloped countries. Significantly, the committee was headed by General William H. Draper, Jr. The Draper Committee concluded that rapid population growth was a major obstacle to economic development and recommended the channeling of foreign aid into population control programs. Although Eisenhower rejected the proposal, the Draper Report succeeded in introducing population control on the agenda of American foreign policy.

It was not until 1965 that the national government under President Johnson fully committed itself to developing a population policy. A major role was assigned to the Agency for International Development (AID). A Population Office was created in AID; millions of dollars were authorized for population activities in AID programs; and a position of special assistant to the secretary of state for population matters was created. On the domestic side, a Center for Population Research was created in the National Institute of Child Health and Human Development to channel federal funds into population research. A Center for Family Planning Services was established in the Health Services and Mental Health Administration Program to fund family-planning services of state and local governments as a part of federal public health activities. A deputy assistant secretary of population affairs was created in the

HEW bureaucracy. At the same time, the War on Poverty's Office of Economic Opportunity was authorized to include family-planning services as part of its community action programs.

Gradually, the funding of population research and family-planning services was shifted from the private sector to the federal government. But the role of the Population Council had been significant in implementing the growing concern of corporate and financial elites about public policy in this field. The Population Council had disposed of over $100 million in the financing of population activities. The Council itself, however, was merely a conduit for money from the Rockefellers, Fords, Scaifes, and others. The Rockefeller funding came from the Rockefeller Brothers' fund, Mrs. John D. Rockefeller, Jr., Mrs. Jean Mauze (a sister of the Rockefeller brothers), John D. Rockefeller III, and other members of the family. The Scaifes are a branch of the Mellon family and major funding came from Mrs. Cornelia Scaife Mauze and Mrs. Allen M. Scaife. Ford money came from the Ford Foundation.

The first presidential message on population was submitted by Richard M. Nixon to the Congress in 1969. The president committed the nation to the support of family planning in all nations and defined the U.S. population problem as unwanted children in poor families:

> It is my view that no American woman should be denied access to family planning assistance because of economic conditions. I believe therefore that we should establish a national goal of the provision of adequate family planning services within the next five years to all those who want them but cannot afford them.

Congressional activity followed in the wake of presidential, corporate, foundation, and university leadership. The first two pieces of significant population legislation were enacted in 1970—the Family Planning Services and Population Research Act of 1970; and an Act to Establish a Commission on Population Growth and the American Future. The Family Planning Services and Population Research Act provided grants to state and local governments for family-planning projects and services. Priority was given to low-income families. Funds were provided for research on developing better means of contraception and providing better family-planning services by the nation.

The Commission on Population Growth in the American Future was established to formally convene top leadership from various sectors of America's society. The commisson was headed by John D. Rockefeller III, and included representatives of corporate and financial institutions, foundations, universities, and the Population Council and Planned

Parenthood, together with representatives of blacks, women, and youth.[5] The Commission was asked to examine population growth and internal migration within the United States to the end of the twentieth century, and to assess the impact of projected population changes on government services, the economy, resources, and the environment; and to make recommendations on how the nation can best cope with these impacts. In short, the Commission's mandate was "to formulate policy for the future."

The Commission made its final report in 1972; it is the strongest statement to date on population control:

> The Commission believes that all Americans regardless of age, marital status, or income, should be enabled to avoid unwanted births. The major efforts should be made to enlarge and improve the opportunity for individuals to control their own fertility, aiming toward the development of a basic ethical principal of only wanted children being brought into the world.
>
> In order to implement this policy, the Commission has formulated the following recommendations:
>
> the elimination of legal restrictions on access to contraceptive information and services, and the development by the states of affirmative legislation to permit minors to receive such information and services.
>
> the elimination of administrative restrictions on access to voluntary sterilization.
>
> the liberalization of state abortion laws along the lines of the New York State Statute.
>
> greater investments and research in the development of improved methods of contraception.

[5] The Commission was an excellent example of a structured forum for elite interaction. Corporate and financial elites were represented, of course, by John D. Rockefeller III as chairman; and by R. B. Hansberger, chairman of the board of Boise-Cascade Corp.; John R. Mire, president of the National Bureau of Economic Research; George D. Woods, director of the First Boston Corp. The foundations were represented by David E. Bell, vice-president of the Ford Foundation; Bernard Berelson, president of the Population Council. The universities were represented by Margaret Bright, Johns Hopkins University; Odis Dudley Duncan, University of Michigan; D. Gale Johnson, University of Chicago. The government was represented by United States Senator Allan Cranston; U.S. Representative John A. Blatnik; Representative John N. Erlenborn; United States Senator Bob Packwood; Representative James H. Scheuer. Civic and cultural groups were represented by Joseph D. Beasley, an M.D. with the Family Health Institute; Marilyn Brant Chandler, Otis Art Institute; Christian N. Ramsey, an M.D. with the Institute for the Study of Health and Society. Black representatives included Arnita Louise Young Boswell; also Paul B. Cornely; and Lawrence A. Davis, president of Arkansas AM&N. In addition to the professional women listed above, women were also represented by Joan F. Flint, a housewife; and Grace Olivarez, who was also active in the Chicano movement. Finally, two students were also named to the Commission.

> full support of all health services related to fertility, programs to improve training for and delivery of these services, an extension of government family planning project grant programs, and the development of a program of family planning education.[6]

These recommendations were developed by a "tight little community." A foundation staff member reported that

> research is a tight little professional community. . . . The determination of priorities is made by members of the professional community in intimate dialogue with one another. . . . Ford and Rockefeller pick up special things that NIH cannot do; for example, the more flexible things. . . . Product research falls in AID. . . . It is directed at contraceptive development and is applied, rather than the basic research that NIH does. . . .[7]

The pattern of interaction is clear:

> . . . there is a movement in and out of one role or another, academia to government, to foundations, etc. . . . Channels of communication develop . . . and can lead to specialization in particular issues. . . . One man can have great influence . . . a "Mafia-like" structure has existed. . . .[8]

The consensus that unites the Rockefellers, intellectuals, corporate leaders, congressmen, organized labor, civic and cultural leaders, universities and foundations, is the liberal notion of improving the quality of life by using government power to control population growth. These people are convinced that rational planning and government action is required to improve conditions of life at home and abroad. They view political stability and reduction in international and domestic violence as desirable by-products of reduced population growth. They believe that lower fertility is an essential requirement for higher levels of individual and societal well-being. Energetic government intervention is seen as essential to achieve the good society. Most (but not all) would prefer to achieve lower fertility through government manipulation of incentives and disincentives, voluntary family planning, and the dissemination of technology, rather than by direct government coercion.

Population policy-making in America also provides a classic example of the *non*-decision. By focusing on population growth as the obstacle to improving the quality of life of the world's population, the more threatening question of inequalities in the distribution of wealth between

[6] *Population and the American Future,* vol. 1. Report of the Commission on Population Growth and the American Future (Washington: U.S. Government Printing Office, 1972), pp. 2–3.

[7] Peter Bachrach and Elihu Bergman, *Power and Choice* (Lexington: D. C. Heath and Co., 1973), p. 79.

[8] Ibid.

rich and poor nations and peoples can be bypassed. Hunger, disease, and violence are portrayed as a product of too many people rather than of inequality in the distribution of resources among people. Some "radical" critics of current population policy argue that fundamental social changes must occur *before* fertility can be reduced. Standards of living of the poor must be raised, wider opportunities for individual fulfillment must be provided, and women must be given a wider variety of roles and opportunities, so that large families will no longer be an economic or psychological necessity. But these questions are seldom addressed by an American elite predisposed to view population growth *within* the established social, economic, and political system.

Many of the nation's most important public policies are made by the Supreme Court rather than the president or Congress. So it was in population policy—the most significant decision about the future of the nation's population was the Supreme Court's momentous decision recognizing abortion as a constitutional right of women. In the historic decisions of *Roe v. Wade* and *Doe v. Bolton* (1974), the Court determined that the fetus is not a "person" within the meaning of the Constitution, and the fetus' right to life is not guaranteed by law. Moreover, the Court held that the liberties guaranteed by the 5th and 14th Amendments encompass the woman's decision about whether or not to terminate her pregnancy. The Supreme Court decided that the Texas criminal abortion statutes prohibiting abortions in any state of pregnancy except to save the life of the mother were unconstitutional; that during the first three months of pregnancy the abortion decision must be left wholly to the woman and her physician; that during the second three months of pregnancy the state may not prohibit abortion but only regulate procedures in ways reasonably related to maternal health; and that only in the final three months of pregnancy may the state prohibit abortion except where necessary for the preservation of life or health of the mother.

In this sweeping decision the Supreme Court established abortion not merely as permissible under law, but as a constitutional right immune from the vagaries of popularly elected legislatures. Abortion, previously regarded as a serious crime, became a constitutional right. Such far-reaching policy declaration would have been unthinkable a few years ago. But the patient efforts of a small group of the nation's top leaders over decades resulted in this startling reversal of traditional policy.

Summary

Pluralist scholars focus their attention on the activities of "the proximate policy-makers"—the president, Congress, and the courts. They observe competition, bargaining, and compromise among and within these public bodies over specific policies and programs. They observe the role of parties, interest groups, and constituents in shaping the decision-making behavior of these proximate policy-makers. But it is possible that the activities of the proximate policy-makers are merely the final phase of a much more complex structure of national policy formation.

Our "oligarchic model" of national policy-making attempts to trace elite interaction in determining the major directions of national policy. It portrays the role of the proximate policy-makers as one of implementing, through law, the policies that have been formulated by a network of elite-financed and elite-directed policy-planning groups, foundations, and universities. The proximate policy-makers act only after the agenda for policy-making has already been set, the major directions of policy changes have been decided, and all that remains is the determination of programmatic specifics.

The initial resources for research, study, planning, and formulation of policy come from corporate and personal wealth. These resources are channeled into foundations, universities, and policy planning groups. Moreover, top corporate elites also sit on the governing boards of these institutions to help determine how their money will be spent. The policy-planning groups—such as the Council on Foreign Relations, the Committee on Economic Development, and the Brookings Institution—play a central role in bringing together individuals at the top of the corporate and governmental worlds, the foundations, the law firms, and the mass media, in order to reach a consensus about policy direction. The mass media, in addition to participating in policy formulation, play a vital role in preparing public opinion for policy change. Special presidential commissions, governmental study groups, or citizens' councils can also be employed to mobilize support for new policies.

Our examination of population control policy was designed to illustrate our oligarchic model. We do not expect every major policy decision to conform to this model. But we believe the model deserves consideration by students of the policy-making process.

Ten

INSTITUTIONAL ELITES IN AMERICA

Institutional Power in America

Power in America is organized into large institutions, private as well as public—corporations, banks, utilities, governmental bureaucracies, broadcasting networks, law firms, universities, foundations, cultural and civic organizations. The nation's resources are concentrated in a relatively few large institutions and control over these institutional resources is the major source of power in society. The people at the top of these institutions—those who are in a position to direct, manage, and guide the programs, policies, and activities of these institutions—compose the nation's elite.

The *systematic* study of the nation's institutional elite is still very exploratory. Although a great deal has been written about "the power elite," much of it has been speculative, impressionistic, and polemical. Serious difficulties confront the social scientist who wishes to move away from anecdote and ideology to serious scientific research on national elites—research that "names names," attempts operational definitions, develops potheses, and produces some reliable information about na- rship.

- .. first task confronting social science is to develop an operational definition of national elite. Such a definition must be consistent with the notion that great power resides in the institutional structure of society; it must also enable us to identify by name and position those individuals who possess great power in America. Our own definition of a national institutional elite produced 5,416 elite positions. Taken collectively, individuals in these positions controlled half of the nation's industrial assets; half of all the assets in communications, transportation, and utilities, half of all banking assets; and two-thirds of all insurance assets; they controlled nearly half of all assets of private foundations and universities; they controlled the television networks, wire services, and major newspaper chains; they controlled the top law firms and the most prestigious civic and cultural associations; they occupied key federal government posts in the executive, legislative and judicial branches and the top military commands.

Our definition of positions of institutional power involved many subjective judgments, but it provided a starting place for a systematic inquiry into the character of America's elite structure. It allowed us to begin investigation into a number of important questions: Who are the people at the top of the institutional structure of America? How did they get there? What are their backgrounds, attitudes, and values? How concentrated or dispersed is their power? Do they agree or disagree on the fundamental goals of society? How much cohesion or competition characterizes their interrelationships? How do they go about making important policy decisions or undertaking new policy directions?

Hierarchy and Polyarchy Among Institutional Elites

Before summarizing our data on institutional elites, it might be helpful to gain some theoretical perspectives on our findings by suggesting *why* we might expect to find evidence of either hierarchy or polyarchy in our results.

European social theorists—notably Weber and Durkheim—provide theoretical explanations of why social structures become specialized in advanced societies, and why coordination mechanisms are required. These theorists suggest that increasing functional *differentiation* of elites occurs with increasing socioeconomic development. In a primitive society, it is difficult to speak of separate economic, political, military, or administrative power roles; in primitive life, these power roles are merged together with other roles, including kinship, religion, and magical roles. But as separate economic, political, bureaucratic, and military institutions develop, and specialized power roles are created within these institutions, separate elite groups emerge at the top of separate institutional structures. The increased division of labor, the scale and complexity of modern social organizations, and specialization in knowledge, all combine to create functional differentiation among institutional elites. This suggests polyarchy among elites in an advanced society such as the United States.

Yet even though specialized elite groups are required to direct relatively autonomous institutional sectors, there must also be some social mechanisms to coordinate the exercise of power by various elites in society. This requirement of *coordination* limits the autonomy of various institutional elites. Thus, specialization acts to bring elites together, as well as to force them apart. Social theory does not necessarily specify *how* coordination of power is to be achieved in modern society. Nor does it specify *how much* unity is required to maintain a relatively stable social system, or how much competition can be permitted. These remain important empirical questions.

Certainly there must be *some* coordination if the parts of the society are to be integrated into a whole. The amount of coordination can vary a great deal, and the mechanism for coordination among elites differs from one society to another.

One means of coordination is to keep the relative size of elite groups small. This smallness itself facilitates communication. There are relatively few people at the top of various institutional structures, and these people have an extraordinary influence on national policy. The small size of these groups means that they are known and accessible to each other. Often the elites of various institutional orders are brought together by policy-planning groups, governmental commissions, and advisory councils, or informal meetings and conferences. But how *small is* America's elite? C. Wright Mills, wisely perhaps, avoids any estimate of the size of "the power elite"; he says only that it is "a handful of men." [1] Floyd Hunter estimates the size of "top leadership" to be "between one hundred and two hundred men." [2] We have already indicated that our definition of the elite produces an estimated size of over 5000 individuals —considerably more than implied in the power elite literature, but still few enough to permit a great deal of personal interaction.

[1] C. Wright Mills, *The Power Elite* (New York: Oxford, 1956), p. 7.

[2] Floyd Hunter, *Top Leadership, U.S.A.* (Chapel Hill: University of North Carolina Press, 1959), p. 176.

Another coordinating mechanism is to be found in the methods by which elites are recruited. The recruitment of elites to different institutional roles from the same social classes with similar educational experiences should provide a basis for understanding and communication. Social homogeneity, kinship links, similarity of educational experience, common membership in clubs and fraternities, common religious and ethnic affiliations, all help to promote unity of outlook. Yet at the same time we know that a certain amount of "circulation of elites" (upward mobility) is essential for the stability of a social system. This means that some heterogeneity in social background must be tolerated. But social theory fails to tell us exactly how much heterogeneity in social background can be expected.

A related mechanism for coordination is common career experiences. If elite members were drawn disproportionately from one career field—let us say industry or finance—there would be greater potential for unity. But again, social theory does not tell us how much, if any, commonality in career lines is functionally requisite for coordination of specialized elites.

Still another form of coordination is general agreement on the rules to govern the resolution of power conflicts and to preserve the stability of the social system itself. Common values serve to unify the elites of various institutional systems. Moreover, agreement among elites themselves on the rule of law and the minimzing of violence has a strong utilitaran motive in preserving stable working arrangements among elite groups. Finally, unifying values also legitimize the exercise of power by elites over masses. So the preservation of the value system performs the dual function of providing the basis of elite unity while at the same time rationalizing and justifying for the masses the exercise of elite power. Unfortunately, social theory does not tell us *how much* consensus is required among elites to facilitate coordination and preserve a stable social system. Social theory tells us that elites must agree on more matters than they disagree, but it fails to specify how broad or narrow the range of issues can be.

Because social theory suggests *both* convergence and differentiation among institutional elites, it is possible to develop competing theoretical models of the social system—models which emphasize either hierarchy or polyarchy. For example, the notion of the "power elite" developed by C. Wright Mills implies *hierarchy* among economic, political, and military power-holders. The idea suggests unity and coordination among leaders of functionally differentiated social institutions. Mills speculates that the need for coordination in large scale, centralized, complex, industrial society necessitates coordination:

> At the pinnacle of each of the three enlarged and centralized domains, there have arisen those higher circles which make up the economic, the political, and the military elites. At the top of the economy, among the corporate rich, there are the chief executives; at the top of the political order, the members of the political directorate; at the top of the military establishment, the elite of soldier-statesmen clustered in and around the Joint Chiefs of Staff in the upper echelon. . . . each of these domains of power—the warlords, the corporation chieftains, the political directorate—tend to come together, to form the power elite of America.[3]

Thus, the hierarchical or "elitist" model rests upon the theoretical proposition that increasing complexity of relations with other societies requires a high degree of coordination and consequently a great concentration of power.

In contrast, the *polyarchical* or "pluralist" model emphasizes differentiation in institutional structures and leadership positions—with different sets of leaders and different institutional sectors of society with little or no overlap, except perhaps by elected officials responsible to the general public. According to this view, elites are largely "specialists," and leadership roles are confined to a narrow range of institutional decisions. These specialists are recruited through separate institutional channels—they are not drawn exclusively from business or finance. Elite groups are viewed as clearly differentiated. They compete for power, with the result that coordination comes about in part through the dynamic equilibrium of compromise. The functional specialization of institutional elites results in competition for power. Competing elites represent and draw their strength from functionally separate systems of society. The argument is that functionally differentiated power structures lead to an equilibrium of competing elites. Resulting checks and balances of competition are considered desirable to prevent the concentration of power and assure the responsibility of elites.

In short, social theory postulates both hierachy *and* polyarchy among elites in the social system. It is the task of systematic social science research to determine just *how much* convergence or differentiation exists among elites in the national system.

Who's Running America? Summary of Findings

Our findings do not all fit neatly into either an hierarchical, elitist model of power, or a polyarchical, pluralist model of power. We find

[3] C. Wright Mills, *The Power Elite* (New York: Oxford, 1956), pp. 8–9.

evidence of both hierarchy and polyarchy in the nation's institutional elite structure. Let us try to summarize our principal findings regarding the questions posed at the beginning of this volume.

1. CONCENTRATION OF INSTITUTIONAL RESOURCES

The nation's resources are concentrated in a relatively small number of large institutions. Half of the nation's industrial assets are concentrated in 100 manufacturing corporations; half of the nation's banking assets are concentrated in the 50 largest banks; half of the nation's assets in transportation, communications, and utilities are concentrated in 33 corporations; two-thirds of the nation's insurance assets are concentrated in just 18 companies; 12 foundations control nearly 40 percent of all foundation assets; 12 universities control 54 percent of all private endowment funds in higher education; 3 network broadcasting companies control 10 percent of the television news, and 10 newspaper chains account for one-third of the daily newspaper circulation. It is highly probable that 30 Wall Street and Washington law firms exercise comparable dominance in the legal field, and that a dozen cultural and civic organizations dominate music, drama, the arts, and civic affairs. Federal government alone now accounts for 21 percent of the gross national product and two-thirds of all government spending. More importantly, concentration of resources in the nation's largest institutions is increasing over time.

In 1950 the largest 100 manufacturing corporations controlled only 39.8 percent of all manufacturing assets, compared to 52.3 percent in 1970. The development of television network broadcasting over the past twenty-five years has concentrated news dissemination in just three corporations. Centralization of governmental functions at the national level has proceeded at a rapid pace since the 1930s. Similar trends in nationalization and concentration of resources in a small number of institutions is evident in other sectors of society.

2. INDIVIDUAL VERSUS INSTITUTIONAL RESOURCES

The resources available to individuals in America are infinitesimal in comparison with the resources available to the nation's largest institutions. The combined personal wealth of all of the nation's centimillionaires amounts to less than one percent of the federal government's budget for a single year. Most of the nation's top wealth-holders acquired their fortune through their connection with large manufacturing or banking institutions. Less than one-fifth of the nation's richest people are "self-made." But personal wealth in itself provides little power; it is only when wealth is associated with top institutional position that it provides the wealth-holder with any significant degree of power.

Managerial elites are gradually replacing owners and stockholders as the dominant influence in American corporations. Most capital investment comes from retained earnings of corporations and bank loans, rather than from individual investors.

Nonetheless, personal wealth in America is unequally distributed: the top fifth of income recipients receive over 40 percent of all income, while the bottom fifth receives about 5 percent. This inequality is lessening very slowly over time.

3. THE SIZE OF THE NATION'S ELITE

Approximately 4000 individuals in 5000 positions exercise formal authority over institutions that control roughly half of the nation's resources in industry, finance, utilities, insurance, mass media, foundations, education, law, and civic and cultural affairs. This definition of the elite is fairly large numerically, yet these individuals constitute an extremely small percentage of the nation's total population—less than two-thousandths of 1 percent. However, this figure is considerably larger than is implied in the "power elite" literature of an even smaller elite.

Perhaps the question of hierarchy or polyarchy depends on whether one wants to emphasize numbers or percentages. To emphasize hierarchy one can comment on the tiny *percentage* of the population that possesses such great authority. To emphasize polyarchy one can comment on the fairly large *number* of individuals at the top of the nation's institutional structure; certainly there is room for competition within so large a group.

4. INTERLOCKING VERSUS SPECIALIZATION

Despite concentration of institutional resources, there is clear evidence of specialization among institutional leaders. Eighty percent of the institutional elites identified in our study were "specialists," holding only one post of the five thousand "top" posts. Of course, many of these individuals held other institutional positions in a wide variety of corporate, civic, and cultural organizations, but these were not "top" positions as we defined them. Governmental leadership is *not* interlocked with the corporate world.

However, the multiple "interlockers"—individuals with six or top posts—turn out to be recognized top leaders in the industrial financial world. Moreover, there is much more "vertical" overlap—of individuals with previous experience in top corporate, governmental, and legal positions—than "horizontal" (concurrent) interlocking. Over one-quarter of governmental elites have held high corporate positions, and nearly 40 percent of the corporate elites have held governmental jobs. Nonetheless, there is evidence of specialization even in the previous leadership experience of elites: most of the leadership experience of corporate elites was derived from corporate positions, and most of the leadership experience of governmental elites was derived from government and law.

There are, however, important concentrations of combined corporate, governmental, and social power in America. These concentrations center about the great, wealthy, entrepreneurial families—the Rockefellers, Mellons, duPonts, Fords. Doubtlessly the most important of these concentrations is in the Rockefeller family group, which has an extensive network in industrial, financial, political, civic, educational, and cultural institutions.

One important linkage between political elites and corporate and personal wealth is in the financing of political campaigns. Top political contributors for both the Democratic and Republican parties are drawn from the corporate and financial world and from the nation's wealthiest stratum of the population.

5. INHERITORS VERSUS CLIMBERS

There is a great deal of upward mobility in American society, as well as "circulation of elites." Only 12 percent of the top corporate elites studied inherited their position and power; the vast majority climbed the rungs of the corporate ladder. Most governmental elites—whether in the executive bureaucracy, Congress, or the courts—also rose from fairly obscure positions. Elected political leaders frequently come from parochial backgrounds and continue to maintain ties with local clubs and groups. Military leaders tend to have the largest percentage of rural, Southern, and lower-social-origin members of any leadership group.

6. SEPARATE CHANNELS OF RECRUITMENT

There are multiple paths to the top. Our top elites were recruited through a variety of channels. Governmental leaders were recruited mainly from law and government; less than one in six were recruited from the corporate world. Military leaders were recruited exclusively through the military ranks, with the exception of the civilian leadership in the Defense Department. Most top lawyers rose through the ranks of the large, well-known law firms, and mass media executives were recruited primarily from newspapers and television. Only in the foundations, universities, and cultural and civic associations was the formal leadership drawn from other sectors of society.

7. SOCIAL CLASS AND ELITE RECRUITMENT

Individuals at the top are overwhelmingly upper- and upper-middle-class in social origin. Even those who climbed the institutional ladder to high position generally started with the advantages of a middle-class upbringing. Nearly all top institutional elite are college-educated, and half hold advanced degrees. Elites are notably "Ivy League": 55 percent of top corporate leaders and 44 percent of top governmental leaders are alumni of just twelve well-known private universities. Moreover, 18 percent of corporate leaders and 6 percent of government leaders attended one of just thirty private "name" prep schools.

Very few top corporate or governmental elites are women, although more women are now being appointed to top corporate boards. More women serve in top positions in the cultural world, but many of these women do so because of their family affiliation.

Only two blacks were identified in the top 5000 positions in 1970. Both of these—Thurgood Marshall and James Farmer—served in government. Since then several blacks have been named to corporate boards. But it is clear that very few blacks occupy any positions of authority in the institutional structure of American society.

Corporate elites are somewhat more "upper-class" in origin than are governmental elites. Governmental elites had lower proportions of private prep school types and Ivy Leaguers than corporate elites, and governmental elites were less Eastern and urban in their origins than corporate elites. Governmental leaders in the study had more advanced professional degrees (generally law degrees) than did corporate elites.

8. CONFLICT AND CONSENSUS AMONG ELITES

Elites in all sectors of American society were seen to share a consensus about the fundamental values of private enterprise, limited government, and due process of law. Moreover, since the Roosevelt era, elites have generally supported liberal, public-regarding, social welfare programs—including social security, fair labor standards, unemployment compensation, a graduated income tax, a federally aided welfare system, government regulation of public utilities, and countercyclical fiscal and monetary policies. Elite consensus also includes a desire to end minority discrimination—and to bring minority Americans into the mainstream of the political and economic system. Today's liberal elite believes that it can change people's lives through the exercise of governmental power—eliminate racism, abolish poverty, uplift the poor, overcome sickness and disease, educate the masses and generally *do good.*

This consensus, which we have labeled the "liberal establishment," extends to top corporate elites, most of which reflect traditionally liberal positions on a wide range of issues. Despite popular images of ultra-conservative or reactionary corporate leadership, available evidence indicates that these leaders share the liberal, public-regarding philosophy: they are prepared within the boundaries set by the profit system to support public-regarding activities, under the rubric of "corporate consciousness" or "social responsibility." Top corporate leaders are interested in maintaining a stable and ordered domestic society. They also favor an end to the Cold War, improved relations with communist nations, less reliance on military solutions to world problems, and increased world trade and technical cooperation.

Elite disagreement occurs *within* this consensus over fundamental values. The range of disagreement is relatively narrow and tends to be confined to means rather than ends. Specific policy disagreements among various elite groups occur over questions such as the oil depletion allowance, federal versus state and local control of social programs, tax reform, government intervention in business and labor disputes, specific energy and environmental protection proposals, and specific measures for dealing with inflation and recession. But general agreement is found that more should be done for the poor, that government should act to counter recessions by increasing spending and providing jobs, that no limits should be placed on individual income earnings, that private enterprise should be the prevailing economic system, and that upward social mobility is a realistic possibility for working-class children.

9. FACTIONALISM AMONG ELITES

Traditional "pluralist" theory emphasizes competition between Democrats and Republicans, liberals and conservatives, labor and management, and other conventional struggles among interest groups. "Elitist" theory emphasizes underlying cohesion among elite groups, but still admits of some factionalism. A recognized source of this factionalism is the emergence of new sources of wealth and new "self-made" men who do not fully share the prevailing values of established elites. In America since World War II new bases of wealth and power have been developed in independent oil-drilling operations, the aerospace industry, computer technology, real estate development in the Sunbelt from Southern California to Florida, and discount drugs and merchandising, fast foods, and low-cost insurance. We have labeled these new elites "the Sunbelt COWBOYS."

The COWBOYS are not as liberal or public-regarding, or as social-welfare-oriented as are YANKEES—the established institutional elites. The COWBOYS tend to think of solutions to social problems in much more individualistic terms; they are generally moderate to conservative on most national policy issues.

The COWBOYS were influential in the administrations of President Lyndon Johnson and Richard Nixon. But the Watergate scandals tended to reinforce the views of established liberal elites that they were inclined to unethical and opportunistic behavior. More importantly, the scandals diminished the national influence of the COWBOYS, and at the same time contributed a great deal to the power of the mass media elite—the most liberal segment of the national leadership.

Despite the view of many new men of wealth, established Eastern institutional wealth and power continues to dominate national life. The rate of new elite formation is lower today than in previous time periods, and new wealth is frequently unstable and highly sensitive to economic fluctuations.

10. AN OLIGARCHIC MODEL OF NATIONAL POLICY-MAKING

Traditional "pluralist" theory focuses attention on the activities of the "proximate policy-makers" in the policy-making process, and the interaction of parties, interest groups, president and Congress, and other public actors in the determination of national policy. In contrast, our "oligarchic model of national policy-making" views the role of "the proximate policy-makers" as one of deciding specific means of implementing major policy goals and directions which have already been determined by elite interaction.

Our "oligarchic model" assumes that the initial resources for research, study, planning, organization, and implementation of national policy-making is derived from corporate and personal wealth. This wealth is channeled into foundations, universities, and policy-planning institutions; and corporate representatives and top wealth-holders sit on the governing boards of these institutions. The foundations provide the initial "seed money" to analyze social problems, to determine national priorities, and to investigate new policy directions. Universities and intellectuals respond to the research emphases determined by the foundations and produce studies that conform to these predetermined emphases. Influential policy-planning groups—notably the Council on Foreign Relations, the Committee on Economic Development and the Brookings Institution—may also use university research on national problems. But their more important function is consensus-building among elites—bringing together individuals at the top of corporate and financial institutions, the universities, the foundations, and the top law firms, as well as the leading intellectuals, the mass media, and influential figures in government. Their goal is to develop action recommendations—explicit policy recommendations have general elite support. These are then communicated to the "proximate policy-makers" directly and through the mass media. At this point federal executive agencies begin "research" in the policy alternatives suggested by the foundations and policy-planning groups; the major burden of research finding is switched to public agencies which endeavor to fill in the details of the policy directions determined earlier. Eventually, the federal executive agencies, in conjunction with the intellectuals, foundation executives, and policy-planning-group representatives, prepare specific legislative proposals, which then begin to circulate among "the proximate policy-makers," notably White House and congressional committee staffs.

The federal law-making process involves bargaining, competition, persuasion, and compromise, as generally set forth in "pluralist" political theory. But this interaction occurs *after* the agenda for policy-making has been established and the major directions of policy changes have already been determined. The decisions of proximate policy-makers are not unimportant, but they tend to center about the *means* rather than the *ends* of national policy.

Who's Running America? Theory and Research

Systematic research on national leadership is still very exploratory. Indeed, most of the serious social science research on elites in America has concentrated on local communities. Frequently analysts have extrapolated the knowledge derived from *community* power studies to *national* power structures. As a result, much of our theorizing about power in America rests on inferences derived from the study of community life. Yet to assure that national elites are comparable to community elites runs contrary to common-sense understanding of the size and complexity of institutions at the national level.

We do not yet have sufficient scientific evidence to confirm or deny the major tenets of "pluralist" or "elitist" models of national power. Our research on institutional elites produces evidence of both hierarchy and polyarchy in the nation's elite structure. If we were forced to summarize our view of the elitist-pluralist debate in the light of our findings, we might compose a few sentences similar in content to a brief statement that appeared near the end of G. William Domhoff's book, *The Higher Circles:*

> If it is true, as I believe, that the power elite consists of many thousands of people rather than several dozen; that they do not meet as a committee of the whole; that there are differences of opinion between them; that their motives are not well known to us beyond such obvious inferences as stability and power; and that they are not nearly so clever or powerful as the ultraconservatives think—it is nonetheless also true, I believe, that the power elite are more unified, more conscious, and more manipulative than the pluralists would have us believe, and certainly more so than any social group with the potential to contradict them. If pluralists ask just how unified, how conscious, and how manipulative, I reply that they have asked a tough empirical question to which they have contributed virtually no data.[4]

But we shall avoid elaborate theorizing about pluralism, polyarchy, elitism, and hierarchy in American society. Unfortunately, theory and conceptualization about power and elites is in such disarray in the social sciences—it is so infected with ideological disputation—that it is really impossible to speculate about the theoretical relevance of our data on institutional leadership without generating endless unproductive debate.

Our purpose has been to present what we believe to be interesting data on national institutional elites. We will leave it to our readers to relate this data to their own theory or theories of power in society. We do believe, however, that systematic understanding of power and elites must begin with operational definitions, testable hypotheses, and reliable data if we ever expect to rise above the level of speculation, anecdote, or polemics in this field of study.

[4] G. William Domhoff, *The Higher Circles* (New York: Random House, 1970), p. 299.

INDEX

D

E

F

G

H

I

J

K

L

M

N

P

R

S

T

U

V

W

Y

Z